Bible Studies
Deuteronomy
Joshua

Second Edition

James Malm

ISBN: 978-1-7753510-9-2
Copyright © 2016 James Malm
All Rights Reserved

Dedication

*This work is dedicated to the Great God whose house is eternity;
the Father and Sovereign of all that exists and the sum of all Truth,
Wisdom, Love, Justice and Mercy.
May God's house be filled with children whose chief joy is to be like
Him!*

Visit Our Website
theshininglight.info

Table of Contents

Deuteronomy 7

- Deuteronomy 1 8
- Deuteronomy 2 14
- Deuteronomy 3 18
- Deuteronomy 4 21
- Deuteronomy 5 28
- Deuteronomy 6 34
- Deuteronomy 7 37
- Deuteronomy 8 42
- Deuteronomy 9 46
- Deuteronomy 10 50
- Deuteronomy 11 53
- Deuteronomy 12 58
- Deuteronomy 13 63
- Deuteronomy 14 67
- Deuteronomy 15 72
- Deuteronomy 16 76
- Deuteronomy 17 81
- Deuteronomy 18 86
- Deuteronomy 19 90
- Deuteronomy 20 93
- Deuteronomy 21 97
- Deuteronomy 22 101
- Deuteronomy 23 108
- Deuteronomy 24 115
- Deuteronomy 25 120
- Deuteronomy 26 124
- Deuteronomy 27 128
- Deuteronomy 28 133
- Deuteronomy 29 140
- Deuteronomy 30 144
- Deuteronomy 31 147
- Deuteronomy 32 152

Deuteronomy 33 159
Deuteronomy 34 167

Joshua **169**

Joshua 1 170
Joshua 2 174
Joshua 3 179
Joshua 4 182
Joshua 5 187
Joshua 6 191
Joshua 7 200
Joshua 8 204
Joshua 9 210
Joshua 10 215
Joshua 11 221
Joshua 12 224
Joshua 13 226
Joshua 14 231
Joshua 15 234
Joshua 16 238
Joshua 17 240
Joshua 18 243
Joshua 19 247
Joshua 20 251
Joshua 21 253
Joshua 23 263
Joshua 24 267

Deuteronomy

Deuteronomy 1

The Fifth Book of Moses is: A WARNING to Judah and to ALL Israel; that the gift of the physical and ultimately the spiritual Promised Land and remaining in that Promised Land. was and is; entirely and totally CONDITIONAL on obedience to every Word of Almighty God!

Because today's Judah does not obey the commandments of God, they will be given one last victory before God allows them to go into one last captivity. Possession of the physical land is NOT permanent; it is CONDITIONAL on obedience to every Word of God!

We are commanded to read through the Book of Deuteronomy during the Feast of Tabernacles on every Sabbatical year (Deu 31:10).

Deuteronomy was the last book authored by Moses, the words being spoken by him and written down by the scribes just before his death and the entrance of the people into the physical promised land.

The book goes over a history of Israel from leaving Egypt [as a type of being called out of sin] and the theme of this book is a profound warning to keep the whole Word of God, and a warning of what will happen if we turn away from doing so, as well as the blessings for being zealous for the Eternal and his Word.

Such a warning is urgently needed today

The Book of Deuteronomy is a very strong indictment of the sinful in physical Israel and of today's lukewarm Spiritual Ekklesia. The Book of

Deuteronomy is a direct message to today's church of God assemblies; which are spiritually lax, lukewarm and sinful, and are now facing strong correction along with the nations of physical Israel.

Moses spoke these words to Israel in his farewell address and scribes recorded them in a book [roll, scroll].

Deuteronomy 1:1 These be **the words which Moses spake unto all Israel** on this side Jordan in the wilderness, in the plain over against the Red sea, between Paran, and Tophel, and Laban, and Hazeroth, and Dizahab.

1:2 (There are eleven days' journey from Horeb by the way of mount Seir unto Kadeshbarnea.)

1:3 And it came to pass in the fortieth year, in the eleventh month, on the first day of the month [after Israel left Egypt], that Moses spake unto the children of Israel, **according unto all that the LORD had given him in commandment unto them;**

These words were and are God's Word's, not Moses' words; Moses was merely the messenger: it was the one who later became flesh as Jesus Christ that sent the message.

1:4 After he had slain Sihon the king of the Amorites, which dwelt in Heshbon, and Og the king of Bashan, which dwelt at Astaroth in Edrei:

1:5 On this side Jordan, in the land of Moab, **began Moses to declare this law**, saying,

Moses began his history from Mt Sinai [Horeb] **1:6** The LORD our God spake unto us in Horeb [Sinai], saying, Ye have dwelt long enough in this mount:

The border of Israel was to be the land of Canaan and up beside Lebanon to the Euphrates including all the land that Abraham had travelled across. This was the border of Israel during the reign of David and Solomon and it will be the millennial borders of Israel in Palestine. During the millennium each tribe will retain its present land across the world and in addition have a representative population in Palestine.

1:7 Turn you, and take your journey, and go to the mount of the Amorites, and unto all the places nigh thereunto, in the plain, in the hills, and in the vale, and in the south, and by the sea side, to the land of the Canaanites, and unto Lebanon, unto the great river, the river Euphrates.

1:8 Behold, I have set the land before you: go in and possess the land **which the LORD sware unto your fathers, Abraham, Isaac, and Jacob, to give unto them and to their seed after them.**

Moses did not speak his own words, he spoke as God instructed him to speak. The law of Moses is really the Law of God, as delivered by God's messenger Moses.

Next Moses speaks of how a system of governance was to be set up and agreed to by all the people. Moses then instructed these leaders to judge fairly and honestly.

1:9 And I spake unto you at that time, saying, I am not able to bear you myself alone: **1:10** The LORD your God hath multiplied you, and, behold, ye are this day as the stars of heaven for multitude. **1:11** (The LORD God of your fathers make you a thousand times so many more as ye are, and bless you, as he hath promised you!)

1:12 How can I myself alone bear your cumbrance, and your burden, and your strife? **1:13** Take you wise men, and understanding, and known among your tribes, and I will make them rulers over you.

1:14 And ye answered me, and said, The thing which thou hast spoken is good for us to do. **1:15** So I took the chief of your tribes, wise men, and known, and **made them heads over you, captains over thousands, and captains over hundreds, and captains over fifties, and captains over tens, and officers among your tribes.**

1:16 And I charged your judges at that time, saying, Hear the causes between your brethren, and judge righteously between every man and his brother, and the stranger that is with him.

1:17 Ye shall not respect persons in judgment; but ye shall hear the small as well as the great; **ye shall not be afraid of the face of man; for the judgment is God's**: and the cause that is too hard for you, bring it unto me, and I will hear it.

1:18 And I commanded you at that time all the things which ye should do.

These judges were to judge the people based on God's Word. Moses then began a history of the journeying in the wilderness. Despite what some claim, NO MAN has any right whatsoever to loose the Word of God; all leaders are to judge the people by the whole Word of God and not by their own ways.

1:19 And when we departed from Horeb, we went through all that great and terrible wilderness, which ye saw by the way of the mountain of the Amorites, as the LORD our God commanded us; and we came to Kadeshbarnea.

1:20 And I said unto you, **Ye are come unto the mountain of the Amorites, which the LORD our God doth give unto us.**

1:21 Behold, the LORD thy God hath set the land before thee: go up and possess it, as the LORD God of thy fathers hath said unto thee; fear not, neither be discouraged.

Spies were sent out to see the land promised to the people, and they brought a bad report discouraging the people from going in. There was no sin in telling the truth about the greatness of the land's inhabitants; the sin was in magnifying the inhabitants above God.

They forgot the might of their Deliverer and considered their own little strength and so became afraid. This is a lesson for us that we must not rely on our own strength, but always to see the awesome power of our Mighty God!

Of course we cannot overcome Satan and sin by our own strength, but if we add to a deep abiding faith in our Mighty One the works of faith, and stand up to FOLLOW HIM whithersoever he goeth; victory is assured by God's Mighty Hand!

1:22 And ye came near unto me every one of you, and said, We will send men before us, and they shall search us out the land, and bring us word again by what way we must go up, and into what cities we shall come.

1:23 And the saying pleased me well: and I took twelve men of you, one of a tribe: **1:24** And they turned and went up into the mountain, and came unto the valley of Eshcol, and searched it out. **1:25** And they took of the fruit of the land in their hands, and brought it down unto us, and brought us word again, and said, It is a good land which the LORD our God doth give us.

1:26 Notwithstanding ye would not go up, but rebelled against the commandment of the LORD your God:

The became afraid and lost sight of and lost faith in, the Great "I AM" and added to that the sin of blaming God for what they had irrationally feared.

Even today many say that God's ways are too hard to for us to keep turning away from any zeal to keep the whole Word of God and following our own false ways; forgetting that we are not alone and that it is God the Almighty who goes before us, if only we would follow him.

1:27 And ye murmured in your tents, and said, Because the LORD hated us, he hath brought us forth out of the land of Egypt, to deliver us into the hand of the Amorites, to destroy us.

1:28 Whither shall we go up? our brethren have discouraged our heart, saying, The people is greater and taller than we; the cities are great and walled up to heaven; and moreover we have seen the sons of the Anakims there.

Moses reminded the people of how he had encouraged them to obey their Husband and possess the land, yet the people had no faith and would not trust God's promises; refusing to enter the land.

1:29 Then I [Moses] said unto you, **Dread not, neither be afraid of them.**

1:30 The LORD your God which goeth before you, he shall fight for you, according to all that he did for you in Egypt before your eyes;

1:31 And in the wilderness, where thou hast seen how that the LORD thy God bare thee, as a man doth bear his son, in all the way that ye went, until ye came into this place.

Brethren, fear not what any man can do; for our Refuge and High Tower of Defense is far greater than all men together, greater even than the grave itself!

1:32 Yet in this thing ye did not believe the LORD your God, **1:33** Who went in the way before you, to search you out a place to pitch your tents in, in fire by night, to shew you by what way ye should go, and in a cloud by day.

1:34 And the LORD heard the voice of your words, and was wroth, and sware, saying, **1:35** Surely there shall not one of these men of this evil generation see that good land, which I sware to give unto your fathers.

1:36 Save Caleb the son of Jephunneh; he shall see it, and to him will I give the land that he hath trodden upon, and to his children, because he hath wholly followed the LORD.

At this point in the narrative, forty years before the people were to finally enter the land and Moses was to die, the leadership was promised to Joshua. It was a choice made by God well in advance.

1:37 Also the LORD was angry with me for your sakes, saying, Thou also shalt not go in thither.

1:38 But **Joshua the son of Nun, which standeth before thee, he shall go in thither: encourage him: for he shall cause Israel to inherit it.**

1:39 Moreover your little ones, which ye said should be a prey, and your children, which in that day had no knowledge between good and evil, they shall go in thither, and unto them will I give it, and they shall possess it.

1:40 But as for you, turn you, and take your journey into the wilderness by the way of the Red sea.

The people then repented of one sin only to rush into another. The problem was in their doing what they thought would be good, rather than following what God had commanded them. Which in the same problem in those calling themselves the people of God today.

1:41 Then ye answered and said unto me, We have sinned against the LORD, we will go up and fight, according to all that the LORD our God commanded us. And when ye had girded on every man his weapons of war, ye were ready to go up into the hill.

1:42 And the LORD said unto me, Say unto them. Go not up, neither fight; for I am not among you; lest ye be smitten before your enemies.

1:43 So I spake unto you; and ye would not hear, but rebelled against the commandment of the LORD, and went presumptuously up into the hill.

1:44 And the Amorites, which dwelt in that mountain, came out against you, and chased you, as bees do, and destroyed you in Seir, even unto Hormah.

1:45 And **ye returned and wept before the LORD; but the LORD would not hearken to your voice, nor give ear unto you**.

Brethren, if we will not heed the Word of God and his warnings now; he will not save us out of the furnace of tribulation even though we turn and cry out to him; then God will accept the sincerely repentant but we will have to prove the sincerity of our repentance by enduring severe trials to keep the Word of God.

1:46 So ye abode in Kadesh many days, according unto the days that ye abode there.

Deuteronomy 2

Deuteronomy 2:1 Then we turned, and took our journey into the wilderness by the way of the Red sea, as the LORD spake unto me: and we compassed mount Seir many days.

At this point God began to lead the people back toward the land after they had been in the wilderness for many years

2:2 And the LORD spake unto me, saying,

2:3 Ye have compassed [camped here] this mountain long enough: turn you northward. **2:4** And command thou the people, saying, Ye are to pass through the coast of your brethren the children of Esau, which dwell in Seir; and they shall be afraid of you: take ye good heed unto yourselves therefore:

2:5 Meddle not with them; for I will not give you of their land, no, not so much as a foot breadth; because I have given mount Seir unto Esau for a possession.

2:6 Ye shall buy meat [food] of them for money, that ye may eat; and ye shall also buy water of them for money, that ye may drink.

2:7 For the LORD thy God hath blessed thee in all the works of thy hand: he knoweth thy walking through this great wilderness: **these forty years the LORD thy God hath been with thee; thou hast lacked nothing.**

2:8 And when we passed by from our brethren the children of Esau, which dwelt in Seir, through the way of the plain from Elath, and from Eziongaber, we turned and passed by the way of the wilderness of Moab.

Israel is commanded not to fight with Esau or Moab.

2:9 And the LORD said unto me, Distress not the Moabites, neither contend with them in battle: for I will not give thee of their land for a possession; because I have given Ar unto the children of Lot for a possession.

2:10 The Emims dwelt therein in times past, a people great, and many, and tall, as the Anakims; **2:11** Which also were accounted giants, as the Anakims; but the Moabites called them Emims.

2:12 The Horims also [first] dwelt in Seir beforetime; but the children of Esau succeeded them [around the time of Job], when they had destroyed them from before them, and dwelt in their stead; as Israel did unto the land of his possession, which the LORD gave unto them.

It was thirty-eight years from their sojourn in Kadesh-barnea until they entered the land East of Jordan.

2:13 Now rise up, said I, and get you over the brook Zered. And we went over the brook Zered.

2:14 And the space in which we came from Kadeshbarnea, until we were come over the brook Zered, **was thirty and eight years;** until all the generation of the men of war were wasted out from among the host, as the LORD sware unto them.

2:15 For indeed the hand of the LORD was against them, to destroy them from among the host, until they were consumed.

Those among today's spiritually called out who lack the faith to diligently live by every Word of God will also be destroyed if they will not repent, and even with sincere repentance today's spiritually lax brethren will be required to endure much to prove themselves.

Israel is forbidden to enter the land of Ammon [Jordan today].

2:16 So it came to pass, when all the men of war were consumed and dead from among the people,

2:17 That the LORD spake unto me, saying, **2:18** Thou art to pass over through Ar, the coast of Moab, this day: **2:19** And when thou comest nigh over against the children of Ammon, distress them not, nor meddle with them: for I will not give thee of the land of the children of Ammon any possession; because I have given it unto the children of Lot for a possession.

2:20 (That also was accounted a land of giants: giants dwelt therein in old time; and the Ammonites call them Zamzummims; **2:21** A people great, and many, and tall, as the Anakims; but the LORD destroyed them before them [Ammon replaced them]; and they succeeded them, and dwelt in their stead: **2:22** As he [the Lord] did to the children of Esau, which dwelt in Seir, when he destroyed the Horims from before them; and they succeeded them, and dwelt in their stead even unto this day: **2:23** And the Avims which dwelt in Hazerim, even unto Azzah, the Caphtorims, which came forth out of Caphtor, destroyed them, and dwelt in their stead.)

Israel is now commanded to begin to destroy the Canaanites; the wicked Canaanites were to be totally destroyed as symbolic examples of the wicked and unrepentant of mankind who are doomed for the lake of fire.

This is only physical symbolism and the Canaanites will be raised up to take part in the main harvest of humanity during the Feast of Tabernacles harvest, and if they do repent they will be brought into the Family of God. However at that time they were adamantly sinful and unrepentant and made a good example of the ultimate fate of such deliberate and willful unrepentant wickedness. In fact we are just as wicked in our nations today, and we will soon be facing a great correction from our God.

2:24 Rise ye up, take your journey, and pass over the river Arnon: behold, I have given into thine hand Sihon the Amorite, king of Heshbon, and his land: begin to possess it, and contend with him in battle.

2:25 This day will I begin to put the dread of thee and the fear of thee upon the nations that are under the whole heaven, who shall hear report of thee, and shall tremble, and be in anguish because of thee.

Moses sent out a proposal for peace in an honourable manner; this left the fate of Heshbon in the hands of its own king.

2:26 And I sent messengers out of the wilderness of Kedemoth unto Sihon king of Heshbon with words of peace, saying,

2:27 Let me pass through thy land: I will go along by the high way, I will neither turn unto the right hand nor to the left. **2:28** Thou shalt sell me meat for money, that I may eat; and give me water for money, that I may drink: only I will pass through on my feet; **2:29** (As the children of Esau which dwell in Seir, and the Moabites which dwell in Ar, did unto me;) until I shall pass over Jordan into the land which the LORD our God giveth us.

2:30 But Sihon king of Heshbon would not let us pass by him: for the LORD thy God hardened his spirit, and made his heart obstinate, that he might deliver him into thy hand, as appeareth this day.

2:31 And the LORD said unto me, Behold, I have begun to give Sihon and his land before thee: begin to possess, that thou mayest inherit his land. **2:32** Then Sihon came out against us, he and all his people, to fight at Jahaz.

2:33 And the LORD our God delivered him before us; and we smote him, and his sons, and all his people. **2:34** And we took all his cities at that time, and utterly destroyed the men, and the women, and the little ones, of every city, we left none to remain: **2:35** Only the cattle we took for a prey unto ourselves, and the spoil of the cities which we took.

2:36 From Aroer, which is by the brink of the river of Arnon, and from the city that is by the river, even unto Gilead, there was not one city too strong for us: the LORD our God delivered all unto us: **2:37** Only unto the land of the children of Ammon thou camest not, nor unto any place of the river Jabbok, nor unto the cities in the mountains, nor unto whatsoever the LORD our God forbad us.

Deuteronomy 3

God began to deliver the wicked Canaanites into the hands of his people

Deuteronomy 3:1 Then we turned, and went up the way to Bashan [Golan]: and Og the king of Bashan came out against us, he and all his people, to battle at Edrei.

3:2 And the LORD said unto me, Fear him not: for I will deliver him, and all his people, and his land, into thy hand; and thou shalt do unto him as thou didst unto Sihon king of the Amorites, which dwelt at Heshbon. **3:3** So the LORD our God delivered into our hands Og also, the king of Bashan, and all his people: and we smote him until none was left to him remaining.

3:4 And we took all his cities at that time, there was not a city which we took not from them, threescore cities, all the region of Argob, the kingdom of Og in Bashan. **3:5** All these cities were fenced with high walls, gates, and bars; beside unwalled towns a great many. **3:6** And we utterly destroyed them, as we did unto Sihon king of Heshbon, utterly destroying the men, women, and children, of every city. **3:7** But all the cattle, and the spoil of the cities, we took for a prey to ourselves.

3:8 And we took at that time out of the hand of the two kings of the Amorites the land that was on this side Jordan, from the river of Arnon unto mount Hermon; **3:9** (Which Hermon the Sidonians call Sirion; and the Amorites call it Shenir;) **3:10** All the cities of the plain, and all Gilead, and all Bashan, unto Salchah and Edrei, cities of the kingdom of Og in Bashan.

3:11 For only Og king of Bashan remained of the remnant of giants; behold his bedstead was a bedstead of iron; is it not in Rabbath of the children of Ammon? nine cubits was the length thereof, and four cubits the breadth of it, after the cubit of a man.

3:12 And this land, which we possessed at that time, from Aroer, which is by the river Arnon, and half mount Gilead, and the cities thereof, **gave I unto the Reubenites and to the Gadites.**

The land of modern Golan and also somewhat to the south and to the east of Golan was taken and given to Manasseh.

Reuben and Gad received the land south of Manasseh down to the Arnon by the Dead sea, which became their border with Ammon.

3:13 And the rest of Gilead, and all Bashan, being the kingdom of Og, gave I unto the half tribe of Manasseh; all the region of Argob, with all Bashan, which was called the land of giants.

3:14 Jair the son of Manasseh took all the country of Argob unto the coasts of Geshuri and Maachathi; and called them after his own name, Bashanhavothjair, unto this day. **3:15** And I gave Gilead unto Machir.

3:16 And unto the Reubenites and unto the Gadites I gave from Gilead even unto the river Arnon half the valley, and the border even unto the river Jabbok, which is the border of the children of Ammon; **3:17** The plain also, and Jordan, and the coast thereof, from Chinnereth even unto the sea of the plain, even the salt sea, under Ashdothpisgah eastward.

These tribes were given this land on condition that they help the other tribes to take their own land on the west side of the Jordan river.

3:18 And I commanded you at that time, saying, The LORD your God hath given you this land to possess it: ye shall pass over armed before your brethren the children of Israel, all that are meet for the war. **3:19** But your wives, and your little ones, and your cattle, (for I know that ye have much cattle,) shall abide in your cities which I have given you; **3:20** Until the LORD have given rest unto your brethren, as well as unto you, and until they also possess the land which the LORD your God hath given them beyond Jordan: and then shall ye return every man unto his possession, which I have given you.

Moses was then allowed to see the promised land from a mountain top and to instruct his successor Joshua. The people are admonished to have no fear and to trust in God and do his will. This ends the prologue of history and Moses now gets into his final warning message to the people.

This history was a precursor to the real meat of this message to physical and to spiritual Israel and all these things were written for our instruction (2 Tim 3:16, 1 Cor 10).

3:21 And I commanded Joshua at that time, saying, Thine eyes have seen all that the LORD your God hath done unto these two kings: so shall the LORD do unto all the kingdoms whither thou passest. **3:22** Ye shall not fear them: for the LORD your God he shall fight for you.

3:23 And I besought the LORD at that time, saying,

3:24 O Lord GOD, thou hast begun to shew thy servant thy greatness, and thy mighty hand: for what God is there in heaven or in earth, that can do according to thy works, and according to thy might? **3:25** I pray thee, let me go over, and see the good land that is beyond Jordan, that goodly mountain, and Lebanon.

3:26 But the LORD was wroth with me for your sakes, and would not hear me: and the LORD said unto me, Let it suffice thee; speak no more unto me of this matter.

3:27 Get thee up into the top of Pisgah, and lift up thine eyes westward, and northward, and southward, and eastward, and behold it with thine eyes: for thou shalt not go over this Jordan.

3:28 But charge Joshua, and encourage him, and strengthen him: for he shall go over before this people, and he shall cause them to inherit the land which thou shalt see.

3:29 So we abode in the valley over against Bethpeor.

Deuteronomy 4

Spiritual Israel, Beloved elect of God; consider this plea and turn back to your Husband your Maker, with the zeal of Joshua and Moses.

Deuteronomy 4:1 Now therefore hearken, O Israel, unto the statutes and unto the judgments, which I teach you, for to do them, that ye may live, and go in and possess the land which the LORD God of your fathers giveth you.

4:2 Ye shall not add unto the word which I command you, neither shall ye diminish ought from it, that ye may keep the commandments of the LORD your God which I command you.

God destroyed all of the people he called out of Egypt who fell into idolatry [idolatry is exalting anything above the Eternal]; and he will destroy all of the spiritually called out of the New Covenant if they follow idols of men or any person who teaches anything other than a passionate zeal to keep the whole Word of God.

Idolatry is not just bowing to a statue; idolatry is obeying anyone contrary to the Word of God and exalting the words of men above the Word of God. If anyone says "I can do this because some man says it is alright" that person is an idolater and will be destroyed from among God's people if they do not repent.

4:3 Your eyes have seen what the LORD did because of Baalpeor: for all the men that followed Baalpeor, **the LORD thy God hath destroyed them from among you.**

God will destroy the idolaters from among the faithful; and God will preserve all those that are zealous to keep the Word and Will of Almighty God.

Unless we quickly repent, this means that the vast majority of today's Spiritual Ekklesia will be destroyed by God for our idolatry of following the false traditions of our idols of men.

4:4 But ye that did cleave unto the LORD your God are alive every one of you this day.

These are God's commandments, laws, statutes, ordinances, precepts and judgments, not those of Moses; Moses merely delivered the message from God to us. These words of God were to be kept in the physical promised land as an instructional allegory that the Word and Will of God must also be fully kept in the spiritual Promised Land of eternity!

4:5 Behold, **I have taught you statutes and judgments, even as the LORD my God commanded me,** that ye should do so in the land whither ye go to possess it.

If we are zealous to keep the Word and Will of God; the Light of our example will shine brilliantly as a beacon of godliness to all peoples! That example being far more effectual than billions spent in preaching.

4:6 Keep therefore and do them; for this is your wisdom and your understanding in the sight of the nations, which shall hear all these statutes, and say, Surely this great nation is a wise and understanding people.

What people are as great as the people who are close to the Eternal God? Who have the ear of the King of the Universe because of their faithful zeal to keep his Word and his Will?

4:7 For what nation is there so great, who hath God so nigh unto them, as the LORD our God is in all things that we call upon him for?

There is nothing so wise and so WONDERFUL as the Word of God!

> **Romans 7:12** Wherefore the law is holy, and the commandment holy, and just, and good.

Deuteronomy 4:8 And what nation is there so great, that hath statutes and judgments so righteous as all this law, which I set before you this day?

4:9 Only take heed to thyself, and keep thy soul diligently, lest thou forget the things which thine eyes have seen, and lest they depart from thy heart all the days of thy life: but teach them thy sons, and thy sons' sons;

Remember God's mighty deeds in delivering Israel out of Egypt and bondage, and remember God's mighty deeds to deliver his spiritual people out of bondage to Satan and sin by living a perfect life and giving that perfect life for his creation so that we might be delivered from the ultimate Adversary: DEATH itself!

4:10 Specially the day that thou stoodest before the LORD thy God in Horeb, when the LORD said unto me, Gather me the people together, and I will make them hear my words, that they may learn to fear me all the days that they shall live upon the earth, and that they may teach their children.

4:11 And ye came near and stood under the mountain; and the mountain burned with fire unto the midst of heaven, with darkness, clouds, and thick darkness.

4:12 And the LORD spake unto you out of the midst of the fire: ye heard the voice of the words, but saw no similitude; only ye heard a voice.

This covenant called by the name of the mediator Moses, was glorious; if only the people had obeyed, but because they did not obey a New Covenant was necessary to replace the Mosaic Covenant.

> **Jeremiah 31:33** But this shall be the covenant that I will make with the house of Israel; After those days, saith the Lord, I will put my law in **their** inward parts, and write it in **their hearts**; and will be **their** God, and they shall be my people.

Deuteronomy 4:13 And he declared unto you his covenant, which he commanded you to perform, **even** [the basic] **ten commandments; and he wrote them upon two tables of stone.**

In addition to the ten commandments:

4:14 And **the LORD commanded me at that time to teach you statutes and judgments, that ye might do them in the land whither ye go over to possess it.**

4:15 Take ye therefore good heed unto yourselves; for ye saw no manner of similitude on the day that the LORD spake unto you in Horeb out of the midst of the fire:

They and we are forbidden to make any likeness of any thing for purpose of worship, but we now have a spiritual covenant and the spirit of this commandment on idolatry, is that we should never allow ANYTHING to ever come between us and God! Today idolatry is mainly the spiritual sin of following anyone in disobedience to God.

4:16 Lest ye corrupt yourselves, and make you a graven image, the similitude of any figure, the likeness of male or female, **4:17** The likeness of any beast that is on the earth, the likeness of any winged fowl that flieth in the air, **4:18** The likeness of any thing that creepeth on the ground, the likeness of any fish that is in the waters beneath the earth:

4:19 And lest thou lift up thine eyes unto heaven, and when thou seest the sun, and the moon, and the stars, even all the host of heaven, shouldest be driven to worship them, and serve them, which the LORD thy God hath divided unto all nations under the whole heaven.

This physical command has as its spiritual intent; that we are to allow NOTHING to come between us and our LORD. We are to follow no man, prophet, apostle or organization that is not diligent for every Word of God.

We are always to be totally loyal to our Master and we are to follow men ONLY as they follow the Creator, and we are to continually test every word of men by the scriptures; remaining steadfastly loyal to our God.

The Eternal has called us out of bondage to sin and delivered us from that spiritual Pharaoh Satan. Therefore let us drink deeply of the Living Waters of the Holy Spirit of God and remain diligent to follow the Lamb of God withersoever he goeth.

4:20 But the LORD hath taken you, and brought you forth out of the iron furnace, even out of Egypt, to be unto him a people of inheritance, as ye are this day.

4:21 Furthermore the LORD was angry with me for your sakes, and sware that I should not go over Jordan, and that I should not go in unto that good land, which the LORD thy God giveth thee for an inheritance: **4:22** But I must die in this land, I must not go over Jordan: but ye shall go over, and possess that good land.

Physical Israel was called out of bondage in Egypt by a Mighty God and she must remain loyal to the Almighty and NOT return back into the sins of ancient Egypt and Babylon, or physical Israel will be cast into strong correction.

Spiritual Israel has been called out of spiritual Egypt of bondage to Satan and sin by God the Father; who has Called us out of spiritual Egypt and into a New Covenant (Jer 31:31), and we have been delivered from bondage to sin by the application of the Atoning Sacrifice of Jesus Christ. Take heed lest you forget your baptismal commitment to God and his Word; lest you be enticed to consider loyalty to any man or group as synonymous with loyalty to the espoused Husband of your baptismal commitment.

For we have a jealous Husband who will not tolerate any emotional and spiritual ADULTERY on our part.

If we exalt any other above him in our affections we are NOT worthy of HIM!

4:23 Take heed unto yourselves, lest ye forget the covenant of the LORD your God, which he made with you [For those people at that time the Mosaic Covenant and for us the New Covenant of Jeremiah 31:31.], **and make you a graven image, or the likeness of any thing, which the LORD thy God hath forbidden thee.**

The Eternal will not hold us guiltless for the spiritual adultery of exalting [obeying] any person or thing above him!

4:24 For the LORD thy God is a consuming fire, even a jealous God.

4:25 When thou shalt beget children, and children's children, and ye shall have remained long in the land, and shall corrupt yourselves, and make a graven image, or the likeness of any thing, and shall do evil in the sight of the LORD thy God, to provoke him to anger:

Possession of the physical promised land was absolutely conditional on complete obedience and loyalty to God.

Our New Covenant relationship with God is completely conditional on our loyalty and obedience to God.

4:26 I call heaven and earth to witness against you this day, that ye shall soon utterly perish from off the land whereunto ye go over Jordan to possess it; ye shall not prolong your days upon it, but shall utterly be destroyed.

Israel's possession of the land was and is, entirely and absolutely, conditionally dependent on obedience to the Eternal.

Today we do NOT live by every Word of God and we will most assuridly be punished for our sins.

Today the New Covenant people of God no longer keep God's Word with any kind of zeal, and we are guilty of gross compromise and laxity in the things of God and the keeping of our Marriage Covenant with Jesus Christ.

We have become organization proud and we are not faithful to the Husband of our baptismal espousal, therefore Jesus Christ will reject those who will not repent. He loves us and he stands at our door knocking and we will not let him in. We "know it all" and we think that we have need of nothing; therefore in order to save the spirit, God is left with no choice except to afflict the flesh. Now it is very late and our correction is in sight, turn to your God oh physical and spiritual Israel for why will you die?

4:27 And **the LORD shall scatter you among the nations, and ye shall be left few in number among the heathen, whither the LORD shall lead you.**

4:28 And there ye shall serve gods, the work of men's hands, wood and stone, which neither see, nor hear, nor eat, nor smell.

Even in great tribulation we may find God; If we sincerely repent and seek him diligently.

4:29 But if from thence thou shalt seek the LORD thy God, thou shalt find him, if thou seek him with all thy heart and with all thy soul.

Dearest Elect of the Eternal, REMEMBER these words. If you find yourself afflicted, RUN quickly to the Eternal God in sincerity and truth.

4:30 When thou art in tribulation, and all these things are come upon thee, even in the latter days, if thou turn to the LORD thy God, and shalt be obedient unto his voice;

4:31 (For the LORD thy God is a merciful God;) he will not forsake thee, neither destroy thee, nor forget the covenant of thy fathers which he sware unto them.

4:32 For ask now of the days that are past, which were before thee, since the day that God created man upon the earth, and ask from the one side of heaven unto the other, whether there hath been any such thing as this great thing is, or hath been heard like it?

4:33 Did ever people hear the voice of God speaking out of the midst of the fire, as thou hast heard, and live? **4:34** Or hath God assayed to go and take him a nation from the midst of another nation, by temptations, by signs, and by wonders, and by war, and by a mighty hand, and by a stretched out arm, and by great terrors, according to all that the LORD your God did for you in Egypt before your eyes?

4:35 Unto thee it was shewed [and recorded for us today], **that thou mightest know that the LORD he is God; there is none else beside him.**

4:36 Out of heaven he made thee to hear his voice, that he might instruct thee: and upon earth he shewed thee his great fire; and thou heardest his words out of the midst of the fire.

4:37 And **because he loved thy fathers** [God has kept his promises to Abraham, Isaac and Jacob], therefore he chose their seed after them, and brought thee out in his sight with his mighty power out of Egypt;

Spiritually the Lamb of God has overcome the Adversary by the mighty deeds of a perfect life and a perfect sacrifice to redeem God's people.

4:38 To drive out nations from before thee greater and mightier than thou art [Satan is mightier than we and God has called us out and delivered us from his bondage and given us his kingdoms of the whole earth, if we faint not.], to bring thee in, to give thee their land for an inheritance, as it is this day.

4:39 Know therefore this day, and consider it in thine heart, that the LORD he is God in heaven above, and upon the earth beneath: there is none else.

4:40 Thou shalt keep therefore his statutes, and his commandments, which I command thee this day, that it may go well with thee, and with thy children after thee, and that thou mayest prolong thy days upon the earth, which the LORD thy God giveth thee, for ever.

Moses then set aside three cities so that an innocent person may flee from anyone seeking revenge and find a fair hearing there. These cities would be like courts or judicial centers today.

4:41 Then Moses severed three cities on this side Jordan toward the sunrising [the east side of Jordan in Golan (Bashan)];

4:42 That the slayer might flee thither, which should kill his neighbour unawares, and hated him not in times past; and that fleeing unto one of these cities he might live:

4:43 Namely, **Bezer** in the wilderness, in the plain country, of the Reubenites; and **Ramoth** in Gilead, of the Gadites; and **Golan** in Bashan, of the Manassites.

4:44 And this is the law which Moses set before the children of Israel: **4:45** These are the testimonies, and the statutes, and the judgments, which Moses spake unto the children of Israel, after they came forth out of Egypt.

4:46 On this side Jordan, in the valley over against Bethpeor, in the land of Sihon king of the Amorites, who dwelt at Heshbon, whom Moses and the children of Israel smote, after they were come forth out of Egypt: **4:47** And they possessed his land, and the land of Og king of Bashan, two kings of the Amorites, which were on this side Jordan toward the sunrising;

4:48 From Aroer, which is by the bank of the river Arnon, even unto mount Sion, which is Hermon, **4:49** And all the plain on this side Jordan eastward, even unto the sea of the plain, under the springs of Pisgah.

Deuteronomy 5

Then Moses began to teach the commandments, laws, statutes, ordinances, precepts and judgments of the Eternal. These things had been dictated by God to Moses who wrote out every word that God spoke to him on Sinai, and now Moses was reminding all Israel in this his last address to the people before he died.

It is not necessary to suppose that Moses spoke and over a million people heard hie words: rather Moses would have directly addressed the Seventy and the Patriarchal elders of the tribes along with the senior priests while scribes would have recorded and written out the words as Moses spoke.

Then these officials would have instructed the people under their care while the scribes maintained these words in writing through the ages.

Deuteronomy 5:1 And Moses called all Israel, and said unto them, **Hear, O Israel, the statutes and judgments which I speak in your ears this day, that ye may learn them, and keep, and do them.**

5:2 The LORD our God made a covenant with us in Horeb [Sinai]. **5:3** The LORD made not this covenant with our fathers, but with us, even us, who are all of us here alive this day.

5:4 The LORD talked with you face to face in the mount out of the midst of the fire, **5:5** (I stood between the LORD and you at that time, to shew you the word of the LORD: for ye were afraid by reason of the fire, and went not up into the mount;) saying,

The commandments were written on tables of stone to show that these people were hard-hearted and lacking in God's Spirit. Those called into the New Covenant of Jeremiah 31:31 are to have the law written on the tables of their hearts and are to internalize every Word of God making it a part of our own nature.

Today, we have become spiritually lax, forgetting our Covenant; and we have departed from God, becoming hearers of the law and NOT doers of God's Word; doing what we think is right instead of what God has commanded.

> **James 1:22** But be ye doers of the word, and not hearers only, deceiving your own selves.
>
> **Romans 2:13** (For not the hearers of the law are just before God, but the doers of the law shall be justified [by the application of the sacrifice of Jesus Christ the Lamb of God].

The sacrifice of Jesus Christ the Lamb of God will only be applied to the sincerely repentant who commit to STOP sinning!

The Ten Commandments

Deuteronomy 5:6 I am the LORD thy God, which brought thee out of the land of Egypt, from the house of bondage.

5:7 Thou shalt have none other gods before me. **5:8** Thou shalt not make thee any graven image, or any likeness of any thing that is in heaven above, or that is in the earth beneath, or that is in the waters beneath the earth:

Brethren, we are commanded by Almighty God to exalt the Eternal above every other thing in existence including men. We must test the words of men against the Word of God (1 Thess 5:21) no matter what title or authority those men claim to have! We must NEVER follow any person contrary to any part of the Word of God! NEVER!

5:9 Thou shalt not bow down thyself unto them, nor serve them: for I the LORD thy God am a jealous God, visiting the iniquity of the fathers upon the children unto the third and fourth generation of them that hate me, **5:10** And shewing mercy unto thousands of them that love me and keep my commandments.

Today, the Spiritual Ekklesia breaks this commandment daily as we exalt our elders and organizations above God's Word. Often excusing our sin by saying "the teacher said it was alright." This IS Idolatry and spiritual ADULTERY; and we will NOT be held guiltless by the Husband of our baptismal commitment.

5:11 Thou shalt not take the name of the LORD thy God in vain: for the LORD will not hold him guiltless that taketh his name in vain.

We take his name in vain every time that we lie saying that we love God when we are not zealous to live by every Word of God. We take his name in vain every time we call ourselves the people of God and then disgrace ourselves by our evil doing.

5:12 Keep the sabbath day to sanctify it, as the LORD thy God hath commanded thee. **5:13** Six days thou shalt labour, and do all thy work:

5:14 But the seventh day is the sabbath of the LORD thy God: in it thou shalt not do any work, thou, nor thy son, nor thy daughter, nor thy manservant, nor thy maidservant, nor thine ox, nor thine ass, nor any of thy cattle, nor thy stranger that is within thy gates; that thy manservant and thy maidservant may rest as well as thou.

5:15 And remember that thou wast a servant in the land of Egypt [to serve Pharaoh in harsh bondage seven days a week], and that the LORD thy God brought thee out thence through a mighty hand and by a stretched out arm: therefore the LORD thy God commanded thee to keep the sabbath day.

We are NOT to do any work of any kind [except that which is specifically permitted or commanded by God], and we are NOT to be responsible for anyone else working on any weekly Sabbath or annual Holy Day.

We are not to become hypocrites by paying others to do what we on moral grounds would not do ourselves, and we are NOT to become thieves by stealing the opportunity for others to have their rest and time with God. We are to allow them the time even if they do not use it wisely.

We are to use the preparation day for all our cooking and work and to rest on God's Sabbaths and Holy Days, spending time with our Creator, learning of him and teaching our families. The vast majority of people in today's Ekklesia call God's Sabbaths holy and then routinely pollute them, breaking this commandment in a regular and flagrant manner.

5:16 Honour thy father and thy mother, as the LORD thy God hath commanded thee; that thy days may be prolonged, and that it may go well with thee, in the land which the LORD thy God giveth thee.

We break this commandment by not honouring God our Father in heaven above all else, and by giving excessive offerings and not properly caring for our parents and the families that God has blessed us with (Mat 15).

5:17 Thou shalt not kill [shed innocent blood].

Yes, in the Ekklesia we do murder; and you ask how do we murder?

We are spiritual murderers when we condemn those who are zealous for God and his commandments, persecuting and attacking them to try and turn them away from their zeal and thereby causing them to sin; and by teaching our children [by words and example] to follow idols of men in place of any zeal to follow the Eternal.

5:18 Neither shalt thou commit adultery.

We commit adultery daily against our espoused Husband; by exalting others in our hearts above his Word. That is emotional and spiritual adultery. How would you feel if you spouse loved others more than he/she loved you?

5:19 Neither shalt thou steal.

Steal? Do we not steal what is God's for ourselves? Many steal God's time on Sabbaths and Holy Days. Many organizations and leaders make merchandise of God's flock and use his sheep for their own advantage, stealing our crowns by leading us away from exalting God into exalting themselves.

5:20 Neither shalt thou bear false witness against thy neighbour.

Today the leaders of the Ekklesia call good, evil; and persecute the righteous. They say that those who follow them above any faithfulness to the Word of God are godly, which is wickedness.

Many elders tell the people not to be [over] righteous twisting the words of Solomon in Ecclesiastes.

They lie and deceive about the Biblical Calendar and many other things, teaching the "Primacy of Peter" lie to exalt themselves above all that is called God. They do not tell the truth and often quote out of context to deceive the brethren about the proper in context meanings, and they spin spin spin both the scriptures and their own actions continually.

5:21 Neither shalt thou desire thy neighbour's wife, neither shalt thou covet [unlawfully desire] thy neighbour's house, his field, or his manservant, or his maidservant, his ox, or his ass, or any thing that is thy neighbour's.

> **Hebrews 13:5** Let your conversation [thoughts and conduct] be without covetousness; and be **content** with such things as ye have: for he hath said, I will never leave thee, nor forsake thee.

Deuteronomy 5:22 These words the LORD spake unto all your assembly in the mount out of the midst of the fire, of the cloud, and of the thick darkness, with a great voice: and he added no more. And he wrote them in two tables of stone, and delivered them unto me.

Moses was chosen as the mediator of the Mosaic Covenant and is a symbolic example of Jesus Christ the Mediator of the New Covenant. Today, Jesus Christ sits in Moses seat!

5:23 And it came to pass, when ye heard the voice out of the midst of the darkness, (for the mountain did burn with fire,) that ye came near unto me, even all the heads of your tribes, and your elders;

5:24 And ye said, Behold, the LORD our God hath shewed us his glory and his greatness, and we have heard his voice out of the midst of the fire: we have seen this day that God doth talk with man, and he liveth.

5:25 Now therefore why should we die? for this great fire will consume us: if we hear the voice of the LORD our God any more, then we shall die. **5:26** For who is there of all flesh, that hath heard the voice of the living God speaking out of the midst of the fire, as we have, and lived?

5:27 Go thou near, and hear all that the LORD our God shall say: and speak thou unto us all that the LORD our God shall speak unto thee; and we will hear it, and do it.

5:28 And the LORD heard the voice of your words, when ye spake unto me; and **the LORD said unto me, I have heard the voice of the words of this people, which they have spoken unto thee: they have well said all that they have spoken.**

The God who later gave up his God-hood to be made flesh as Jesus Christ longs for a converted heart in his bride, so that she would obey him and seek to please him out of a sincere and passionate love for him. He again states that possession of the land is absolutely conditional on obedience to the Word and Will of God.

The same condition applies to entrance into the resurrection to eternal life. Just as Israel could not remain in the physical Promised Land without obedience, we cannot remain in the New Covenant without obedience to the Word and Will of God.

Take heed lest you be rejected for disobedience and lack of zeal to live by every Word of God (Rev 3:16).

God is working to place an obedient faithful heart in his New Covenant called out, but we have strayed very far from him: for this cause he will afflict our flesh in the hope that the spirit might be saved.

> **Jeremiah 31:33** But this shall be the covenant that I will make with the house of Israel; After those days, saith the Lord, I will put my law in their inward parts, and write it in their hearts; and will be their God, and they shall be my people.

Deuteronomy 5:29 O that there were such an heart in them, that they would fear me, and keep all my commandments always, that it might be well with them, and with their children for ever!

Moses recalls that Israel was sent away while Moses heard the Word of the LORD on the mount, which Word Moses then gave to Israel. These are not the laws of Moses; they are the Word of Almighty God given through the messenger, the intermediary, Moses.

5:30 Go say to them, Get you into your tents again. **5:31** But as for thee, stand thou here by me, and **I will speak unto thee all the commandments, and the statutes, and the judgments, which thou shalt teach them, that they may do them in the land which I give them to possess it.**

5:32 Ye shall observe to do therefore as the LORD your God hath commanded you: ye shall not turn aside to the right hand or to the left.

5:33 Ye shall walk in all the ways which the LORD your God hath commanded you, that ye may live, and that it may be well with you, and that ye may prolong your days in the land which ye shall possess.

Brethren, no man has any right to change, add to or diminish from the Word of God!

Neither the pope nor ANY other person has the right to loose the Word of God; rather all persons are to bind and loose judgments in human disputes according to the Word of God: We are NOT to try to change God's Word according to our own opinions.

Deuteronomy 6

Deuteronomy 6:1 Now these are the commandments, the statutes, and the judgments, which the LORD your God commanded to teach you, that ye might do them in the land whither ye go to possess it:

6:2 That thou mightest fear the LORD thy God, to keep all his statutes and his commandments, which I command thee, thou, and thy son, and thy son's son, all the days of thy life; and that thy days may be prolonged.

6:3 Hear therefore, O Israel, [BOTH physical Israel and the spiritual New Covenant brethren] and observe to do it; that it may be well with thee, and that ye may increase mightily, as the LORD God of thy fathers hath promised thee, in the land that floweth with milk and honey.

The physical promised land is a type of an even better spiritual Promised Land of eternal life in the Family of God, pictured by the Feast of The Ingathering of Nations [Feast of Tabernacles].

Just as possession of the physical promised land is absolutely dependent on obedience to every Word of God; so, entry into the spiritual Promised Land of eternal life is utterly dependent on faithful obedience to every Word of God.

6:4 Hear, O Israel: The LORD our God is one LORD

The God family is united as one God family, into which will be added the children of God as they are changed to spirit.

Now comes the greatest commandment, as Jesus himself said (Mat 22:37).

6:5 And **thou shalt love the LORD thy God with all thine heart, and with all thy soul, and with all thy might.**

6:6 And **these words, which I command thee this day, shall be in thine heart: 6:7 And thou shalt teach them diligently unto thy children, and shalt talk of them when thou sittest in thine house, and when thou walkest by the way, and when thou liest down, and when thou risest up.**

6:8 And **thou shalt bind them for a sign upon thine hand** [keep them with the deeds of our hands], **and they shall be as frontlets between thine eyes** [in our minds as Jesus taught Mat 22:37] .

6:9 And **thou shalt write them upon the posts of thy house, and on thy gates.**

We must always remain faithful to the God (Elohim) Family of YHVH [the Great I AM] our Mighty One!

6:10 And it shall be, when the LORD thy God shall have brought thee into the land which he sware unto thy fathers, to Abraham, to Isaac, and to Jacob, to give thee great and goodly cities, which thou buildedst not,

6:11 And houses full of all good things, which thou filledst not, and wells digged, which thou diggedst not, vineyards and olive trees, which thou plantedst not; when thou shalt have eaten and be full;

When we think that we are full of spiritual things and have need of nothing (Rev 3:15-22); beware, because pride will cause us to stumble and depart from our God.

6:12 Then **beware lest thou forget the LORD, which brought thee forth out of the land of Egypt, from the house of bondage.**

6:13 Thou shalt fear the LORD thy God, and serve him, and shalt swear by his name.

We are not to follow idols of men as others do; we are not to accept the "Primacy of Peter" Nicolaitane church governance system; we are NOT to exalt men above the Word of God as today's Spiritual Ekklesia has done; this is absolutely forbidden by Jesus Christ.

6:14 Ye shall not go after other gods, of the gods of the people which are round about you;

6:15 (For the LORD thy God is a jealous God among you) lest the anger of the LORD thy God be kindled against thee, and destroy thee from off the face of the earth.

6:16 Ye shall not tempt the LORD your God, as ye tempted him in Massah (Ex 17:1-7).

6:17 Ye shall diligently keep the commandments of the LORD your God, and his testimonies, and his statutes, which he hath commanded thee. 6:18 And thou shalt do that which is right and good in the sight of the LORD [through living by every Word of God]: that it may be well with thee, and that thou mayest go in and possess the good land which the LORD sware unto thy fathers.

If we are diligently faithful to keep every Word of God; he will deliver us from bondage to Satan, sin and the grave, into eternal life.

6:19 To cast out all thine enemies from before thee, as the LORD hath spoken.

6:20 And when thy son asketh thee in time to come, saying, What mean the testimonies, and the statutes, and the judgments, which the LORD our God hath commanded you?

Ancient Egypt was used by God as an example of bondage to Satan and sin; and physical Israel being Called Out of Egypt was a type of spiritual Israel being Called Out of bondage to Satan, sin and death. The New Covenant Called to God through Christ are a spiritual Israel.

We are to explain to our families [especially on Passover] how God delivered ancient Israel from slavery and how God will also deliver us from bondage to Satan, sin and death if we are diligent to follow God on the road to life eternal.

6:21 Then thou shalt say unto thy son, We were Pharaoh's bondmen in Egypt; and the LORD brought us out of Egypt with a mighty hand:

6:22 And the LORD shewed signs and wonders, great and sore, upon Egypt, upon Pharaoh, and upon all his household, before our eyes: **6:23** And he brought us out from thence, that he might bring us in, to give us the land which he sware unto our fathers.

6:24 And **the LORD commanded us to do all these statutes, to fear the LORD our God, for our good always, that he might preserve us alive** [The promise of physical life and freedom to ancient Israel was an allegorical promise of eternal life for the faithful spiritual overcomers.], as it is at this day [the day this was written].

Living by every Word of God; is the biblical definition of godly righteousness.

6:25 And **it shall be our righteousness, if we observe to do all these commandments before the LORD our God, as he hath commanded us.**

Deuteronomy 7

Just as God caused Israel to destroy or drive many of the wicked Canaanites out of the Promised Land and later God removed Israel for their sins: God will also severely correct modern physical and spiritual Israel for breaking the commandments of God.

What applies to physical Israel also applies to the spiritual Israel of the New Covenant; if we are not passionate to live by every Word of God in Christ-like zeal; we will also be rejected by our LORD.

Deuteronomy 7:1 When the LORD thy God shall bring thee into the land whither thou goest to possess it, and hath cast out many nations before thee, the Hittites, and the Girgashites, and the Amorites, and the Canaanites, and the Perizzites, and the Hivites, and the Jebusites, seven nations greater and mightier than thou;

The wicked Canaanites were used as a type of the unrepentant wicked and the command to completely destroy the Canaanites was an instructional allegory, and an object lesson for us; that in due time God will destroy all the unrepentant wicked.

7:2 And when the LORD thy God shall deliver them before thee; **thou shalt smite them, and utterly destroy them; thou shalt make no covenant with them, nor shew mercy unto them**:

The forbidding of marriages with the Canaanites is a prohibition against marriages with the unconverted. The godly are not to marry and become one with those who have no zeal to live by every Word of God. Why?

7:3 Neither shalt thou make marriages with them; thy daughter thou shalt not give unto his son, nor his daughter shalt thou take unto thy son. **7:4** For **they will turn away thy son from following me, that they may serve other gods: so will the anger of the LORD be kindled against you, and destroy thee suddenly**.

The Canaanites worshiped fertility with odious orgies intended to arouse the gods to bring fertility to the earth. They and every trace of their religion was to be wiped out from the earth.

7:5 But thus shall ye deal with them; ye shall destroy their altars, and break down their images, and cut down their groves [fertility trees like the Christmas tree and also phallic symbols of obelisks], and burn their graven images with fire.

Today's Judaeo Anglo Saxon society is just as wicked as the Canaanites were, with our rampant fornication, homosexuality and adultery while denying God.

Today's Spiritual Ekklesia who are supposed to be the salt that makes this wicked world endurable to God, are just as wicked in both the physical and the spiritual sense as well. Today the assemblies are full of physical sexual sin, and we are also full of spiritual adultery against the Husband of our baptismal espousal, by following idols of men instead of being passionately zealous for our LORD.

7:6 For thou art an holy people unto the LORD thy God: the LORD thy God hath chosen thee to be a special people unto himself, above all people that are upon the face of the earth.

If physical Israel without God's Spirit was holy to God; how much more Holy to God are those with the New Covenant gift of God's Spirit? Therefore we ought to behave in holiness and godliness and we should be Holy as God is Holy.

> **1 Peter 2:9** But ye are a chosen generation, a royal priesthood, an **holy** nation, a peculiar [special] **people**; that ye should shew forth the praises of him who hath called you out of darkness into his marvellous light;

Deuteronomy 7:7 The LORD did not set his love upon you, nor choose you, because ye were more in number than any people; for ye were the fewest of all people:

7:8 But **because the LORD loved you, and because he would keep the oath which he had sworn unto your fathers**, hath the LORD brought you out with a mighty hand, and redeemed you out of the house of bondmen, from the hand of Pharaoh king of Egypt.

God is faithful to keep his Word and he has called out a certain first fruits, not because we are good and deserving, but because he is full of mercy and love and keeps his promises.

7:9 Know therefore that the LORD thy God, he is God, the faithful God, which keepeth covenant and mercy with them that love him and keep his commandments to a thousand generations;

7:10 And repayeth them that hate [those who rebel and refuse to keep his Word and Will] him to their face, to destroy them: he will not be slack to him that hateth [those who refuse to faithfully live by every Word of God and resist and rebel against God] him, he will repay him to his face.

7:11 Thou shalt therefore keep the commandments, and the statutes, and the judgments, which I command thee this day, to do them.

The Lord's blessing on the FAITHFUL who are zealous to live by every Word of God

7:12 Wherefore it shall come to pass, **if ye hearken to these judgments, and keep, and do them**, that the LORD thy God shall keep unto thee the covenant [both the Mosaic Covenant and the New Covenant of Jeremiah 31:31] and the mercy which he sware unto thy fathers:

These physical blessings for faithfulness to the Mosaic Covenant have their spiritual blessing counterparts in the New Covenant

7:13 And he will love thee, and bless thee, and multiply thee: he will also bless the fruit of thy womb, and the fruit of thy land, thy corn, and thy wine, and thine oil, the increase of thy kine, and the flocks of thy sheep, in the land which he sware unto thy fathers to give thee.

7:14 Thou shalt be blessed above all people: there shall not be male or female barren among you, or among your cattle. **7:15** And the LORD will take away from thee all sickness, and will put none of the evil diseases of Egypt, which thou knowest, upon thee; but will lay them upon all them that hate thee.

7:16 And thou shalt consume [in the Kingdom of God, the wicked will be destroyed] all the people which the LORD thy God shall deliver thee; thine eye shall have no pity upon them: neither shalt thou serve their gods; for that will be a snare unto thee.

The driving of the wicked out of the land was an analogy of us driving sin out of our lives with the help of our Deliverer; and a prophecy of the final death of the unrepentant wicked!

7:17 If thou shalt say in thine heart, These nations are more than I; how can I dispossess them?

7:18 Thou shalt not be afraid of them: but shalt well remember what the LORD thy God did unto Pharaoh, and unto all Egypt;

7:19 The great temptations which thine eyes saw, and the signs, and the wonders, and the mighty hand, and the stretched out arm, whereby the LORD thy God brought thee out: so shall the LORD thy God do unto all the people [the wicked] of whom thou art afraid.

7:20 Moreover the LORD thy God will send the hornet among them, until they that are left, and hide themselves from thee, be destroyed.

We need not fear Satan the god-king of this world, for the Almighty shall defeat him just like HE defeated the god-king of Egypt; and our Deliverer will also deliver his spiritually Called Out and grant them victory over Satan, sin and the grave.

If we follow the lead of God and live by his every Word with passionate love and zeal, God will help us until we drive every last sin out of our lives.

Just as God promised to drive out the wicked Canaanites; he has also promised to drive all sin out of sincerely repentant persons, strengthening them to overcome and to drive out all sin.

Do not fear the temptations and persecutions of the wicked:

7:21 Thou shalt not be affrighted at them: for **the LORD thy God is among you, a mighty God and terrible.**

Just as God gave the physical promised land to physical Israel; he will give the spiritual Promised Land of eternal life in peace and harmony with God and man to those faithful to live by every Word of God; and God will drive out all sin and wickedness out of us if we will only turn from our sin and follow HIM!

Just as Israel could not overcome the Canaanites on their own, we cannot overcome all sin on our own, but God will NOT leave us alone! As long as we follow HIM; he will go before us to guarantee the victory!

7:22 And the LORD thy God will put out those nations before thee by little and little: thou mayest not consume them at once, lest the beasts of the field increase upon thee.

7:23 But the LORD thy God shall deliver them unto thee, and shall destroy them with a mighty destruction, until they be destroyed.

7:24 And he shall deliver their kings into thine hand, and thou shalt destroy their name from under heaven: there shall no man be able to stand before thee, until thou have destroyed them.

God's New Covenant called out are to utterly detest and abhor idolatry including idols of men, or any other thing! If any man tells you it is alright to hire catered meals on God's Holy Sabbath's he is a wicked deceiver; do not make an idol of him by obeying him and disobeying Almighty God.

7:25 The graven images of their gods shall ye burn with fire: thou shalt not desire the silver or gold that is on them, nor take it unto thee, lest thou be snared therin: for it is an abomination to the LORD thy God.

7:26 Neither shalt thou bring an abomination [any idolatry] into thine house, lest thou be a cursed thing like it: but thou shalt utterly detest it, and thou shalt utterly abhor it; for it is a cursed thing.

Deuteronomy 8

The spiritually Called Out of the New Covenant must overcome all sin and enthusiastically live by every Word of God in order to be chosen to enter the spiritual Promised Land of eternal life at peace with God.

8:1 All the commandments which I command thee this day shall ye observe to do, that ye may live, and multiply, and go in and possess the land which the LORD sware unto your fathers.

We must be HUMBLE before our God and we must do whatever God commands, not being lifted up with pride and doing what we think is right.

8:2 And thou shalt remember all the way which the LORD thy God led thee these forty years in the wilderness, **to humble thee, and to prove [test] thee, to know what was in thine heart, whether thou wouldest keep his commandments, or no.**

The manna from heaven was a type of the Bread of Life, Jesus Christ and the whole Word of God

8:3 And he humbled thee, and suffered thee to hunger, and fed thee with manna, which thou knewest not, neither did thy fathers know; that he might make thee know **that man doth not live by bread only, but by every word that proceedeth out of the mouth of the LORD doth man live.**

God used physical hunger and thirst to teach them and us how we are to hunger and thirst after the righteousness of God. The word righteousness means "to be right" and in the scriptural sense means to be like God and to live as Christ lived, to live by every Word of God.

We know John tells us that Jesus is the Logos the Word of God, who inspired the entirety of Holy Scriptures, and we see in the Exodus study that God gave Israel manna to eat and living waters from the rock to drink in the wilderness.

This manna was an allegorical type that God would feed spiritual Israel with the whole Word of God which is the Bread of Life; Jesus Christ in print.

This manna was sweet like honey:

> **Exodus 16:31** And the house of Israel called the name thereof Manna: and it was like coriander seed, white; and the taste of it was like **wafers made with honey.**

David teaches us that God's Word is sweeter than honey like the Manna; and like honey God's Word is the sweetest thing, more to be desired than great physical treasure!

> **Psalm 19:7** The law of the Lord is perfect, converting the soul: the testimony of the Lord is sure, making wise the simple.
>
> **19:8** The statutes of the Lord are right, rejoicing the heart: the commandment of the Lord is pure, enlightening the eyes.
>
> **19:9** The fear of the Lord is clean, enduring for ever: the judgments of the Lord are true and righteous altogether.
>
> **19:10** More to be desired are they than gold, yea, than much fine gold: sweeter also than honey and the honeycomb.
>
> **John 6:35** And Jesus said unto them, I am the bread of life: he that cometh to me shall never hunger; and he that believeth on me shall never thirst.

Jesus also said that he was the Fountain of Living Waters of the Holy Spirit of God, on the last day of the Feast of Tabernacles.

> Jesus said: **Matthew 5:6** Blessed are they which do hunger and thirst after righteousness: for they shall be filled.

Deuteronomy 8:4 Thy raiment waxed not old upon thee, neither did thy foot swell, these forty years.

The LORD chastens those who fall astray to save us out of our pride and sin because of his great love for us, just as a good father chastens a wayward child.

8:5 Thou shalt also consider in thine heart, that, **as a man chasteneth his son, so the LORD thy God chasteneth thee.**

8:6 Therefore **thou shalt keep the commandments of the LORD thy God, to walk in his ways, and to fear him.**

8:7 For the LORD thy God bringeth thee into a good land, a land of brooks of water, of fountains and depths that spring out of valleys and hills; **8:8** A land of wheat, and barley, and vines, and fig trees, and pomegranates; a land of oil olive, and honey; **8:9** A land wherein thou shalt eat bread without scarceness, thou shalt not lack any thing in it; a land whose stones are iron, and out of whose hills thou mayest dig brass.

8:10 When thou hast eaten and art full, then thou shalt bless the LORD thy God for the good land which he hath given thee.

Both physical Israel and Judah have rejected living by every Word of God [despite their lip-service to godliness] and are now ripe for another final correction; and unless we quickly and sincerely repent our judgment will now come very quickly.

Today's Spiritual New Covenant Ekklesia has also turned aside from God and has fallen away into idolizing men and corporate entities as we were warned against in 2 Thessalonians 2:3, Jude and many other scriptures.

How can we speak the word "God" and yet forget him? By forgetting to do what God has commanded us to do!

8:11 Beware that thou forget not the LORD thy God, in not keeping his commandments, and his judgments, and his statutes, which I command thee this day:

8:12 Lest when thou hast eaten and art full, and hast built goodly houses, and dwelt therein; **8:13** And when thy herds and thy flocks multiply, and thy silver and thy gold is multiplied, and all that thou hast is multiplied;

Spiritually; Beware of becoming proud and beginning to think that we have all understanding and have need of nothing (Rev 3:14-22), lest we turn from our zeal to live by every Word of God and lean to our own ways.

8:14 Then **thine heart be lifted up, and thou forget the LORD thy God**, which brought thee forth out of the land of Egypt, from the house of bondage; **8:15** Who led thee through that great and terrible wilderness, wherein were fiery serpents, and scorpions, and drought, where there was no water; who brought thee forth water out of the rock of flint; **8:16** Who fed thee in the wilderness with manna, which thy fathers knew not, that he might humble thee, and that he might prove thee, to do thee good at thy latter end;

Just as God gave strength and many blessings of physical wealth to the faithful of the Mosaic Covenant; it is God Almighty who gives spiritual power to get the spiritual wealth of knowledge and understanding in the New Covenant.

In either case, those who become full of pride in what they have and forsake their God; shall be forsaken by God and will fall into serious correction.

8:17 And thou say in thine heart, **My power and the might of mine hand hath gotten me this wealth.**

8:18 But **thou shalt remember the LORD thy God: for it is he that giveth thee power to get wealth, that he may establish his covenant** which he sware unto thy fathers, as it is this day.

Those who forget to keep the commandments of the Eternal will once again be sternly corrected until they learn their lesson and sincerely repent: Then a revival of godliness greater than that of the time of Ezra will come!

Judah has forgotten the law of her God and has filled the land with all manner of abominations; therefore Judah will face one last correction to be humbled and made ready for the coming of Messiah!

Make no mistake! A soon coming final correction of Judah, including both physical and spiritual Israel is at hand.

Today's apostate Spiritual Ekklesia will also be rejected by Jesus Christ and cast into great tribulation to afflict the flesh in the hope that the spirit might be saved (Rev 3:15-22).

8:19 And it shall be, if thou do at all forget the LORD thy God, and walk after other gods, and serve them, and worship them, I testify against you this day that ye shall surely perish.

8:20 As the nations which the LORD destroyeth before your face, so shall ye perish; because ye would not be obedient unto the voice of the LORD your God.

Deuteronomy 9

Say not; "God blesses us because we are good righteous folks." No, God has blessed us and allowed us a period of blessing to keep his promises to his friends in ancient times.

Deuteronomy 9:1 Hear, O Israel: Thou art to pass over Jordan this day, to go in to possess nations greater and mightier than thyself, cities great and fenced up to heaven, **9:2** A people great and tall, the children of the Anakims, whom thou knowest, and of whom thou hast heard say, Who can stand before the children of Anak!

Just as God gave them victory over the wicked as long as they faithfully followed the Eternal; so God will give us victory over sin [and ultimately victory over death itself] as long as we faithfully follow him!

9:3 Understand therefore this day, that the LORD thy God is he which goeth over before thee; as a consuming fire he shall destroy them, and he shall bring them down before thy face: so shalt thou drive them out, and destroy them quickly, as the LORD hath said unto thee.

It is NOT because of our righteousness that God has called us out of bondage to sin; it is because **God is righteous and keeps HIS promises** which he made to his servants the prophets.

Today physical Israel and the Ekklesia of spiritual Israel are full to the top and running over with pride in ourselves as we follow our own ways and turn aside from the Word of God. For this apostasy we will surely be afflicted one last time.

9:4 Speak not thou in thine heart, after that the LORD thy God hath cast them out from before thee, saying, For my righteousness the LORD hath brought me in to possess this land: but for the wickedness of these nations the LORD doth drive them out from before thee.

9:5 Not for thy righteousness, or for the uprightness of thine heart, dost thou go to possess their land: but for the wickedness of these nations the LORD thy God doth drive them out from before thee, and that he may perform the word which the LORD sware unto thy fathers, Abraham, Isaac, and Jacob.

Physical Israel continually provoked the Eternal, and today's spiritual New Covenant Ekklesia has provoked our LORD by our continual idolatry in following idols of men away from the Husband of our baptismal commitment.

9:6 Understand therefore, that the LORD thy God giveth thee not this good land to possess it for thy righteousness; for thou art a stiffnecked [stubborn self-willed] people.

9:7 Remember, and forget not, how thou provokedst the LORD thy God to wrath in the wilderness: from the day that thou didst depart out of the land of Egypt, until ye came unto this place, ye have been rebellious against the LORD.

9:8 Also in Horeb ye provoked the LORD to wrath [with the gold calf (an Egyptian god) at Sinai], so that the LORD was angry with you to have destroyed you.

9:9 When I was gone up into the mount to receive the tables of stone, even the tables of the covenant which the LORD made with you, then I abode in the mount forty days and forty nights, I neither did eat bread nor drink water:

9:10 And the LORD delivered unto me two tables of stone written with the finger of God; and on them was written according to all the words, which the LORD spake with you in the mount out of the midst of the fire in the day of the assembly.

9:11 And it came to pass at the end of forty days and forty nights, that the LORD gave me the two tables of stone, even the tables of the covenant.

9:12 And the LORD said unto me, Arise, get thee down quickly from hence; for thy people which thou hast brought forth out of Egypt have corrupted themselves; they are quickly turned aside out of the way which I commanded them; they have made them a molten image.

9:13 Furthermore the LORD spake unto me, saying, I have seen this people, and, behold, it is a stiffnecked people:

9:14 Let me alone, that I may destroy them, and blot out their name from under heaven: and I will make of thee a nation mightier and greater than they.

9:15 So I turned and came down from the mount, and the mount burned with fire: and the two tables of the covenant were in my two hands.

God would have destroyed Israel already at Sinai, but he was merciful because of his promises to the ancients and because of the intercession of Moses.

Just as Moses was the only intercessor between God and man in the Mosaic Covenant; even so, Jesus Christ has become the ONLY Mediator between man and God in the New Covenant.

> **1 Timothy 2:5** For there is one God, and one mediator between God and men, the man [while in the flesh] Christ Jesus; [NOT Mary, or any man]

Deuteronomy 9:16 And I looked, and, behold, ye had sinned against the LORD your God, and had made you a molten calf [idol]: ye had turned aside quickly out of the way which the LORD had commanded you.

9:17 And I took the two tables, and cast them out of my two hands, and brake them before your eyes.

The tables were broken to demonstrate that exalting anything between us and God breaks our covenant with him.

Mosaic Covenant Israel said "here is your god" referring to the idols of calves; so today the elders and leaders of the Ekklesia say to the people that they should live by the words of men in place of any zeal to live by every Word of God. Today the golden calves of the Ekklesia are idols of men and corporate entities.

Moses repented on behalf of the people and asked God to save the people alive.

9:18 And I fell down before the LORD, as at the first, forty days and forty nights: **I did neither eat bread, nor drink water**, because of all your sins which ye sinned, in doing wickedly in the sight of the LORD, to provoke him to anger. **9:19** For I was afraid of the anger and hot displeasure, wherewith the LORD was wroth against you to destroy you. But the LORD hearkened unto me at that time also.

9:20 And the LORD was very angry with Aaron to have destroyed him: and I prayed for Aaron also the same time.

9:21 And I took your sin, the calf which ye had made, and burnt it with fire, and stamped it, and ground it very small, even until it was as small as dust: and I cast the dust thereof into the brook that descended out of the mount.

Today Jesus Christ is about to destroy our golden calves of corporate entities and false teachers; grinding them to dust in the great correction which is now at the very door.

9:22 And at Taberah, and at Massah, and at Kibrothhattaavah, ye provoked the LORD to wrath.

9:23 Likewise when the LORD sent you from Kadeshbarnea, saying, Go up and possess the land which I have given you; then ye rebelled against the commandment of the LORD your God, and ye believed him not, nor hearkened to his voice.

9:24 Ye have been rebellious against the LORD from the day that I knew you.

9:25 Thus I fell down before the LORD forty days and forty nights, as I fell down at the first; because the LORD had said he would destroy you.

Today's Spiritual Ekklesia, like ancient Israel, is worthy of complete destruction for our idolatry of men and corporations against our God; but those who sincerely repent will be saved.

9:26 I prayed therefore unto the LORD, and said, O Lord GOD, destroy not thy people and thine inheritance, which thou hast redeemed through thy greatness, which thou hast brought forth out of Egypt with a mighty hand.

9:27 Remember thy servants, Abraham, Isaac, and Jacob; look not unto the stubbornness of this people, nor to their wickedness, nor to their sin: **9:28** Lest the land whence thou broughtest us out say, Because the LORD was not able to bring them into the land which he promised them, and because he hated them, he hath brought them out to slay them in the wilderness.

9:29 Yet they are thy people and thine inheritance, which thou broughtest out by thy mighty power and by thy stretched out arm.

Deuteronomy 10

God's ten basic commandments were again written by God on a second two tables of stone.

Deuteronomy 10:1 At that time the LORD said unto me, Hew thee two tables of stone like unto the first, and come up unto me into the mount, and make thee an ark of wood. **10:2** And **I will write on the tables the words that were in the first tables which thou brakest,** and thou shalt put them in the ark.

10:3 And I made an ark of shittim [Acacia wood] wood, and hewed two tables of stone like unto the first, and went up into the mount, having the two tables in mine hand. **10:4** And **he** [God] **wrote on the tables**, according to the first writing, the ten commandments, which the LORD spake unto you in the mount out of the midst of the fire in the day of the assembly: and the LORD gave them unto me.

10:5 And I turned myself and came down from the mount, and put the tables in the ark which I had made; and there they be, as the LORD commanded me.

A short inset about the death of Aaron

>**10:6** And the children of Israel took their journey from Beeroth of the children of Jaakan to Mosera: there Aaron died, and there he was buried; and Eleazar his son ministered in the priest's office in his stead.

10:7 From thence they journeyed unto Gudgodah; and from Gudgodah to Jotbath, a land of rivers of waters.

Moses continues to speak about Mt Sinai

10:8 At that time [at Mt Sinai] the LORD separated the tribe of Levi, to bear the ark of the covenant of the LORD, to stand before the LORD to minister unto him, and to bless in his name, unto this day. **10:9** Wherefore Levi hath no part nor inheritance with his brethren; the LORD is his inheritance, according as the LORD thy God promised him.

10:10 And **I stayed in the mount, according to the first time**, forty days and forty nights; and the LORD hearkened unto me at that time also, and the LORD would not destroy thee.

Moses speaks about the journey of Israel after the Passover of the second year at Sinai.

> **Numbers 9:1** And the LORD spake unto Moses in the wilderness of Sinai, **in the first month of the second year after they were come out of the land of Egypt, saying,**

Deuteronomy 10:11 And the LORD said unto me, Arise, take thy journey before the people, that they may go in and possess the land, which I sware unto their fathers to give unto them.

Below, is what God requires of all his people! BOTH the physically called out of Egypt of the Mosaic Covenant, Judah/Israel; and the spiritually called out of the New Covenant!

10:12 And now, Israel, **what doth the LORD thy God require of thee, but to fear the LORD thy God, to walk in all his ways, and to love him, and to serve the LORD thy God with all thy heart and with all thy soul,**

10:13 To keep the commandments of the LORD, and his statutes, which I command thee this day for thy good?

10:14 Behold, the heaven and the heaven of heavens is the LORD's thy God, the earth also, with all that therein is.

God took delight in Abraham and therefore called Abraham's descendants out of Egypt according to his promises. God has also called us to become the spiritual children of Abraham, calling us to become like faithful Abraham; therefore let us also sincerely repent of our idolatry of men.

> **Galatians 3:7** Know ye therefore that **they which are of faith, the same are the children of Abraham.**

Galatians 3:29 And if ye be Christ's, then are ye **Abraham's seed,** and heirs according to the promise.

Deuteronomy 10:15 Only the LORD had a delight in thy fathers to love them, and he chose their seed after them, even you above all people, as it is this day.

10:16 Circumcise therefore the foreskin of your heart [let us also sincerely repent of our idolatry and rebellion against our LORD], **and be no more stiffnecked** [stubborn and self-willed to resist God].

10:17 For **the LORD your God is God of gods, and Lord of lords, a great God, a mighty, and a terrible, which regardeth not persons, nor taketh reward: 10:18** He doth execute the judgment of the fatherless and widow, and loveth the stranger, in giving him food and raiment.

10:19 Love ye therefore the stranger: for ye were strangers in the land of Egypt.

10:20 Thou shalt fear the LORD thy God; him shalt thou serve, and to him shalt thou cleave, and swear by his name.

The Eternal is the Mighty God who alone saves; therefore let us leave off this exalting of idols of men and their false traditions, and our rejection of any zeal to keep the Word of God.

10:21 He is thy praise, and he is thy God, that hath done for thee these great and terrible things, which thine eyes have seen.

10:22 Thy fathers went down into Egypt with threescore and ten [male] persons; and now the LORD thy God hath made thee as the stars of heaven for multitude.

Deuteronomy 11

Deuteronomy 11:1 Therefore **thou shalt love the LORD thy God, and keep his charge, and his statutes, and his judgments, and his commandments, always.**

God has done many mighty deeds to deliver physical Israel from bondage in Egypt, and he has done many mighty deeds to deliver the New Covenant brethren out from bondage to Satan, sin and eternal death.

These mighty deeds of God in delivering physical Israel were recorded to encourage the Spiritual Ekklesia that our Mighty One is faithful and powerful to keep all of his promises of salvation, if we will only follow him in dedicated zeal.

11:2 And know ye this day: for I speak not with your children which have not known, and which have not seen the chastisement of the LORD your God, his greatness, his mighty hand, and his stretched out arm, **11:3** And his miracles, and his acts, which he did in the midst of Egypt unto Pharaoh the king of Egypt, and unto all his land;

Just as God destroyed Pharaoh the god-king of Egypt; God will also destroy Satan the god-king of the wicked. And the sincerely repentant who are passionate to follow the Lamb of God whithersoever he goeth will rise up from the grave in total victory over Satan, sin and death; just like physical Israel came up out of the grave of the Red Sea.

11:4 And what he did unto the army of Egypt, unto their horses, and to their chariots; how he made the water of the Red sea to overflow them as they pursued after you, and how the LORD hath destroyed them unto this day;

Remember God's correction on the stubborn self-willed among physical Israel; because God will not hold back from also correcting the spiritually called out when they go astray from him.

11:5 And what he did unto you in the wilderness, until ye came into this place; **11:6** And what he did unto Dathan and Abiram, the sons of Eliab, the son of Reuben: how the earth opened her mouth, and swallowed them up, and their households, and their tents, and all the substance that was in their possession, in the midst of all Israel:

These things were recorded for our instruction so that we might learn to live by every Word of God, and enter the Promised Land of eternal life.

11:7 But your eyes have seen all the great acts of the LORD which he did.

11:8 Therefore shall ye keep all the commandments which I command you this day, that ye may be strong, and go in and possess the land, whither ye go to possess it; **11:9** And that ye may prolong your days in the land, which the LORD sware unto your fathers to give unto them and to their seed, a land that floweth with milk and honey.

All of these things were recorded for our instruction and we have indeed seen many miracles of deliverance in our own lives.

We should be full of faith in our God and his power to deliver us out of ALL our trials. We should know to run to our High Tower of Strength and our Deliverer in times of stress; and we should NEVER seek to prevent persecution from the wicked by hiding our light of zeal for our Great God, or by compromising with our faithfulness.

We should personally and as groups, practice what we preach and boldly declare and dedicatedly live by every Word of the LORD; without compromise or watering down to avoid offending the wicked.

11:10 For the land, whither thou goest in to possess it, is not as the land of Egypt, from whence ye came out, where thou sowedst thy seed, and wateredst it with thy foot [a foot pump, used for irrigation], as a garden of herbs:

Today the land is not as it was; yet once the people sincerely repent and turn to godliness as the Kingdom of God begins; God's blessings will again rain down on the land.

11:11 But the land, whither ye go to possess it, is a land of hills and valleys, and drinketh water of the rain of heaven:

11:12 A land which the LORD thy God careth for: the eyes of the LORD thy God are always upon it, from the beginning of the year even unto the end of the year.

A good land is promised to the people who live by every Word of God; and a wonderful eternity with God is promised to those who overcome and keep the Spiritual New Covenant of Marriage with Jesus Christ and very Lamb of God.

Physical blessings for obedience; all of which have their spiritual counterparts

11:13 And it shall come to pass, **if ye shall hearken diligently unto my commandments which I command you this day, to love the LORD your God, and to serve him with all your heart and with all your soul,**

11:14 That I will give you the rain of your land [spiritually, God's Spirit will rain down upon the faithful] in his due season, the first rain and the latter rain [The seasonal spring and fall rains are a type of God pouring his Spirit first on the early first fruits faithful, and later on the sincerely repentant main fall harvest of humanity.], that thou mayest gather in thy corn [grain], and thy wine, and thine oil [as a type that God will gather in the harvest of humanity].

The faithful to live by every Word of God will produce much spiritual fruit through the blessings of God's Spirit.

11:15 And I will send grass in thy fields for thy cattle, that thou mayest eat and be full.

When we are blessed we must be careful not to become filled with pride and so thinking ourselves wise depart from our zeal to follow our God, and begin to go our own ways following idols of men as is done in the Ekklesia today.

11:16 Take heed to yourselves, that your heart be not deceived, and ye turn aside, and serve other gods, and worship them;

Just as God shuts up the rain on the land for wickedness; he will also withhold his Holy Spirit from those who are not zealous to live by his Word.

11:17 And then the LORD's wrath be kindled against you, and he shut up the heaven, that there be no rain, and that the land yield not her fruit; and lest ye perish quickly from off the good land which the LORD giveth you.

11:18 Therefore shall ye lay up these my words in your heart and in your soul, and bind them for a sign upon your hand [keep and live by the Word of God, fulfilling God's Word in our every deed], that they may be as frontlets between your eyes [keep God's Word always in our minds and hearts].

The duty of parents

11:19 And ye shall teach them [diligently teach God's Word] **your children, speaking of them when thou sittest in thine house, and when thou walkest by the way, when thou liest down, and when thou risest up.**

11:20 And thou shalt write them upon the door posts of thine house, and upon thy gates: [God's Word should always be foremost in our thoughts, and everywhere we look God's Word should come to mind.]

11:21 That your days may be multiplied, and the days of your children, in the land which the LORD sware unto your fathers to give them, as the days of heaven upon the earth.

Let our meditation be upon the things of God day and night, as it was with the Lord's beloved David (Psalm 119).

11:22 For **if ye shall diligently keep all these commandments which I command you, to do them, to love the LORD your God, to walk in all his ways, and to cleave unto him;**

If the New Covenant called out are diligent to zealously live by every Word of God, then through the power of God we will be given total victory over Satan and bondage to sin and the grave.

11:23 Then will the LORD drive out all these nations [after their sins came to the full, the Canaanites became symbolic of Satanic wickedness] from before you, and ye shall possess greater nations and mightier than yourselves.

In the spiritual sense; if we are faithful to follow the Lamb of God, God will drive out all sin from within us and defeat Satan and his supporters who oppress us, and we shall inherit eternal life and a place in The Eternal Kingdom of God.

The millennial borders of the physical promised land in the Middle East; to which will be added the additional lands that the nations of Israel have been given through the ancient blessings.

11:24 Every place whereon the soles of your feet shall tread shall be yours: from the wilderness and Lebanon, from the river, the river Euphrates, even unto the uttermost sea shall your coast be.

Spiritually speaking, neither Satan nor any of his supporters can prevail against us on the spiritual plane; no not even the grave can conquer those who are zealously faithful followers of God the Father and the Lamb of God!

11:25 There shall no man be able to stand before you: for the LORD your God shall lay the fear of you and the dread of you upon all the land that ye shall tread upon, as he hath said unto you.

The physical promised land and Theocracy of Israel was a type of the eternal Kingdom of God!

Possession of the spiritual Promised Land of eternal life with God is CONDITIONAL on our faithful obedience to HIM; just as possession of the physical promised land by Israel is CONDITIONAL on their faithful obedience to God.

The blessings for the faithful to God and the curses for following idols of men to do what seems right in our own eyes.

Each of these points has its spiritual counterpart.

11:26 Behold, I set before you this day a blessing and a curse;

11:27 A blessing, if ye obey the commandments of the LORD your God, which I command you this day:

Today's Spiritual Ekklesia obeys men and not God; we have gone after other gods, making men our idol gods in place of the Eternal

11:28 And a curse, if ye will not obey the commandments of the LORD your God, but turn aside out of the way which I command you this day, to go after other gods, which ye have not known.

11:29 And it shall come to pass, when the LORD thy God hath brought thee in unto the land whither thou goest to possess it, that **thou shalt put the blessing upon mount Gerizim, and the curse upon mount Ebal.**

11:30 Are they not on the other side Jordan, by the way where the sun goeth down [on the west side of Jordan in the land], in the land of the Canaanites, which dwell in the champaign over against Gilgal, beside the plains of Moreh?

11:31 For ye shall pass over Jordan to go in to possess the land which the LORD your God giveth you, and ye shall possess it, and dwell therein.

11:32 And ye shall observe to do all the statutes and judgments which I set before you this day.

Deuteronomy 12

Deuteronomy 12:1 These are the statutes and judgments, which ye shall observe to do in the land, which the LORD God of thy fathers giveth thee to possess it, all the days that ye live upon the earth.

This is what God requires of us for all eternity: To utterly destroy all sin and evil, and to live by every Word of God always; without even a hint of compromise.

Just as God commanded physical Israel to destroy all idolatry; the spiritually called out are to destroy all spiritual idolatry; which also includes idols of men and corporate entities. We are to follow the Eternal God the Father and Jesus Christ only: Proving the words of men by the Word of God and following only the Word of God!

1 Thessalonians 5:21 Prove all things; hold fast that which is good

The pagans often worshiped by green [evergreen] trees, which were regarded as fertility symbols and as symbols of everlasting life; a prime example being the Christmas tree.

Deuteronomy 12:2 Ye shall utterly destroy all the places, wherein the nations which ye shall possess served their gods, upon the high mountains, and upon the hills, and under every green tree:

12:3 And ye shall overthrow their altars, and break their pillars, and burn their groves with fire; and ye shall hew down the graven images of their gods, and destroy the names of them out of that place.

We must NOT worship our God as others worship their gods; instead we must worship GOD in the way that God commands us! We must NOT do what is right in our own eyes; we must DO what God has commanded us!

12:4 Ye shall not do so unto the LORD your God.

We are to seek God alone and to worship him through living by every Word of God.

12:5 But unto the place which the LORD your God shall choose out of all your tribes to put his name there, even unto his habitation shall ye seek, and thither thou shalt come:

God chose to place his presence in the tabernacle until he later chose Jerusalem during the days of David and Solomon.

12:6 And thither ye shall bring your burnt offerings, and your sacrifices, and your tithes, and heave offerings of your hand, and your vows, and your freewill offerings, and the firstlings of your herds and of your flocks: **12:7** And there ye shall eat before the LORD your God, and ye shall rejoice in all that ye put your hand unto, ye and your households, wherein the LORD thy God hath blessed thee.

At this point the tabernacle had been set up and it is assumed that they would be entering the land immediately. Once the tabernacle was set up, sacrifices were to be made at the tabernacle before God, and they could no longer offer sacrifices anywhere they wanted.

12:8 Ye shall not do after all the things that we do here this day, every man whatsoever is right in his own eyes. 12:9 For ye are not as yet come to the rest and to the inheritance, which the LORD your God giveth you. **12:10** But when ye go over Jordan, and dwell in the land which the LORD your God giveth you to inherit, and when he giveth you rest from all your enemies round about, so that ye dwell in safety;

Speaking of the future religious activities in the promised land, not coming before the Eternal at his tabernacle/temple while claiming to worship God by sacrificing elsewhere was a symbolic type of deciding for ourselves to do as we please.

It is because there is no temple today that physical sacrifices are not to be offered until the new Ezekiel Temple is built by Messiah when he comes.

12:11 Then there shall be a place which the LORD your God shall choose to cause his name to dwell there; thither shall ye bring all that I

command you; your burnt offerings, and your sacrifices, your tithes, and the heave offering of your hand, and all your choice vows which ye vow unto the LORD:

12:12 And ye shall rejoice before the LORD your God, ye, and your sons, and your daughters, and your menservants, and your maidservants, and the Levite that is within your gates; forasmuch as he hath no part nor inheritance with you.

Sacrifices could ONLY be made at the tabernacle or later the temple in Jerusalem.

12:13 Take heed to thyself that thou offer not thy burnt offerings in every place that thou seest:

12:14 But in the place which the LORD shall choose in one of thy tribes, there thou shalt offer thy burnt offerings, and there thou shalt do all that I command thee [regarding sacrifices and the tabernacle / temple service].

12:15 Notwithstanding thou mayest kill and eat flesh in all thy gates, whatsoever thy soul lusteth after, according to the blessing of the LORD thy God which he hath given thee: the unclean and the clean may eat thereof, as of the roebuck, and as of the hart.

12:16 Only ye shall not eat the blood; ye shall pour it upon the earth as water.

> We must NOT eat any blood in any way. We must be very careful to avoid such things as bloody unwashed meat or so called supplements containing hemoglobin or other blood and blood components.

This next instruction is about the Festival tithes and vows. Remember that the Levites were a tribe in Israel with their own widows, orphans and handicapped; this is not talking about giving gifts to already paid elders. The Levitical priesthood of the Mosaic Covenant was done away by the death of Christ; who upon his resurrection was exalted to the restored spirit high priesthood of Melchizedek.

A new priesthood of Levi will yet be called into the New Covenant and serve in the physical things of the Ezekiel Temple.

On the other hand we should remember to share with the unpaid faithful elders, deacons and volunteer brethren who do so much for the brethren out of a real and sincere love, many of whom may well be in genuine need.

The festival tithe and freewill offerings

12:17 Thou mayest not eat within thy gates the tithe of thy corn [grain], or of thy wine, or of thy oil, or the firstlings of thy herds or of thy flock, nor any of thy vows which thou vowest, nor thy freewill offerings, or heave offering of thine hand:

12:18 But thou must eat them before the LORD thy God in the place which the LORD thy God shall choose, thou, and thy son, and thy daughter, and thy manservant, and thy maidservant, and the Levite that is within thy gates: and thou shalt rejoice before the LORD thy God in all that thou puttest thine hands unto.

12:19 Take heed to thyself that thou forsake not the Levite as long as thou livest upon the earth.

People are allowed to kill and eat meat anywhere, but the official sacrifices must still be made ONLY at the temple in Jerusalem.

12:20 When the LORD thy God shall enlarge thy border, as he hath promised thee, and thou shalt say, I will eat flesh, because thy soul longeth to eat flesh; thou mayest eat flesh, whatsoever thy soul lusteth [lawfully desires] after.

I would expect that during the millennium instead of the whole population of the earth going up to Jerusalem three times a year.

The festivals would be observed locally including the eating of meat, but official delegations from all nations would go up to Jerusalem where the sacrifices would be made to God for the Festivals.

12:21 If the place which the LORD thy God hath chosen to put his name there be too far from thee, then thou shalt kill of thy herd and of thy flock, which the LORD hath given thee, as I have commanded thee, and thou shalt eat in thy gates whatsoever thy soul lusteth after. **12:22** Even as the roebuck and the hart is eaten, so thou shalt eat them: the unclean and the clean shall eat of them alike.

12:23 Only be sure that thou eat not the blood: for the blood is the life; and thou mayest not eat the life with the flesh. 12:24 Thou shalt not eat it; thou shalt pour it upon the earth as water. 12:25 Thou shalt not eat it; that it may go well with thee, and with thy children after thee, when thou shalt do that which is right in the sight of the LORD.

12:26 Only thy holy things [the animals for sacrifice must be taken to the temple at Jerusalem to be offered to God] which thou hast, and thy [the sacrifices of the Nazarites] vows, **thou shalt take, and go unto the place which the LORD shall choose:**

12:27 And **thou shalt offer thy burnt offerings, the flesh and the blood, upon the altar of the LORD thy God: and the blood of thy sacrifices shall be poured out upon the altar of the LORD thy God, and thou shalt eat the flesh.**

12:28 Observe and hear all these words which I command thee, that it may go well with thee, and with thy children after thee for ever, when thou doest that which is good and right in the sight of the LORD thy God.

12:29 When the LORD thy God shall cut off the nations from before thee, whither thou goest to possess them, and thou succeedest them, and dwellest in their land;

We must NOT add to or diminish from God's Word. Be very careful to prove ALL things by the Word of God and hold fast that which is scripturally proven.

God's Word must be our standard: NOT the words of any man. Do not follow idols of men who try to deceive us into turning aside from any zeal for God with smooth words and clever reasoning's.

12:30 Take heed to thyself that thou be not snared by following them, after that they be destroyed from before thee; and that thou enquire not after their gods, saying, How did these nations serve their gods? even so will I do likewise.

12:31 Thou shalt not do so unto the LORD thy God: for every abomination to the LORD, which he hateth, have they done unto their gods; for even their sons and their daughters they have burnt in the fire to their gods.

12:32 What thing soever I command you, observe to do it: thou shalt not add thereto, nor diminish from it.

Deuteronomy 13

Miracles and fulfilled predictions are not proof of godliness or that anyone is a messenger from God. God's messengers often foretell events and do perform miracles by the power of God, but Satan's agents can also do these things.

God tells Moses and he tells us how to discern the difference between the true man of God and Satan's counterfeits.

Deuteronomy 13:1 If there arise among you a prophet, or a dreamer of dreams, and giveth thee a sign or a wonder [makes a prediction, or performs a miracle],

13:2 And the sign or the wonder come to pass, whereof he spake unto thee, saying, Let us go after [exalts anything including any person, rather than the Eternal] other gods, which thou hast not known, and let us serve them;

13:3 Thou shalt not hearken unto the words of that prophet, or that dreamer of dreams: for the LORD your God proveth [is testing us] you, **to know whether ye love the LORD your God with all your heart and with all your soul.**

God Tests His People!

God wants to know just how much we really love HIM! Do we truly love God enough to do what God says; or will we be turned aside by every person who claims to be from God?

13:4 Ye shall walk after the LORD your God, and fear him, and keep his commandments, and obey his voice, and ye shall serve him, and cleave unto him.

Those who seek to dominate the brethren and cause people to follow after themselves and their false traditions in place of the Word of Almighty God will be destroyed by the Eternal if they do not sincerely repent.

Brethren, that means that nearly every church of God leader and elder is facing rejection by Jesus Christ (Rev 3:15-22) and stern correction in the soon coming great tribulation for exalting idols of men and false traditions above the Word of God.

13:5 And that prophet, or that dreamer of dreams, **shall be put to death; because he hath spoken to turn you away from the LORD your God,** which brought you out of the land of Egypt, and redeemed you out of the house of bondage, to thrust thee out of the way which the LORD thy God commanded thee to walk in. So shalt thou put the evil away from the midst of thee.

Miracles and fulfilled prophecy are not proof of whether a man is of God or not: the proof that a person is godly is their zeal and faithfulness to live by and to teach others to live by, every Word of God.

Anyone who waters down or diminishes, or adds to God's Word; is to be rejected as if he does not exist for us. We are not to make idols of any person or thing to put them before God, not even a member of our own family.

> **Matthew 10:37** He that loveth father or mother more than me is not worthy of me: and he that loveth son or daughter more than me is not worthy of me.

Deuteronomy 13:6 If thy brother, the son of thy mother, or thy son, or thy daughter, or the wife of thy bosom, or thy friend, which is as thine own soul [body] , entice thee secretly, saying, Let us go and serve other gods, which thou hast not known, thou, nor thy fathers;

We are not to follow anyone to make an idol of them and obey them in place of obeying God; and we are not to conceal those who seek to deceive the brethren into following themselves or anything other than the Eternal, but we are commanded by Almighty God to reveal this wickedness and to warn the brethren.

We have become soft hearted about wickedness and evil deceitful men! Almighty God is outraged at such misguided pity for those who would steal our crowns and our potential eternal lives!

13:7 Namely, of the gods of the people which are round about you, nigh unto thee, or far off from thee, **from the one end of the earth even unto the other end of the earth;**

13:8 Thou shalt not consent unto him, nor hearken unto him; neither shall thine eye pity him, neither shalt thou spare, **neither shalt thou conceal him**:

13:9 But thou shalt surely kill him; thine hand shall be first upon him to put him to death, and afterwards the hand of all the people. **13:10** And thou shalt stone him with stones, that he die; because he hath sought to thrust [or to deceive] thee away from the LORD thy God, which brought thee out of the land of Egypt, from the house of bondage.

13:11 And all Israel shall hear, and fear, and shall do no more any such wickedness as this is among you.

In the New Covenant such people are to be publicly brought before the people with proof and then they are to be rejected by all of the brethren (Titus 3:10).

Do you dabble in Astrology, or celebrate birthdays in the pagan manner, or go to Easter or Christmas celebrations instead of keeping the Biblical Festivals of God? Do you allow crosses [symbols of Tammuz] or pictures of Saturn falsely labeled Christ in your home?

Do we call God's Sabbath's holy and then pollute them because some man says it is alright to do so? Do we claim to be observing God's High Days as we observe dates other than what God has commanded? Do we idolize men and false traditions above the Word of God, cleaving to them and justifying our sin of rejecting godly knowledge?

How much do we exalt the words of men and do the things that Almighty God hates? How can we claim to love God when we do what God hates?

See how serious God is about apostasy!

13:12 If thou shalt hear say in one of thy cities, which the LORD thy God hath given thee to dwell there, saying,

13:13 Certain men, the children of Belial, are gone out from among you, and have withdrawn the inhabitants of their city, saying, Let us go and serve other gods, which ye have not known;

13:14 Then shalt thou enquire, and make search, and ask diligently; and, behold, if it be truth, and the thing certain, that such abomination is wrought among you;

The New Covenant called out are to reject all false teachers who would demand that we exalt them above the Word of God; and we are to reject all those who would commit idolatry by following such wicked men.

13:15 Thou shalt surely smite the inhabitants of that city with the edge of the sword, destroying it utterly, and all that is therein, and the cattle thereof, with the edge of the sword.

13:16 And thou shalt gather all the spoil of it into the midst of the street thereof, and shalt burn with fire the city, and all the spoil thereof every whit, for the LORD thy God: and it shall be an heap for ever; it shall not be built again.

13:17 And there shall cleave nought of the cursed thing to thine hand: that the LORD may turn from the fierceness of his anger, and shew thee mercy, and have compassion upon thee, and multiply thee, as he hath sworn unto thy fathers;

13:18 When thou shalt hearken to the voice of the LORD thy God, to keep all his commandments which I command thee this day, to do that which is right in the eyes of the LORD thy God.

Deuteronomy 14

If we have committed ourselves to live by every Word of God, God will dwell in us through his Holy Spirit and we will become the temple or dwelling place of God. Therefore we are to keep ourselves pure from any sin and we are to treat our bodies with respect as the dwelling place or temple of God!

> **1 Corinthians 3:16** Know ye not that ye are the temple of God, and that the Spirit of God dwelleth in you? **3:17 If any man defile the temple of God, him shall God destroy; for the temple of God is holy, which temple ye are.**

Deuteronomy 14:1 Ye are the children of the LORD your God: ye shall not cut yourselves, nor make any baldness between your eyes for the dead.

14:2 For thou art an holy people unto the LORD thy God, and the LORD hath chosen thee to be a peculiar [special] people unto himself, above all the nations that are upon the earth.

> **1 Peter 1:16** Because it is written, **Be ye holy**; for I am **holy**.

What we consume becomes a part of us; the same is true mentally and spiritually. We are to learn to guard what we allow to enter our minds by guarding what we take into our bodies.

The clean thing is a picture of godliness, while the unclean thing is a picture of that which is evil or polluted by evil.

The law of the clean and the unclean is to teach us to put a difference between the holy and the profane, between the godly and the ungodly.

In the New Covenant this commandment is to be kept physically and expanded to be kept spiritually.

The clean and the unclean are a physical lesson to teach a spiritual reality: We are not to pollute ourselves with sin, nor are we to tempt ourselves by thinking the forbidden thing to be desirable. We are to keep the law in BOTH the letter AND the spirit.

Deuteronomy 14:3 Thou shalt not eat any abominable thing.

14:4 These are the beasts which ye shall eat: the ox, the sheep, and the goat, **4:5** The hart, and the roebuck, and the fallow deer, and the wild goat, and the pygarg, and the wild ox, and the chamois. **14:6** And every beast that parteth the hoof, and cleaveth the cleft into two claws, and cheweth the cud among the beasts, that ye shall eat.

14:7 Nevertheless these ye shall not eat of them that chew the cud, or of them that divide the cloven hoof; as the camel, and the hare, and the coney: for they chew the cud, but divide not the hoof; therefore they are unclean unto you.

14:8 And the swine, because it divideth the hoof, yet cheweth not the cud, it is unclean unto you: ye shall not eat of their flesh, nor touch their dead carcase.

This also forbids the use of the skins and furs or any other part of any dead unclean creature.

14:9 These ye shall eat of all that are in the waters: all that have [both] fins and scales shall ye eat: **14:10** And whatsoever hath not fins and scales ye may not eat; it is unclean unto you.

An <u>extensive list of clean products</u>. Certainly does not contain all products.

A <u>list of clean and unclean animals</u>.

Be careful of Jewish Kosher certifying agencies as there are different ones with different standards, some not biblical. They tend to twist the command not to even touch the dead bodies of the unclean thing into a simple "do not eat the meat," thereby supposedly justifying the use of extractions, gelatin etc; and the use and wearing of forbidden unclean skins and furs.

Note that the shed hair of living animals is not unclean, only the dead body. Therefore the shorn hair or wool of living camels, llamas etc is clean.

14:11 Of all clean birds ye shall eat.

14:12 But these are they of which ye shall not eat: the eagle, and the ossifrage, and the ospray, **14:13** And the glede, and the kite, and the vulture after his kind, **14:14** And every raven after his kind, **14:15** And the owl, and the night hawk, and the cuckow, and the hawk after his kind, **14:16** The little owl, and the great owl, and the swan, **14:17** And the pelican, and the gier eagle, and the cormorant, **14:18** And the stork, and the heron after her kind, and the lapwing, and the bat. **14:19** And every creeping thing [such as insects which walk and fly like house flies] that flieth is unclean unto you: they shall not be eaten.

14:20 But of all clean fowls ye may eat.

The characteristics and features of clean birds can be determined from the scripturally known clean birds; namely the dove (turtledove), pigeon, and quail (Leviticus 1:14-17, 12:8, 14:22, 15:14-15; Psalm 105:40; Matthew 3:16, 21:12; Mark 1:10, 11:15; Luke 2:24, 3:22; John 1:32, 2:14-16).

The turtledove and pigeon are clean birds as they were used in sacrifices and only clean creatures could be used for sacrifices (Leviticus 1:14-17, 12:8, 14:22, 15:14-15).

The Holy Spirit descended upon Yeshua (Jesus) in the form of a dove, illustrating that doves are clean birds (Matthew 3:16; Mark 1:10; Luke 3:22; John 1:32). Doves were sold along with oxen and sheep in the Israeli marketplace, further indicating that doves are clean birds (Matthew 21:12; Mark 11:15; John 2:14-16). Quails are clean birds as the Lord provided them to the Hebrews for food after the Hebrew exodus from Egypt (Psalm 105:40).

Clean birds have all of the following characteristics:

- they are foragers and are not birds of prey or scavengers
- they have crops a gizzard with a double lining which can easily be separated
- they have three front toes with an elongated middle front toe and a hind toe
- they spread three front toes on one side of a perch and their hind toe on the other side
- they do not eat in flight, landing to eat.

Unclean birds lack one or more of the characteristics of clean birds. The characteristics and features of unclean birds can be determined from the list of unclean birds listed in Scripture.

Unclean birds include those that are:

- birds of prey
- carrion-eating scavenger birds
- ratite birds [having a flat breastbone without a keel, and so unable to fly including the mostly large, flightless birds with a ratite breastbone, i.e. the ostrich, rhea, emu, cassowary, and kiwi]- web-footed, and zygodactyl-footed [two front and two back toes] birds
- waterfowl [ducks, swans and geese]
- flying mammals (bats)

The pelican and the seagull are listed in Scripture among the unclean birds. The pelican and seagull possess webbed feet, as do ducks, geese, and swans. Ducks, geese, and swans are unclean because they lack some of the characteristics and features of clean birds – they do not have crops, they have different body structures than clean birds do, their body fat is intertwined with their flesh and they have webbed feet.

14:21 Ye shall not eat of anything that dieth of itself: thou shalt give it unto the stranger that is in thy gates, that he may eat it; or thou mayest sell it unto an alien: for thou art an holy people unto the LORD thy God.

Thou shalt not seethe a kid in his [own] mother's milk [a pagan fertility rite].

Festival Tithing

14:22 Thou shalt truly tithe all the increase of thy seed, that the field bringeth forth year by year. **14:23** And **thou shalt eat** [the tithe] **before the LORD thy God, in the place which he shall choose to place his name there,** the tithe of thy corn [grain], of thy wine, and of thine oil, and the firstlings of thy herds and of thy flocks; that thou mayest learn to fear the LORD thy God always.

14:24 And if the way be too long for thee, so that thou art not able to carry it; or if the place be too far from thee, which the LORD thy God shall choose to set his name there, when the LORD thy God hath blessed thee:

14:25 Then shalt thou turn it into money, and bind up the money in thine hand, and shalt go unto the place which the LORD thy God shall choose:

14:26 And thou shalt bestow that money for whatsoever thy soul lusteth [lawfully desires] after, for oxen, or for sheep, or for wine, or for strong drink, or for whatsoever thy soul desireth: and thou shalt eat there before the LORD thy God, and thou shalt rejoice, thou, and thine household,

14:27 And the Levite that is within thy gates; thou shalt not forsake him; for he hath no part nor inheritance with thee.

The Tithe For The Poor

14:28 At **the end of three years** thou shalt bring forth all the tithe of thine increase the same year [during that one year], and shalt lay it up within thy gates:

14:29 And the Levite [this is not referring to paid elders but to the poor of the tribe of Levi], (because he hath no part nor inheritance with thee,) and the stranger, and the fatherless, and the widow, which are within thy gates, shall come, and shall eat and be satisfied; that the LORD thy God may bless thee in all the work of thine hand which thou doest.

It is robbing the poor and robbing God to give the poor fund money to an already paid elder for his own personal use or for any corporate use other than helping the destitute.

Deuteronomy 15

The Sabbatical year of debt release goes together with the Sabbath of the land from cultivation Leviticus 25; the release of debt coming at the END of every Sabbatical year land Sabbath.

This law is in reference to personal debt that impoverishes the people; not commercial debt to finance factories, or other big projects. That said I do think that a totally new banking and financial system [different from today's banking system] that does not impoverish individuals and still provides a means to finance big projects will be established in the kingdom of God.

Deuteronomy 15:1 At the end of every seven years thou shalt make a release.

15:2 And this is the manner of the release: Every creditor that lendeth ought unto his neighbour shall release it; he shall not exact it of his neighbour, or of his brother; because it is called the LORD's release.

Spiritually this command is to be kept by the Ekklesia; with the brethren forgiving all debts owed within the spiritual Israel of the New Covenant called out; while remaining able to collect from the unconverted who do not keep these commandments.

15:3 Of a foreigner thou mayest exact it again: but that which is thine with thy brother thine hand shall release;

The following does not mean that this command will end; it means that when there are no poor [no one in debt] then this law will not be applicable since there will be no personal debt to forgive.

15:4 Save when there shall be no poor among you; for the LORD shall greatly bless thee in the land which the LORD thy God giveth thee for an inheritance to possess it:

Again, blessings and possession of the promised land are totally CONDITIONAL on obedience to every Word of God. This is also true of entry into the spiritual Promised Land of the resurrection to eternal life as spirit.

God's blessings will only come if we are zealously diligent to live by every Word of God.

15:5 Only if thou carefully hearken unto the voice of the LORD thy God, to observe to do all these commandments which I command thee this day.

15:6 For the LORD thy God blesseth thee, as he promised thee: and thou shalt lend unto many nations, but thou shalt not borrow; and thou shalt reign over many nations, but they shall not reign over thee.

We are to help others most especially our brethren in the faith. This does not mean that we are to subsidize the lazy but we are not to refuse the requests of those in genuine personal need through no fault of their own.

15:7 If there be among you a poor man of one of thy brethren within any of thy gates in thy land which the LORD thy God giveth thee, **thou shalt not harden thine heart, nor shut thine hand from thy poor brother:**

15:8 But **thou shalt open thine hand wide unto him, and shalt surely lend him sufficient for his need, in that which he wanteth** [what he lacks in the way of survival necessities].

We cannot lawfully refuse to help those who are suffering through no fault of their own, however we should not give what we do not have.

15:9 Beware that there be not a thought in thy wicked heart, saying, The seventh year, the year of release, is at hand; and thine eye be evil against thy poor brother, and thou givest him nought; and he cry unto the LORD against thee, and it be sin unto thee.

When we help the poor among the Ekklesia we are not loaning to men, we are giving to God!

15:10 Thou shalt surely give him, and thine heart shall not be grieved when thou givest unto him: because that **for this thing the LORD thy**

God shall bless thee in all thy works, and in all that thou puttest thine hand unto.

15:11 For the poor shall never cease out of the land: therefore **I command thee, saying, Thou shalt open thine hand wide unto thy brother, to thy poor, and to thy needy, in thy land.**

The following speaks of servitude for a debt. Such debt servants are to be well treated just like we would treat our own sons and daughters who serve us.

It was the custom to repay a debt by serving the debt holder or by being "sold" into service. Here God puts a limit on such service.

15:12 And if thy brother, an Hebrew man, or an Hebrew woman, be sold unto thee, and serve thee six years; then **in the seventh year thou shalt let him go free from thee.**

15:13 And **when thou sendest him out free from thee, thou shalt not let him go away empty**:

15:14 Thou shalt furnish him liberally out of thy flock, and out of thy floor, and out of thy winepress: of that wherewith the LORD thy God hath blessed thee thou shalt give unto him.

15:15 And **thou shalt remember that thou wast a bondman in the land of Egypt, and the LORD thy God redeemed thee: therefore I command thee this thing to day.**

15:16 And it shall be, if he say unto thee, I will not go away from thee; because he loveth thee and thine house, because he is well with thee; **15:17** Then thou shalt take an aul, and thrust it through his ear unto the door, and he shall be thy servant for ever. And also unto thy maidservant thou shalt do likewise.

15:18 It shall not seem hard unto thee, when thou sendest him away free from thee; for he hath been worth a double hired servant to thee, in serving thee six years: and the LORD thy God shall bless thee in all that thou doest.

The first born males of the flocks and the herds is to be eaten at the Feasts and is not to be worked or sheared, the first born is set apart to God.

If it is without blemish it may be sacrificed as the Passover or at the fall Feast; and is to be eaten by the offeror. If it is blemished it is NOT to be sacrificed because it is not a suitable symbol of Jesus Christ; the blemished first born may be eaten at home.

15:19 All the **firstling males** that come of thy herd and of thy flock thou shalt sanctify unto the LORD thy God: thou shalt do no work with the firstling of thy bullock, nor shear the firstling of thy sheep. **15:20** Thou shalt eat it before the LORD thy God year by year **in the place which the LORD shall choose**, thou and thy household.

15:21 And **if there be any blemish therein, as if it be lame, or blind, or have any ill blemish, thou shalt not sacrifice it unto the LORD thy God. 15:22 Thou shalt eat it within thy gates**: the unclean and the clean person shall eat it alike, as the roebuck, and as the hart. **15:23 Only thou shalt not eat the blood thereof; thou shalt pour it upon the ground as water.**

Deuteronomy 16

Deuteronomy 16 goes through the Holy Days which are studied in depth, in articles available at the Festival Categories on the right hand sidebar.

Deuteronomy 16:1 Observe the month of Abib, and keep the passover unto the LORD thy God: for in the month of Abib the LORD thy God brought thee forth out of Egypt by night.

The Passover

The Passover as with all other sacrifices may only be killed at the tabernacle or temple; which is why we cannot sacrifice the Passover lamb today.

In the millennium those privileged to visit the Ezekiel Temple in Jerusalem will sacrifice there including the Passover lamb; while those around the world will have a Passover service locally with the Unleavened Bread and Wine but without the lamb as we do today.

I add that with modern technology after Christ comes the services at Jerusalem throughout the Festivals could be broadcast worldwide for all the world to see,

Imagine watching Jesus Christ, Moses, Ezra, Paul and many others speaking directly and personally, live to the whole earth from the Ezekiel Temple at Jerusalem!

16:2 Thou shalt therefore sacrifice the passover unto the LORD thy God, of the flock and the herd, in the place which the LORD shall choose to place his name there.

16:3 Thou shalt eat no leavened bread with it; seven days shalt thou eat unleavened bread therewith, even the bread of affliction; for thou camest forth out of the land of Egypt in haste: that thou mayest remember the day when thou camest forth out of the land of Egypt all the days of thy life.

A brief inset about the Feast of Unleavened Bread before returning to the Passover

16:4 And **there shall be no leavened bread seen with thee in all thy coast seven days;** neither shall there any thing of the flesh, which thou sacrificedst the first day at even, remain all night until the morning.

Returning to the Passover

16:5 Thou mayest not sacrifice the passover within any of thy gates, which the LORD thy God giveth thee:

Here we find the word "even" or "evening" clearly defined as sunset. This is solid proof that the Passover is to be sacrificed at and after sunset. See the Passover book or the Passover articles at the Spring Festivals category.

16:6 But at the place which the LORD thy God shall choose to place his name in, there **thou shalt sacrifice the passover at even, at the going down of the sun**, at the season that thou camest forth out of Egypt. **16:7** And thou shalt roast and eat it in the place which the LORD thy God shall choose: and thou shalt turn in the morning, and go unto thy tents.

While God permitted the preparing of food on that emergency situation when Israel was marching out of Egypt; here we see the commandment to do NO WORK on these Holy Days.

No WORK, includes food preparation which is to be done on the previous day, the preparation day; as mentioned by John.

Jesus was killed on Passover day, which is the preparation day for the first High Day of the Feast of Unleavened Bread and the Jews along with the followers of Christ understood that they must complete preparations before sunset ending Passover day, since no work was to be done on the Holy Day.

The sanctity and no work command regarding the Holy Day was why the disciple put Jesus in the tomb Wednesday afternoon without further preparation. They then waited until after the High Day which was on Thursday that year to purchase the spices on Friday and then waited until after the weekly Sabbath before returning to anoint the body on Sunday morning.

> **John 19:31** The Jews therefore, because it **was** the preparation, that the bodies should not remain upon the cross on the **sabbath** day, (for that **sabbath** day **was an high day,**) besought Pilate that their legs might be broken, **and** that they might be taken away

The Feast of Unleavened Bread

Deuteronomy 16:8 Six days thou shalt eat unleavened bread: and on the seventh day shall be a solemn assembly to the LORD thy God: thou shalt do no work therein.

> **Leviticus 23:6** And on the fifteenth day of the same month is the feast of unleavened bread unto the LORD: seven days ye must eat unleavened bread.
>
> **23:7** In the **first day ye shall have an holy convocation: ye shall do no servile work** [work of any kind] **therein.**
>
> **23:8** But ye shall offer an offering made by fire unto the LORD seven days: **in the seventh day is an holy convocation: ye shall do no servile work** [work of any kind] **therein.**

The count to Pentecost

Deuteronomy 16:9 Seven weeks shalt thou number unto thee: begin to number the seven weeks from such time as thou beginnest to put the sickle to the corn [grain; The Sunday Wave Offering during Unleavened Bread].

Pentecost is on the fiftieth day after the Wave Offering on the Sunday during the Feast of Unleavened Bread [the next day after the completion of a seven week count].

16:10 And **thou shalt keep the feast of weeks unto the LORD thy God with a tribute of a freewill offering of thine hand, which thou shalt give unto the LORD thy God, according as the LORD thy God hath blessed thee:**

16:11 And **thou shalt rejoice before the LORD thy God**, thou, and thy son, and thy daughter, and thy manservant, and thy maidservant, and the Levite that is within thy gates, and the stranger, and the fatherless, and the widow, that are among you, in the place which the LORD thy God hath chosen to place his name there.

16:12 And thou shalt remember that thou wast a bondman in Egypt: and thou shalt observe and do these statutes.

The Feast of Tabernacles

16:13 Thou shalt observe the feast of tabernacles seven days, after that thou hast gathered in thy corn [grain] and thy wine: **16:14 And thou shalt rejoice in thy feast, thou, and thy son, and thy daughter, and thy manservant, and thy maidservant, and the Levite, the stranger, and the fatherless, and the widow, that are within thy gates.**

16:15 Seven days shalt thou keep a solemn feast unto the LORD thy God in the place which the LORD shall choose: because the LORD thy God shall bless thee in all thine increase, and in all the works of thine hands, therefore thou shalt surely rejoice.

The Feast's of Unleavened Bread and Tabernacles are both to be kept with daily services for a full seven days; they [and Pentecost] are pilgrim Feasts to be observed in a place chosen by God, which was the tabernacle or later the temple at Jerusalem.

No work of any kind including cooking is permitted on the Weekly Sabbaths and Annual High Days, the other intermediate days are appointed times to be observed, yet without the restrictions on work necessary for the Feast, like cleaning clothes, cooking etc.

There are three pilgrim Feast's during the year and one offering is required at each.

It is clear that some members of a family might not attend because of illness, age, or advanced pregnancy, or some kind of uncleanness; and that some would be needed on the farm to care for livestock etc. However it is God's intention that as many as possible gather together for the three pilgrim Feasts.

In the future it will be impossible for billions of people from around the earth to gather at the Ezekiel Temple in Jerusalem; then the Feast's will have to be observed locally with delegations representing all peoples going up to the temple at Jerusalem.

16:16 Three times in a year shall all thy males appear before the LORD thy God in the place which he shall choose; in the feast of unleavened bread, and in the feast of weeks, and in the feast of tabernacles: and they shall not appear before the LORD empty:

16:17 Every man shall give as he is able, according to the blessing of the LORD thy God which he hath given thee.

Only three annual offerings are commanded, not seven offerings as some falsely teach.

God Commands Justice

Now God commands that justice be served by honest just judges; judging according to the Word of God and not loosing God's Word for their own opinions. See the Binding and Loosing article.

16:18 Judges and officers shalt thou make thee in all thy gates, which the LORD thy God giveth thee, throughout thy tribes: and **they shall judge the people with just judgment.**

16:19 Thou shalt not wrest judgment; thou shalt not respect persons, neither take a gift: for a gift doth blind the eyes of the wise, and pervert the words of the righteous.

16:20 That which is altogether just shalt thou follow, that thou mayest live, and inherit the land which the LORD thy God giveth thee.

We must NOT believe one person over another because they are wealthy, or poor, or because they are elders or layman. All judgments must be fair, honest and just by the Word of God, and we must not be respecters of persons. This is a commandment that is routinely broken in today's Ekklesia, as brethren put organizations and elders on a pedestal.

Idolatry

Pagan altars were placed under green [evergreen] trees because such green trees were regarded as fertility symbols.

16:21 Thou shalt not plant thee a grove of any trees near unto the altar of the LORD thy God, which thou shalt make thee. **16:22** Neither shalt thou set thee up any image; which the LORD thy God hateth.

The pagans worshiped their gods, setting up their altars in groves of trees, which trees like the modern Christmas tree, were regarded as symbols of fertility and eternal life.

Sometimes trees had their branches removed to represent the upright male organ of fertility [obelisks are a form of phallic symbol; an example of which is the Masonic Washington Memorial, which to the initiated in masonry represents the virility of the nation].

Pagan images would include crosses [the symbol of Tammuz], fish [the symbol of Dagon] and so called pictures of Christ which are really stylized pictures of the pagan god Saturn.

Deuteronomy 17

The sacrificial animals represent the various aspects of the sacrifice of Christ the Lamb of God, and they must be perfect, symbolizing the perfection and total innocence of Messiah from any blemish of sin. See the articles on the sacrificial system.

Deuteronomy 17:1 Thou shalt not sacrifice unto the LORD thy God any bullock, or sheep, wherein is blemish, or any evilfavouredness: for that is an abomination unto the LORD thy God.

Sacrificial animals are types of Jesus Christ the Lamb of God and should mirror his perfection. To sacrifice an imperfect animal is to symbolize Christ as imperfect; such imperfections are types of sin.

The sin of idolatry

17:2 If there be found among you, within any of thy gates which the LORD thy God giveth thee, man or woman, that hath wrought wickedness in the sight of the LORD thy God, **in transgressing his covenant,**

Today many brethren do worship idols of men and follow them contrary to the Word of God; which is the same sin of idolatry.

17:3 And hath gone and served other gods, and worshipped them, either the sun, or moon, or any of the host of heaven, which I have not commanded;

The key term here is "which I have not commanded;" God DID command us to use the sun and moon to establish natural divisions of time and a calendar, however we are NOT to worship those bodies!

This command forbidding astrology, forbids thinking that the heavenly bodies influence events on earth and people's lives. In other words people worship these bodies by obeying or following the advice of the astrologers. This is NOT referring the observance of sunset or the phases of the moon as a measurement of time which God has commanded for us.

17:4 And it be told thee, and thou hast heard of it, and enquired diligently, and, behold, it be true, and the thing certain, that such abomination is wrought in Israel:

Just as God has commanded that all idolaters be stoned to death; so the New Covenant called out who make idols of men and corporate entities to love and obey them more than they love and obey Almighty God, will also be rejected by Christ (Rev 3:15-22).

Today the brethren have been given over to the strong delusion that blind unquestioning obedience to men, is obedience to God: IT IS NOT! Those who blindly follow men will be strongly corrected in the fire of affliction for our idolatry!

17:5 Then shalt thou bring forth that man or that woman, which have committed that wicked thing, unto thy gates, even that man or that woman, and shalt stone them with stones, till they die.

A minimum of two or three witnesses in required to establish any thing.

17:6 At the mouth of two witnesses, or three witnesses, shall he that is worthy of death be put to death; but at the mouth of one witness he shall not be put to death.

17:7 The hands of the witnesses shall be first upon him to put him to death, and afterward the hands of all the people. So thou shalt put the evil away from among you.

It takes two or more witnesses to establish guilt or to prove any matter.

17:8 If there arise a matter too hard for thee in judgment, between blood and blood, between plea and plea, and between stroke and stroke, being matters of controversy within thy gates: then shalt thou arise, and get thee up into the place which the LORD thy God shall choose;

We are to go to godly priests/ministry for just judgment, because they supposedly know God's Word and will judge fairly by the Word of God.

When the priests/ministry go astray, justice departs from the land; and when the elders and priests are zealous for the Word of God there is justice.

17:9 And thou shalt come unto the priests the Levites, and unto the judge that shall be in those days, and enquire; and they shall shew thee the sentence of judgment:

17:10 And thou shalt do according to the sentence, which they of that place which the LORD shall choose shall shew thee; and thou shalt observe to do according to all that they inform thee:

The priests were to be the ultimate judges in Israel and when they went astray the people were led astray. All judgments MUST be made, based on and consistent with every Word of God.

All of today's New Covenant brethren are people "in training" to eventually be resurrected to become [if they pass the course] priests and kings after the order of Jesus Christ; in God's coming kingdom.

Even the Levites were to be questioned and checked against the scriptures, and we are required to "prove all things" and hold fast to every Word of God (1 Thess 5:22). We must judge all matters faithfully by the Word of God.

17:11 According to the sentence of the law [The duty of the ministry is to faithfully teach the judgments in the Word of God.] which they shall teach thee, and according to the judgment which they shall tell thee, thou shalt do: thou shalt not decline from the sentence which they shall shew thee, to the right hand, nor to the left.

17:12 And the man that will do presumptuously, and will not hearken unto the priest that standeth to minister there before the LORD thy God, or unto the judge, [The person who will not be subject to the Word of God.] even that man shall die: and thou shalt put away the evil from Israel.

17:13 And all the people shall hear, and fear, and do no more presumptuously.

Moses prophesies of a coming king

17:14 When thou art come unto the land which the LORD thy God giveth thee, and shalt possess it, and shalt dwell therein, and shalt say, **I will set a king over me**, like as all the nations that are about me; **17:15** Thou shalt in any wise **set him king over thee, whom the LORD thy God shall choose**: one from among thy brethren shalt thou set king over thee: thou mayest not set a stranger over thee, which is not thy brother.

In the New Covenant, the faithfully obedient to God brethren, must choose to follow the man who demonstrates by his fruits that God has chosen him!

That person MUST be a person who is a brother in the faith and has proven by his fruits to be the choice of God (Mat 7).

Today we have been led far astray because we have not questioned and proved by their fruits from the scriptures, the men whom we follow! We have broken this commandment in Deuteronomy as well as the many commandments on the subject in the New Testament.

A great many of the leaders in the various groups of today's Spiritual Ekklesia have proven by their fruits and their lack of zeal to live by every Word of God with their compromising with God's Word; that they are NOT godly men.

We have been led astray because we have been willing to blindly and without question, follow anyone who makes some grand claim and gives lip-service to the faith, while doing whatever they please instead of doing as God has commanded.

Neither physical nor spiritual leaders are to use their positions to feed themselves and not the flock. They are NOT to take the best things for themselves nor are they to seek the exaltation of the people.

They are to be faithful to the Eternal in all things; to exalt the Eternal and to obey him in all things; to faithfully serve the Eternal by feeding the flock sound doctrine and a good knowledge of every Word of God: They are to speak the Word of God before all peoples without fear or compromise.

17:16 But he shall not multiply horses [make himself personally rich] to himself, nor cause the people to return to Egypt [A ruler must not lead the people into sin and bondage to enrich himself.], to the end that he should multiply horses: forasmuch as the LORD hath said unto you, Ye shall henceforth return no more that way.

The ruler or leader must not exercise his office for personal gain.

17:17 Neither shall he multiply wives to himself, that his heart turn not away: neither shall he greatly multiply to himself silver and gold.

The leaders of the people both secular and spiritual, and the elders must have a personal copy of the Word of God and study it every day of their lives to learn it and to live by it.

Every one of us has been called to become a priest and or a king [ruler]; and we are all to have personal copies of God's Word; and we are to study it, to learn it and to live by it, all the days of our lives.

17:18 And it shall be, when he sitteth upon the throne of his kingdom, **that he shall write him a copy of this law in a book out of that which is before the priests the Levites:**

17:19 And **it shall be with him, and he shall read therein all the days of his life: that he may learn to fear the LORD his God, to keep all the words of this law and these statutes, to do them:**

17:20 That his heart be not lifted up [in pride] **above his brethren, and that he turn not aside from the commandment, to the right hand, or to the left:** to the end that he may prolong his days in his kingdom, he, and his children, in the midst of Israel.

Deuteronomy 18

Wages for the Temple service

The Levites including the priests who are serving in the Temple are to have a portion of those sacrifices which are not totally burned in the fire. These offerings are explained in the book of instruction for the Levites: Leviticus.

Deuteronomy 18:1 The priests the Levites, and all the tribe of Levi, shall have no part nor inheritance with Israel: **they shall eat the offerings of the LORD made by fire**, and his inheritance.

18:2 Therefore shall they have no inheritance among their brethren: the LORD is their inheritance, as he hath said unto them.

The term Levites is used to include the priests and all those who officiate in making the sacrifices at the Temple. All priests are Levites, but all Levites are not priests.

18:3 And **this shall be the priest's due from the people, from them that offer a sacrifice, whether it be ox or sheep; and they shall give unto the priest the shoulder, and the two cheeks, and the maw.**

18:4 The **firstfruit also of thy corn [grain], of thy wine, and of thine oil, and the first of the fleece of thy sheep, shalt thou give him.**

18:5 For the LORD thy God hath chosen him out of all thy tribes, **to stand to minister in the name of the LORD, him and his sons for ever.**

When Christ comes and the Ezekiel Temple is built, the descendants of Zadok will be converted to the New Covenant and they will then serve in the physical things and sacrifices in that temple (Ezek 40-48); while those called out and changed to spirit will serve as priests in a spiritual capacity around the whole earth teaching all nations to live by every Word of God.

The Priests and Levites would come from their villages to serve in the temple, and David later set up courses for different groups of Levites to come for two weeks of service each year, plus all of them serving together at the Festivals.

18:6 And if a Levite come from any of thy gates out of all Israel, where he sojourned, and come with all the desire of his mind unto the place which the LORD shall choose; **18:7** Then he shall minister in the name of the LORD his God, as all his brethren the Levites do, which stand there before the LORD.

The Levites [priests] must share equally in the rewards of their temple service, but each person may keep what comes from his ordinary work outside of the temple service.

18:8 They shall have like portions to eat, beside that which cometh of the sale of his patrimony.

Instructions to reject all idolatry and methods of idolatrous worship

18:9 When thou art come into the land which the LORD thy God giveth thee, thou shalt not learn to do after the abominations of those nations.

18:10 There shall not be found among you any one that maketh his son or his daughter to pass through the fire, or that useth divination [using signs like reading tea leaves, or reading entrails, or dropping arrows to see which way they point, in order to make a decision], or an observer of times [astrologer], or an enchanter [someone who uses belief in spells and potions], or a witch [anyone who rebels against obedience to every Word of God].

18:11 Or a charmer, or a consulter with familiar spirits, or a wizard, or a necromancer.

18:12 For all that do these things are an abomination unto the LORD: and because of these abominations the LORD thy God doth drive them out from before thee.

We are to worship the Eternal perfectly according to his Word, and we are not to follow the ways, teachings or prognostications of idols of men.

18:13 Thou shalt be perfect with the LORD thy God.

18:14 For these nations, which thou shalt possess, hearkened unto observers of times [listened to and followed astrologers], and unto diviners: **but as for thee, the LORD thy God hath not suffered thee so to do.**

Moses was the mediator of the Mosaic Covenant, and here he prophesies of the New Covenant and its Mediator, Messiah the Christ.

18:15 The LORD thy God will raise up unto thee a Prophet from the midst of thee, of thy brethren, like unto me; unto him ye shall hearken;

That Prophet, Messiah the Christ, has replaced Moses and is the ONLY New Covenant Mediator [High Priest] with God the Father.

18:16 According to all that thou desiredst of the LORD thy God in Horeb in the day of the assembly, saying, Let me not hear again the voice of the LORD my God, neither let me see this great fire any more, that I die not.

18:17 And the LORD said unto me, They have well spoken that which they have spoken.

Jesus Christ the Messiah would not speak his own words but would teach everything that God the Father tells him to speak.

18:18 I will raise them up a Prophet from among their brethren, like unto thee, and will put my words in his mouth; and he shall speak unto them all that I shall command him.

Just as Moses was the mediator of the Mosaic Covenant, Jesus Christ is the Mediator of the New Covenant. Please see the vital Hebrews study in the Epistles category.

18:19 And it shall come to pass, that whosoever will not hearken unto my words which he shall speak in my name, I will require it of him.

All those who reject the Messiah will be corrected and if they remain adamantly unrepentant they will be destroyed: And the man who presumptuously declares his own personal thoughts to be from God to gain a personal following, declaring false things in "the name of The LORD" as certain men have done; is worthy of death.

Anyone who exalts himself as an idol of the brethren to demand zeal for themselves and who minimizes any zeal for keeping the Word of God, as is commonly done in today's Spiritual Ekklesia will surely die for his great sin; unless he did it ignorantly and quickly repents.

18:20 But the prophet, which shall presume to speak a word in my name, which I have not commanded him to speak, or that shall speak in the name of other gods, even that prophet shall die.

Any person who presumes to speak "in the name of the LORD," things which the LORD has not spoken, is worthy of death. Spiritually, if such men refuse to sincerely repent when their minds are opened to a good understanding and given the opportunity, they will be destroyed in the lake of fire.

18:21 And if thou say in thine heart, **How shall we know the word which the LORD hath not spoken?**

18:22 When a prophet speaketh in the name of the LORD, if the thing follow not, nor come to pass, that is the thing which the LORD hath not spoken, but the prophet hath spoken it presumptuously: thou shalt not be afraid [We must not have any respect for such a person; yet such a presumption man who made many failed prophecies in "the name of the LORD" is worshiped as an idol in today's Ekklesia.] **of him.**

A false prophet is one who speaks "In the name of the Lord" when the Lord has NOT spoken, and what he says fails to come to pass. This is not referring to discussion or speculation by anyone; it is referring to presuming to speak "by the authority of God" or "in the name of the Lord."

A false prophet is also anyone who would water down God's ways and lead the people into sinning through compromising with God's Word, rejecting any zeal to live by every Word of God in favor of a zeal to follow the false traditions of idols of men; as many leaders of the major churches do today.

Deuteronomy 19

Judicial Cities

Deuteronomy 19:1 When the LORD thy God hath cut off the nations, whose land the LORD thy God giveth thee, and thou succeedest them, and dwellest in their cities, and in their houses;

Three judicial cities were to be established as centers of justice with courts for the hearing of crimes and disputes.

19:2 Thou shalt separate three cities for thee in the midst of thy land, which the LORD thy God giveth thee to possess it.

19:3 Thou shalt prepare thee a way, and divide the coasts of thy land, which the LORD thy God giveth thee to inherit, into three parts, that every slayer may flee thither.

19:4 And this is the case of the slayer, which shall flee thither, that he may live: Whoso **killeth his neighbour ignorantly**, whom he hated not in time past;

19:5 As when a man goeth into the wood with his neighbour to hew wood, and his hand fetcheth a stroke with the axe to cut down the tree, and the head slippeth from the helve, and lighteth upon his neighbour, that he die; he shall flee unto one of those cities, and live:

19:6 Lest the avenger of the blood pursue the slayer, while his heart is hot, and overtake him, because the way is long, and slay him; whereas he was not worthy of death, inasmuch as he hated him not in time past.

19:7 Wherefore I command thee, saying, Thou shalt separate three cities for thee.

19:8 And **if the LORD thy God enlarge thy coast**, as he hath sworn unto thy fathers, and give thee all the land which he promised to give unto thy fathers;

19:9 If thou shalt keep all these commandments to do them, which I command thee this day, to love the LORD thy God, and to walk ever in his ways; **then shalt thou add three cities more for thee, beside these three:**

19:10 That innocent blood be not shed in thy land, which the LORD thy God giveth thee for an inheritance, and so blood be upon thee.

The proven murderer must die for his murder

19:11 But if any man hate his neighbour, and lie in wait for him, and rise up against him, and smite him mortally that he die, and fleeth into one of these cities:

19:12 Then the elders of his city shall send and fetch him thence, and deliver him into the hand of the avenger of blood, that he may die.

19:13 Thine eye shall not pity him, but thou shalt put away the guilt of innocent blood from Israel, that it may go well with thee.

The following is one of the reasons that Judah will once again go into a captivity (Hosea 5:10).

19:14 Thou shalt not remove thy neighbour's landmark, which they of old time have set in thine inheritance, which thou shalt inherit in the land that the LORD thy God giveth thee to possess it.

Repeated here is the requirement for several witness to prove any matter; this includes using several witness to sight the new moon to avoid any possibility of a mistake and to discern any trouble maker making a false report.

19:15 One witness shall not rise up against a man for any iniquity, or for any sin, in any sin that he sinneth: **at the mouth of two witnesses, or at the mouth of three witnesses, shall the matter be established.**

The law of false witnesses

19:16 If a false witness rise up against any man to testify against him that which is wrong;

19:17 Then both the men, between whom the controversy is, shall stand before the LORD, before the priests and the judges, which shall be in those days;

19:18 And **the judges shall make diligent inquisition: and, behold, if the witness be a false witness, and hath testified falsely against his brother;**

19:19 Then shall ye do unto him, as he had thought to have done unto his brother: so shalt thou put the evil away from among you.

19:20 And those which remain shall hear, and fear, and shall henceforth commit no more any such evil among you.

19:21 And thine eye shall not pity; but life shall go for life, eye for eye, tooth for tooth, hand for hand, foot for foot.

Deuteronomy 20

Deuteronomy 20:1 When thou goest out to battle against thine enemies, and seest horses, and chariots, and a people more than thou, be not afraid of them: for the LORD thy God is with thee, which brought thee up out of the land of Egypt. **20:2** And it shall be, when ye are come nigh unto the battle, . . .

The job of the ministry is to boldly set a godly example and teach God's ways with zeal, to encourage the people to fight the good fight against sin and to rely on the Eternal, and to NEVER FEAR what any enemy can do.

We fight spiritual battles almost daily and we need to KNOW and to be filled with COURAGEOUS FAITH in our Deliverer. We need to remember and understand that the battle is the LORD's, and that we are NOT alone in our struggles.

. . . that the priest shall approach and speak unto the people,

Let the uncommitted and the faithless be separated out; so that the spiritually faithful, courageous and zealous may be delivered.

That is exactly what the Master Builder is doing at this time; separating out the faithful from the faithless, the zealous from the lax and lukewarm. Today the courageous who will stand on the Rock of their Salvation, are being separated from the weak and fearful who compromise to avoid trials or for supposed personal gain.

Brethren, we are in a great WAR against bondage to Satan, sin and eternal death.

Fear not! Be strong and courageous for the fight, because we are not alone in the battle: Our Mighty God goes before us to give all who faithfully zealously follow him; complete absolute victory!

20:3 And shall say unto them, **Hear, O Israel, ye approach this day unto battle against your enemies: let not your hearts faint, fear not, and do not tremble, neither be ye terrified because of them;**

20:4 For the LORD your God is he that goeth with you, to fight for you against your enemies, to save you.

If any are not willing to fight the good fight for godliness, feeling committed to some other thing they should not assemble together with the courageous fighters against sin and keepers of the Word of God. Why? Because they do not fight the good fight themselves and therefore are a discouragement to others.

20:5 And the officers shall speak unto the people, saying, What man is there that hath built a new house, and hath not dedicated it? let him go and return to his house, lest he die in the battle, and another man dedicate it.

20:6 And what man is he that hath planted a vineyard, and hath not yet eaten of it? let him also go and return unto his house, lest he die in the battle, and another man eat of it.

20:7 And what man is there that hath betrothed a wife, and hath not taken her? let him go and return unto his house, lest he die in the battle, and another man take her.

20:8 And the officers shall speak further unto the people, and they shall say, **What man is there that is fearful and fainthearted? let him go and return unto his house, lest his brethren's heart faint as well as his heart.**

20:9 And it shall be, when the officers have made an end of speaking unto the people that they shall make captains of the armies to lead the people.

The laws of war

20:10 When thou comest nigh unto a city to fight against it, then proclaim peace unto it.

20:11 And it shall be, if it make thee answer of peace, and open unto thee, then it shall be, that all the people that is found therein shall be tributaries unto thee, and they shall serve thee.

20:12 And if it will make no peace with thee, but will make war against thee, then thou shalt besiege it:

20:13 And when the LORD thy God hath delivered it into thine hands, thou shalt smite every male thereof with the edge of the sword:

20:14 But the women, and the little ones, and the cattle, and all that is in the city, even all the spoil thereof, shalt thou take unto thyself; and thou shalt eat the spoil of thine enemies, which the LORD thy God hath given thee.

20:15 Thus shalt thou do unto all the cities which are very far off from thee, which are not of the cities of these [Canaanite nations representing sin which are appointed to destruction] nations.

20:16 But of the cities of these people [the Canaanites in Palestine], which the LORD thy God doth give thee for an inheritance, **thou shalt save alive nothing that breatheth:**

The Canaanites having become extremely wicked were used as an example of what Jesus Christ will do to all unrepentant people who refuse to STOP sinning and or justify their sins as is done in today's Ekklesia.

Brethren, in today's Spiritual Ekklesia we are spiritually greater sinners than the ancient Canaanites were because we are supposed to have God's Spirit, we are supposed to know better; and yet we are full up to overflowing with idolatry and spiritual adultery against the Husband of our baptismal commitment.

Just as those wicked people of Canaan were to be destroyed, so today's apostate spiritually called out will be severely corrected if we refuse to repent.

20:17 But thou **shalt utterly destroy them;** namely, the Hittites, and the Amorites, the Canaanites, and the Perizzites, the Hivites, and the Jebusites; as the LORD thy God hath commanded thee: **20:18** That they teach you not to do after all their abominations, which they have done unto their gods; so should ye sin against the LORD your God.

Fruit trees are not to be destroyed in a siege; which is an allegory that those who bear spiritual fruit will not be destroyed by God but will be saved in the judgment.

20:19 When thou shalt besiege a city a long time, in making war against it to take it, **thou shalt not destroy the trees thereof by forcing an axe against them: for thou mayest eat of them, and thou shalt not cut them down (for the tree of the field is man's life) to employ them in the siege:**

20:20 Only the trees which thou knowest that they be not trees for meat, thou shalt destroy and cut them down; and thou shalt build bulwarks against the city that maketh war with thee, until it be subdued.

Deuteronomy 21

When a dead person is found lying alone, a sacrifice is to be made by the people of the city closest to a man found murdered as an indication that they did not commit this killing and that they do not know who did the deed, which is the reason that the guilty person cannot be apprehended and required to die for his crime. This is the only exception to the commandment that all sacrifices be made at the temple.

Deuteronomy 21:1 If one be found slain in the land which the LORD thy God giveth thee to possess it, lying in the field, and it be not known who hath slain him:

21:2 Then thy elders and thy judges shall come forth, and they shall measure unto the cities which are round about him that is slain:

21:3 And it shall be, that the city which is next unto the slain man, even the elders of that city shall take an heifer, which hath not been wrought with, and which hath not drawn in the yoke; **21:4** And the elders of that city shall bring down the heifer unto a rough valley, which is neither eared nor sown, and shall strike off the heifer's neck there in the valley:

This displays the Theocratic nature of the Mosaic Covenant and the mediatorial nature of the priesthood in interceding between men and God.

21:5 And the priests the sons of Levi shall come near; for them the LORD thy God hath chosen to minister unto him, and to bless in the name of the LORD; and by their word [based on every Word of God] shall every controversy and every stroke be tried:

21:6 And all the elders of that city, that are next unto the slain man, shall wash their hands over the heifer that is beheaded in the valley:

21:7 And they shall answer and say, **Our hands have not shed this blood, neither have our eyes seen it.**

21:8 [The priests must then say] "Be merciful, O LORD, unto thy people Israel, whom thou hast redeemed, and lay not innocent blood unto thy people of Israel's charge." And the blood shall be forgiven them. **21:9 So shalt thou put away the guilt of innocent blood from among you, when thou shalt do that which is right in the sight of the LORD.**

The following law of war is meant to mitigate the actions of the nations in their abuse of captives, especially female captives. This is in reference to captives of nations "far off" and not to the local Canaanites who were to be totally destroyed as examples concerning the end of the unrepentant.

The instruction here is that if a man desires a female captive he must take her in proper marriage giving her all the rights of a wife; and he must not just use and abuse female prisoners in rapacious lust and then sell them as slaves.

This law must also take into account that inter-religious marriage is forbidden, and that therefore the woman must be willing to accept the religion of Israel like Ruth the Moabite did.

21:10 When thou goest forth to war against thine enemies, and the LORD thy God hath delivered them into thine hands, and thou hast taken them captive,

21:11 And seest among the captives a beautiful woman, and hast a desire unto her, that thou wouldest have her to thy wife;

21:12 Then thou shalt bring her home to thine house, and she shall shave her head, and pare her nails;

21:13 And she shall put the raiment of her captivity from off her, and shall remain in thine house, and bewail her father and her mother a full month: and after that thou shalt go in unto her, and be her husband, and she shall be thy wife.

From there she is to be treated and have all the rights of a lawful wife.

21:14 And **it shall be, if thou have no delight in her, then thou shalt let her go whither she will; but thou shalt not sell her at all for money, thou shalt not make merchandise of her, because thou hast humbled her.**

God winked at polygamy before the New Covenant because of the hardness of the unconverted heart, but this was never intended by the

Creator, as Jesus Christ explained; for he explained that "they two shall be one flesh." If polygamy were to be tolerated in the Mosaic Covenant, then rules regulating the matter needed to be put in place to bring as much peace and fairness as possible.

21:15 If a man have two wives, one beloved, and another hated, and they have born him children, both the beloved and the hated; and if the firstborn son be hers that was hated:

This law goes beyond the issue of polygamy [having more than one wife at the same time] and is applicable to the man who has divorced and remarried. A man may not mistreat his own children because of any bad feelings towards his former wife the mother of his child.

21:16 Then it shall be, when he maketh his sons to inherit that which he hath, that he may not make the son of the beloved firstborn before the son of the hated, which is indeed the firstborn:

21:17 But he shall acknowledge the son of the hated for the firstborn, by giving him a double portion of all that he hath: for he is the beginning of his strength; the right of the firstborn is his.

A rebellious disobedient son who will not be subject to the Word of God [the duty of parents being to teach obedience to the Word of God] is worthy of death if he remains unrepentant after much patient instruction.

This law applies spiritually to the brethren being corrected by God the Father, who as called out sons of God the Father fall away from loving and keeping God's Word. If after they have been patiently warned and corrected, they continue to reject the Word of God for their own ways; the rebellious will be destroyed by God.

21:18 If a man have a stubborn and rebellious son, which will not obey the voice of his father, or the voice of his mother, and that, when they have chastened him, will not hearken unto them:

21:19 Then shall his father and his mother lay hold on him, and bring him out unto the elders of his city, and unto the gate of his place;

21:20 And they shall say unto the elders of his city, This our son is stubborn and rebellious, he will not obey our voice; he is a glutton, and a drunkard.

21:21 And all the men of his city shall stone him with stones, that he die: so shalt thou put evil away from among you; and all Israel shall hear, and fear.

Judgment is not to be made by any one person alone but by the duly constituted authorities.

The following law sets the conditions for Christ to be buried on the same day that he was killed.

21:22 And if a man have committed a sin worthy of death, and he be to be put to death, and thou hang him on a tree: **21:23 His body shall not remain all night upon the tree, but thou shalt in any wise bury him that day**; (for he that is hanged is accursed of God;) that thy land be not defiled, which the LORD thy God giveth thee for an inheritance.

Deuteronomy 22

These next two statutes refer to practical love for our neighbor. This law while explicitly referring to livestock should also be applied to anything which another loses, from his animal to his car or wallet.

Deuteronomy 22:1 Thou shalt not see thy brother's ox or his sheep go astray, and hide thyself from them: thou shalt in any case bring them [return them] again unto thy brother.

22:2 And if thy brother be not nigh unto thee, or if thou know him not, then thou shalt bring it unto thine own house, and it shall be with thee until thy brother seek after it, and thou shalt restore it to him again.

22:3 In like manner shalt thou do with his ass; and **so shalt thou do with his raiment; and with all lost thing of thy brother's, which he hath lost, and thou hast found**, shalt thou do likewise: thou mayest not hide thyself.

We are not to hide what we have found and so unlawfully keep what is not rightly ours, even if it is a great treasure.

We are also to help others in order to prevent any loss, even if they are our personal enemies.

> **Romans 12:20** Therefore if thine enemy hunger, feed him; if he thirst, give him drink: for in so doing thou shalt heap coals of fire on his head [shame his mind and conscience concerning his mistreatment of us].

Deuteronomy 22:4 Thou shalt not see thy brother's ass or his ox fall down by the way, and hide thyself from them: thou shalt surely help him to lift them up again.

The following restriction refers more to deliberately attempting to appear as the opposite sex, than to the idea of women wearing pants for example. Articles of dress are different across the world and this command merely forbids anyone to attempt to appear as a different sex other than our born sex.

This law prevents a homosexual bent of mind from being publicly displayed as an evil example. Almighty God forbids cross dressing and calls doing so an abomination: Cross dressing by either sex for the purpose of sexual titillation is an abomination and absolutely forbidden by God.

22:5 The woman shall not wear that which pertaineth unto a man, neither shall a man put on a woman's garment: for all that do so are abomination unto the LORD thy God.

This is one of the conservation laws of God, after the prohibition of cutting fruit bearing trees for war.

Taking the eggs allows the mother to live and continue to reproduce while taking the mother would prevent her future reproduction and also causes the eggs and young to die being uncared for. Hunting of adult birds should only take place outside of breeding-rearing seasons.

22:6 If a bird's nest chance to be before thee in the way in any tree, or on the ground, whether they be young ones, or eggs, and the dam sitting upon the young, or upon the eggs, **thou shalt not take the dam with the young:**

22:7 But thou shalt in any wise let the dam go, and take the young to thee; that it may be well with thee, and that thou mayest prolong thy days.

The following is another law of love for others.

These laws are also principles of godly behaviour; to fence in a flat roof also clearly implies the fencing off of any deep pit or cliff or similar danger.

22:8 When thou buildest a new house, then thou shalt make a battlement [guard railing] for thy roof, that thou bring not blood upon thine house, if any man fall from thence.

This mainly refers to seed of the same KIND but of different TYPES which could cross pollinate: For example different types of grain in the same field. This does not refer to growing grain in the same field as an olive tree.

22:9 Thou shalt not sow thy vineyard with divers seeds: **lest the fruit of thy seed which thou hast sown, and the fruit of thy vineyard, be defiled** [by cross pollination with other varieties].

God cares about his people far more then about asses. This is a practical physical law since the two animals here are of different strength and inclinations.

This is also a practical spiritual principle that we are not to yoke the spiritually clean with the spiritually unclean. We are not to knowingly marry an unconverted person, nor are we to take part in unclean unconverted actions, polluting ourselves with the evildoing of others by participating with them in their unclean [sinful] activities.

We are to keep ourselves HOLY and we are not to try to mix holiness with the profane, for the unclean thing makes the clean holy thing, unclean.

Do we not know what Paul means; that we are to purge out the leaven of sin?

Brethren, Paul means that we are to STOP sinning when we see that we are wrong! We read this every Passover without comprehending that we need to STOP breaking the Word of God because some man said it was alright; we need to STOP polluting God's Holy Sabbaths; we need to STOP being zealous for idols of men and corporations and we need to ignite the fire of passion to learn and to live by every Word of God.

We need to be zealous to live by every Word of God, as Moses repeats over and over in this book of Deuteronomy!

> **1 Corinthians 5:6** Your glorying is not good. Know ye not that a little leaven leaveneth the whole lump? **5:7** Purge out therefore the old leaven, that ye may be a new lump
>
> **Haggai 2:11** Thus saith the Lord of hosts; Ask now the priests concerning the law, saying,
>
> **2:12** If one bear holy flesh in the skirt of his garment, and with his skirt do touch bread, or pottage, or wine, or oil, or any meat, shall it be holy? And the priests answered and said, No.
>
> **2:13** Then said Haggai, If one that is unclean by a dead body touch any of these, shall it be unclean? And the priests answered and said, It shall be unclean.

We are not to try and bind in marriage a spiritually clean person with an unconverted person and we are not to try and mix true teachings with false teachings. Bear in mind that the ox is a clean animal while the ass is an unclean animal and the two are not to be yoked together.

Deuteronomy 22:10 Thou shalt not plow with an ox [the clean] and an ass [the unclean] together.

The instruction below refers to a blend of materials and not to a separate attachment in the same garment; for example an elastic waistband on a garment is acceptable. The fine pure white linen is symbolic of the righteousness of the saints and we are to be dressed in a pure garment to represent spiritual purity.

> **Revelation 19:8** And to her was granted that she should be arrayed in fine linen, **clean and white: for the fine linen is the righteousness of saints.**

Linen should not be mixed with other materials and thereby made impure; signifying some impurity in the saints. The issue of mixing types of threads to make cloth is about purity and impurity, and by extension the spiritual purity required of God within his people.

We are not to join together with the false religious doctrines and prophecies of unrepentant rebels against God and the Word of God. We are not to mix false ways with true religion and we are not to be joined in marriage with unbelievers as Solomon was, and as many do today.

Jesus Christ will NEVER tolerate any sin in his people; he will help us to overcome any sin; however if we justify and continue in our sin he will take his Spirit from us and consign us to severe correction.

Contrary to what is being taught about a false love which tolerates sin; a little leaven does leaven the whole lump (1 Cor 5:6;) and the leaven of sin will not be tolerated by God. We must repent of sin and turn away from it; we must never tolerate even a very small amount of any sin!

All of these statutes have their spiritual applications and lessons; even those which appear hard to understand, even in the physical context.

Deuteronomy 22:11 Thou shalt not wear a garment of divers sorts, as of woollen and linen together.

Fringes or Zit Zit

These fringes were to be a reminder of God's law.

After Israel had sinned, God commanded them:

> **Numbers 15:38** Speak unto the children of Israel, and bid them that they make them fringes in the borders of their garments throughout their generations, and that they put upon the fringe of the borders a ribband of blue:

15:39 And it shall be unto you for a fringe, that **ye may look upon it, and remember all the commandments of the LORD, and do them** ; and that ye seek not after your own heart and your own eyes, after which ye use to go a whoring: **15:40** That ye may remember, and do all my commandments, and be holy unto your God.

Under the New Covenant, the law is written in our hearts by sincere repentance and a diligent study of God's Word with the aid of God's Spirit, which the Mosaic Covenant did not contain any promise of. This particular statute is now fulfilled by God's Holy Spirit to which we are to listen, rather than looking at **a tzit tzit** [fringe or tassel] on our garment which did not seem to help the people keep the commandments in the past.

Deuteronomy 22:12 Thou shalt make thee fringes upon the four quarters of thy vesture, wherewith thou coverest thyself.

The following refers to testing an accusation of a fraudulent marriage, through false claims of a lack of virginity.

22:13 If any man take a wife, and go in unto her, and hate [the modern word "hate" is too strong, this means to be dissatisfied finding her not a virgin as was claimed] her,

I point out that virginity means that NOTHING has ever penetrated. If a finger or any other object [including for medical reasons] penetrates, even though she has not had a man; she is still not a virgin. If she is not wholly intact she must clearly inform her intended before any marriage plans are made.

22:14 And give occasions of speech against her, and bring up an evil name upon her, and say, I took this woman, and when I came to her, I found her not a maid:

22:15 Then shall the father of the damsel, and her mother, take and bring **forth the tokens of the damsel's virginity** [It was the custom in those days for a virgin to wipe any blood from first intercourse with a cloth, however if the virgin is properly slightly stretched with the husband's finger before intercourse there will be little or no bleeding.] unto the elders of the city in the gate:

22:16 And the damsel's father shall say unto the elders, I gave my daughter unto this man to wife, and he hateth her;

22:17 And, lo, he hath given occasions of speech against her, saying, **I found not thy daughter a maid** [virgin]; and yet these are the tokens of my daughter's virginity. And they shall spread the cloth before the elders of the city.

This was at times a matter of life and death for the woman; because if she is guilty of fornication she must die. In principle this also outlaws prostitution and proscribes the death sentence for whoredom.

This severe punishment is an allegory that Jesus Christ is a jealous God and that he will sternly correct all those who have made a baptismal commitment of espousal to him; and then followed others instead of being absolutely zealous to faithfully follow him withersoever he goeth, and to keep the whole Word of God.

22:18 And the elders of that city shall take that man and chastise him;

22:19 And they shall amerce him in a [fine him] hundred shekels of silver, and give them unto the father of the damsel, because he hath brought up an evil name upon a virgin of Israel: and she shall be his wife; he may not put her away all his days.

22:20 But **if this thing be true, and the tokens of virginity be not found for the damsel**:

22:21 Then they shall bring out the damsel to the door of her father's house, and the men of her city **shall stone her with stones that she die**: because she hath wrought folly in Israel, **to play the whore** in her father's house: so shalt thou put evil away from among you.

Adultery is punishable by death: this is also the punishment for spiritual adultery [loving and obeying anyone other than God the Father and our espoused Husband Jesus Christ], which is death on an eternal spiritual level.

Those who exalt any man or organization above our espoused Husband; who say that "we can do this or that unlawful thing, because some man or corporate church says so" are guilty of idolatry and spiritual adultery.

All those who do not base their conduct on a passionate love for the scriptures and the things of our Husband: Will not be joined with Messiah in marriage to him and will not be in the resurrection of the chosen. They are showing Jesus Christ how little they love him, by not diligently studying the scriptures to prove all things and to follow the whole Word of God.

By obeying others and exalting others above God and our Husband, they are committing spiritual adultery and are worthy of death, if they do not repent.

22:22 If a man be found lying with a woman married to an husband, then they shall both of them die, both the man that lay with the woman, and the woman: so shalt thou put away evil from Israel.

22:23 If a damsel that is a virgin be betrothed unto an husband, and a man find her in the city, and lie with her;

22:24 Then ye shall bring them both out unto the gate of that city, and ye shall stone them with stones that they die; **the damsel, because she cried not**, being in the city; and the man, because he hath humbled his neighbour's wife: so thou shalt put away evil from among you.

Now comes in the law concerning rape. A virgin is not to be considered guilty if she has cried out and fought her attacker.

22:25 But if a man find a betrothed damsel in the field, and the man force her, and lie with her: then the man only that lay with her shall die.

22:26 But unto the damsel thou shalt do nothing; there is in the damsel no sin worthy of death: for as when a man riseth against his neighbour, and slayeth him, even so is this matter:

22:27 For he found her in the field, and the betrothed damsel cried, and there was none to save her.

If a man rape a virgin not married or betrothed, then he must marry her **with her father's consent**, as well as pay a penalty which is the usual value of presents given at a betrothal.

The following is a reminder of the law in Exodus 22:16. Notice in the law that the father has the right to reject the marriage; providing a safety net for the lady if she has been truly forced and the deed was not one of passion on both sides.

> **Exodus 22:16** And if a man entice a maid that is not betrothed, and lie with her, he shall surely endow her to be his wife. **23:17 If her father utterly refuse to give her unto him, he shall pay money according to the dowry of virgins.**

Deuteronomy 22:28 If a man find a damsel that is a virgin, **which is not betrothed**, and lay hold on her, and lie with her, and they be found;

22:29 Then the man that lay with her shall give unto the damsel's father fifty shekels of silver, and she shall be his wife; because he hath humbled her, he may not put her away all his days.

No man may have his own mother or the wife of his father because they are one flesh with his father.

22:30 A man shall not take his father's wife, nor discover his father's skirt.

Deuteronomy 23

In reference to verse one below: Persons being excluded from assembling at the Holy Place in the presence of God because of physical imperfections has a spiritual counterpart in that the willfully sinful and spiritually imperfect sinners will be excluded from the resurrection of the faithful; not being holy as God is holy, having no zeal to live by every Word of God.

> **John 15:2** Every branch in me that beareth not fruit he taketh away: and every branch that beareth fruit, he purgeth it, that it may bring forth more fruit.

Christ said that we must abide in Christ to bear fruit (See John 15); and this contains two issues: First we MUST abide in Christ fully and follow others ONLY as they follow Christ; and second we MUST GROW spiritually and bear fruit in terms of becoming holy as God is holy.

That is, we must GROW and multiply understanding and righteousness through enthusiastic study and the faithful application of every Word of God; internalizing the very nature of God through following the lead of the Holy Spirit to live by every Word of God.

We are to be holy as God is holy, and we are to be perfect as God is perfect, internalizing the nature of God by the power of the Spirit of God.

Those people barred from entering the physical temple because of physical flaws are an instructional example for us that imperfect people will not be in the resurrection to spirit. Nevertheless these physically imperfect people are only an allegorical lesson and they will later be resurrected physically and receive an opportunity to enter the congregation of New Covenant Spiritual Israel.

Deuteronomy 23:1 He that is wounded in the stones, or hath his privy member cut off, shall not enter into the congregation of the LORD.

This is an instructional reference to being unable to bear fruit indicating that those who do not bear spiritual fruit will not be a part of the New Covenant Ekklesia.

Lessons in Obedience to God

The term "bastard" in the physical sense refers to an illegitimate child. In the spiritual sense it refers to one called out to become a child of God, who rejects our heavenly Father's instruction and correction.

> **Hebrews 12:5** And ye have forgotten the exhortation which speaketh unto you as unto children, My son, despise not thou the chastening of the Lord, nor faint when thou art rebuked of him: **12:6** For whom the Lord loveth he chasteneth [corrects], and scourgeth every son whom he receiveth. **12:7** If ye endure [accept God's correction] chastening, God dealeth with you as with sons; for what son is he whom the father chasteneth not? **12:8** But if ye be without [if we refuse God's correction and insist on our own ways] chastisement, whereof all are partakers, then are ye bastards, and not sons.

There are those who believe that they have the authority to decide for themselves whether to bind or to loose the Word of God. For a thorough study into this subject please see the Salvation articles.

Deuteronomy 23:2 A bastard shall not enter into the congregation of the LORD; even to his tenth generation shall he not enter into the congregation of the LORD.

The descendants of Ammon and Moab could not enter into Israel for ten generations from the day that Israel entered the promised land. This was a physical matter because of their sins at that time; once the resurrection of the main harvest comes, they will have their opportunity to enter New Covenant Spiritual Israel.

In those days Moab and Ammon had heard what God had done in Egypt and knew about God revealing himself and entering into a Covenant with Israel at Sinai; and they chose to resist Israel and so resist the God who led Israel, not allowing passage through their land and refusing to sell food and water to Israel.

Then they compounded their resistance to God Almighty by hiring Balaam to curse them. And as if that wickedness was not sufficient; when God refused to allow the curse of Balaam and turned it to a blessing, they conspired to lead Israel into sin so that God would reject his own called out people!

Brethren this is exactly what Satan has done to the Ekklesia today! Being unable to resist God and God's purpose for his called out, Satan has led today's Spiritual Ekklesia into sin with the purpose of causing God to destroy his own called out people of New Covenant Spiritual Israel!

Whereas those who sinned sexually with the daughters of Moab in physical Israel were destroyed; in today's Spiritual Israel those who are sinning by committing spiritual adultery against the Husband of our baptismal commitment by making little gods and idols of men; will be cast into the furnace of great tribulation to afflict the flesh in the hope that the spirit might be saved after having learned a great eternal lesson.

Almighty God the All Wise, is using this latter day situation in the Ekklesia to teach us vital lessons about spiritual adultery against Him and idolatry of men, so that we will learn to exalt and follow God above all else; while ancient Moab and Ammon are instructional examples to help us learn this lesson.

23:3 An Ammonite or Moabite shall not enter into the congregation of the LORD; **even to their tenth generation shall they not enter into the congregation of the LORD for ever:**

23:4 Because they met you not with bread and with water in the way, when ye came forth out of Egypt; and because they hired against thee Balaam the son of Beor of Pethor of Mesopotamia, to curse thee.

23:5 Nevertheless the LORD thy God would not hearken unto Balaam; but the LORD thy God turned the curse into a blessing unto thee, because the LORD thy God loved thee.

23:6 Thou shalt not seek their peace [as a type of God not extending mercy to the adamantly unrepentant wicked] nor their prosperity all thy days for ever.

Prophetically Ammon and Moab will be subject to millennial Israel (Zeph 2:9).

We should always have respect for the Edomites [Turks, Turkmens] and the Egyptians.

23:7 Thou shalt not abhor an Edomite; for he is thy brother: thou shalt not abhor an Egyptian; because thou wast a stranger in his land.

23:8 The children that are begotten of them shall enter into the congregation of the LORD in their third generation.

The Holy God will not co-dwell with any physical or spiritual uncleanness. All physical uncleanness was to be removed from the military camp of Mosaic Israel as well as from any Holy Place.

This is an object lesson for us that the SPIRITUAL uncleanness of sin is to be removed from us: There must be no sin polluting us because God will not co-dwell with sin in us.

> **1 Corinthians 3:16** Know ye not that ye are the temple of God, and that the Spirit of God dwelleth in you? **3:17 If any man defile the temple of God** [with the uncleanness of sin], **him shall God destroy**; for the temple of God is holy, which temple ye are.

Brethren, those who teach self-justification, or that Christ will wink at sin so we need not be concerned, or that we should tolerate willful sin in our assembles: Are sons of wickedness like Balaam; seeking to lead us into sin so that God will destroy his people!

> Any man who says that he is a servant of Jesus Christ and can do anything he wants and God must back him up: Is a LIAR! For Jesus taught: **John 8:34** Jesus answered them, Verily, verily, I say unto you, Whosoever committeth sin [breaks the Word of God] is the servant of sin [and therefore is NOT the servant of Jesus Christ but a bastard (Heb 12:8)].

Deuteronomy 23:9 When the host goeth forth against thine enemies, then keep thee from every wicked thing.

23:10 If there be among you any man, that is not clean by reason of uncleanness that chanceth him by night, then shall he go abroad out of the camp, he shall not come within the camp:

Here we see the evening associated with sun set

23:11 But it shall be, **when evening cometh on**, he shall wash himself with water: and **when the sun is down**, he shall come into the camp again.

23:12 Thou shalt have a place also without the camp, whither thou shalt go forth abroad: **23:13** And thou shalt have a paddle upon thy weapon; and it shall be, when thou wilt ease [eliminate] thyself abroad, thou shalt dig therewith, and shalt turn back and cover that which cometh from thee:

The regulations concerning physical uncleanness have their spiritual counterpart. God will not dwell in the presence of sin. God's Spirit will LEAVE the self-justifying willful sinner.

Let me be absolutely clear: If we make excuses for ourselves to justify continuing in sin; God's Spirit will be withdrawn from us.

23:14 **For the LORD thy God walketh in the midst of thy camp, to deliver thee, and to give up thine enemies before thee; therefore shall thy camp be holy: that he see no unclean thing in thee, and turn away from thee.**

Laws on escaped slaves, usury and prostitution

This refers to a person who has escaped from a foreign land and is God's refugee law. Nevertheless the refugee must sincerely repent of all past sin and pledge to keep the laws of Israel [the laws of God]; and then he may choose his own city or place to dwell at.

23:15 Thou shalt not deliver unto his master the servant which is escaped from his master unto thee: **23:16** He shall dwell with thee, even among you, in that place which he shall choose in one of thy gates, where it liketh him best: thou shalt not oppress him.

All sexual promiscuity is forbidden; including homosexuality and prostitution, as well as adultery, fornication and cross dressing for sexual reasons. All of these things pervert the sanctity of marriage, which is an allegory of the complete loyal unity which God desires with his faithful people.

23:17 **There shall be no whore of the daughters of Israel, nor a sodomite of the sons of Israel.**

The commandments below are blatantly and shamelessly flouted in the Israelite nations and Judah today. Because of these sins they shall yet go into another captivity.

Money gotten through evil deeds is forbidden to be brought into the Temple of God because it is the fruits of sin. Anything that is even associated with sin is unclean and not to be taken into the presence of God.

23:18 Thou shalt not bring the hire of a whore, or the price of a dog [dogs will try to mount anything including their own males and are a biblical type for homosexuals], into the house of the LORD thy God for any vow: for even both these are abomination unto the LORD thy God.

This is referring to personal necessities loans and not to commercial loans for the purpose of earning income. Loaning a billion dollars to build a huge skyscraper or a bridge is a far different matter from loaning a person a few dollars so he may buy bread for his family.

This is not about the supporting the lazy, the object here is to relieve the personal poverty of those destitute or suffering through no fault of their own.

23:19 Thou shalt not lend upon usury to thy brother; usury of money, usury of victuals, usury of any thing that is lent upon usury: **23:20** Unto a stranger thou mayest lend upon usury; but **unto thy brother thou shalt not lend upon usury**: that the LORD thy God may bless thee in all that thou settest thine hand to in the land whither thou goest to possess it.

It is better NOT to make a vow, than to make a vow and not keep it.

This actually has to do with lying to or before God by making unkept promises. Our baptismal Marriage Covenant was a type of promise or vow to God to live by every Word of God. If we make that commitment and then seek excuses to compromise and avoid passionate obedience to God; we are breaking our baptismal commitment [vow] to God the Father and to Jesus Christ.

23:21 When thou shalt vow a vow unto the LORD thy God, thou shalt not slack to pay it: for the LORD thy God will surely require it of thee; and it would be sin in thee.

23:22 But if thou shalt forbear to vow, it shall be no sin in thee.

23:23 That which is gone out of thy lips thou shalt keep and perform; even a freewill offering [The vow beinga type of our free will baptismal pledge to follow the Lamb of God whithersoever he goeth and to live by every Word of God.], according as thou hast vowed unto the LORD thy God, which thou hast promised with thy mouth.

The law of gleaning

This is the law that the disciples of Christ followed in gleaning a few ears of grain as they walked through a field on Sabbath. This is the same as picking an apple as one walks through an orchard on the Sabbath; this in no way justifies paying for goods and services or cooking on a Sabbath. No payment was made and no preparation, cooking or carrying away was done by the disciples. We may take what is necessary for the immediate filling of an immediate need, we may NOT steal another man's harvest.

23:24 When thou comest into thy neighbour's vineyard, then **thou mayest eat grapes thy fill at thine own pleasure; but thou shalt not put any in thy vessel** [to take away to our home].

23:25 When thou comest into the standing corn [grain] of thy neighbour, then thou mayest pluck the ears with thine hand; but thou shalt not move a sickle [harvest in quantity] unto thy neighbour's standing corn [grain].

Deuteronomy 24

Laws of Divorce

These laws were given to mitigate suffering in a spiritually unconverted society, but God never intended divorce. For the instructions of Christ on the spiritual intent of these laws see this article.

One may NOT remarry his divorced wife, who has since that divorce been the wife of another.

God allowed divorce because of the unconverted hardness of heart. This was an act of mercy to provide those trapped in an intolerable situation with an abusive spouse a means of relief. Divorce was NEVER God's intention and in the New Covenant where both spouses have God's Spirit, divorce is NOT lawful (Mat 19**).**

Deuteronomy 24:1 When a man hath taken a wife, and married her, and it come to pass that she find no favour in his eyes, because he hath found some uncleanness in her: then let him write her a bill of divorcement, and give it in her hand, and send her out of his house.

24:2 And when she is departed out of his house, she may go and be another man's wife.

24:3 And if the latter husband hate her, and write her a bill of divorcement, and giveth it in her hand, and sendeth her out of his house; or if the latter husband die, which took her to be his wife;

24:4 Her former husband, which sent her away, may not take her again to be his wife, after that she is defiled; for that is abomination before the LORD: and thou shalt not cause the land to sin, which the LORD thy God giveth thee for an inheritance.

God gives newlyweds a one year honeymoon from government service.

24:5 When a man hath taken a new wife, he shall not go out to war, neither shall he be charged with any business: but he shall be free at home one year, and shall cheer up his wife which he hath taken.

We must not take a man's tools for any debt, because they are his life and livelihood.

24:6 No man shall take the nether or the upper millstone to pledge: for he taketh a man's life to pledge.

Death for enslaving another in Israel

The making of merchandise of the brethren by the elders of today's Ekklesia also carries a death penalty. Those men who seek personal followings and make merchandise of the brethren will NOT be in the resurrection to life eternal, unless they sincerely repent.

24:7 If a man be found stealing any of his brethren of the children of Israel, and maketh merchandise of him, or selleth him; then that thief shall die; and thou shalt put evil away from among you.

Leprosy

Biblical leprosy referred to any growing skin blemish, not necessarily that which is called the disease of leprosy today. The biblical term leprosy was a reference to skin blemishes which disfigured and therefore made the victim unclean.

Biblical leprosy is a broader term than the leprosy (Hansen's disease) that we know today. The Hebrew *tsara'ath* included a variety of ailments and is most frequently seen in Leviticus, where it referred primarily to uncleanness or imperfections according to biblical standards.

A person with any scaly skin blemish was *tsara'ath*. The symbolism extended to any rot or mold on leather, the walls of a house, and on woven cloth. Other Old Testament references to leprosy are associated with punishment or the consequences of sin.

The recent discovery of a highly toxic mold (*Stachybotrys sp.*), which contaminates buildings and causes respiratory distress, memory loss, and rash, lends support to the translation of *tsara'ath* to include "mold." As noted, *tsara'ath* incorporates a collection of contemporary terms, including Hansen's disease, infectious skin diseases, and mold or mildew.

The symbolism of biblical leprosy is similar to the symbolism of leaven; which may be very small at first, but which grows and grows until the whole body is covered, or the whole lump is leavened. Leaven and leprosy are types of sin which pollutes the whole body.

> **1 Corinthians 5:6** Your glorying [in tolerating a sinner in the assembly] is not good. Know ye not that a little leaven leaveneth the whole lump? **5:7** Purge out therefore the old leaven [sincerely repent from all sin, casting it out and STOP sinning], that ye may be a new [a new sin free spiritual person in Christ] lump, as ye are unleavened. For even Christ our passover is sacrificed for us: **5:8** Therefore let us keep the feast, not with old leaven [continuing in our sins], neither with the leaven of malice and wickedness; but with the unleavened bread of [purity from sin] sincerity and truth.

Deuteronomy 24:8 Take heed in the plague of leprosy, that thou observe diligently, and do according to all that the priests the Levites shall teach you: as I commanded them, so ye shall observe to do.

24:9 Remember what the LORD thy God did unto Miriam by the way, after that ye were come forth out of Egypt.

Love Thy Neighbour Laws

We must not take back again by force that which we have lent for immediate personal needs, but must wait until the person is able to repay.

24:10 When thou dost lend thy brother any thing, thou shalt not go into his house to fetch his pledge. **24:11** Thou shalt stand abroad [outside], and the man to whom thou dost lend shall bring out the pledge abroad unto thee.

We must not hold any personal collateral against loans for personal necessities beyond the day's sun set regardless of whether he is able to repay.

24:12 And if the man be poor, thou shalt not sleep with his pledge:

24:13 In any case **thou shalt deliver him the pledge again when the sun goeth down, that he may sleep in his own raiment**, and bless thee: and it shall be righteousness unto thee before the LORD thy God.

We must pay wages to our workers at the time agreed and without any delay.

24:14 Thou shalt not oppress an hired servant that is poor and needy, whether he be of thy brethren, or of thy strangers that are in thy land within thy gates:

24:15 At his [appointed pay day] day thou shalt give him his hire, neither shall the sun go down upon it; for he is poor, and setteth his heart upon it: lest he cry against thee unto the LORD, and it be sin unto thee.

Every person is to be held responsible for his own conduct; to receive his reward or punishment.

The same law is true spiritually. When we stand before God we will be held responsible for our own actions for good or for bad. We will not be able to shirk saying "I was only following this or that person." What will you answer when you are asked why you followed some person and did not fully follow the whole Word of God? You will be speechless before your judge who will say to you:

> **Matthew 7:23** And then will I profess unto them, I never knew you: depart from me, ye that work iniquity. **7:24** Therefore whosoever heareth these sayings of mine, **and doeth them**, I will liken him unto a wise man, which built his house upon a rock: **7:25** And the rain descended, and the floods came, and the winds blew, and beat upon that house; and it fell not: for it was founded upon a rock.
>
> **7:26** And every one that heareth these sayings of mine, **and doeth them not**, shall be likened unto a foolish man, which built his house upon the sand: **7:27** And the rain descended, and the floods came, and the winds blew, and beat upon that house; and it fell: and great was the fall of it.

Deuteronomy 24:16 The fathers shall not be put to death for the children, neither shall the children be put to death for the fathers: **every man shall be put to death for his own sin.**

All judgment is to be fair and just and equal for all.

24:17 Thou shalt not pervert the judgment of the stranger, nor of the fatherless; nor take a widow's raiment to pledge:

24:18 But thou shalt remember that thou wast a bondman in Egypt, and the LORD thy God redeemed thee thence: therefore I command thee to do this thing.

We are to be merciful and generous to the needy in our everyday dealings

24:19 When thou cuttest down thine harvest in thy field, and hast forgot a sheaf in the field, thou shalt not go again to fetch it: it shall be for the stranger, for the fatherless, and for the widow: that the LORD thy God may bless thee in all the work of thine hands.

24:20 When thou beatest thine olive tree [shake the branches to harvest the berries], thou shalt not go over the boughs again: it shall be for the stranger, for the fatherless, and for the widow.

24:21 When thou gatherest the grapes of thy vineyard, thou shalt not glean it afterward: it shall be for the stranger, for the fatherless, and for the widow.

24:22 And thou shalt remember that thou wast a bondman in the land of Egypt: therefore I command thee to do this thing.

Deuteronomy 25

Sundry Laws

A maximum of forty lashes is proscribed for corporal punishment, and a fair and honest judgment must be rendered to all.

Deuteronomy 25:1 If there be a controversy between men, and they come unto judgment, that the judges may judge them; then **they shall justify the righteous, and condemn the wicked.**

> **Proverbs 17:15** He that justifieth the wicked, and he that condemneth the just, even they both are abomination to the Lord.

Deuteronomy 25:2 And it shall be, if the wicked man be worthy to be beaten, that the judge shall cause him to lie down, and to be beaten before his [in front of the judge] face, according to his fault, by a certain number.

25:3 Forty stripes he may give him, and not exceed: lest, if he should exceed, and beat him above these with many stripes, then thy brother should seem vile unto thee.

The laborer is worthy of wages, and he should receive according to his efforts. especially those that labor in sound doctrine.

> **1 Corinthians 9:9** For it is written in the law of Moses, thou shalt not muzzle the mouth of the ox that treadeth out the corn. Doth God take care for oxen?

9:10 Or saith he it altogether for our sakes? For our sakes, no doubt, this is written: that he that ploweth should plow in hope; and that he that thresheth in hope should be partaker of his hope.

9:11 If we have sown unto you spiritual things, is it a great thing if we shall reap your carnal things?

1 Timothy 5:17 Let the elders that rule well be counted worthy of double honour, especially they who labour in the word and doctrine. **5:18** For the scripture saith, thou shalt not muzzle the ox that treadeth out the corn. And, The labourer is worthy of his reward.

Deuteronomy 25:4 Thou shalt not muzzle the ox when he treadeth out the corn [grain].

The counterbalance to this rule is that the ox who eats greedily will lose his job and quite likely be slaughtered. Deuteronomy 25:4 is often wrongly used to excuse the taking of more than is right by religious organizations or elders.

A man should provide a son for his dead childless brother. This is because the land was given to each family as a permanent inheritance; and the inheritance genealogy needed to be maintained.

25:5 If brethren dwell together, and one of them die, and have no child, the wife of the dead shall not marry without unto a stranger: her husband's brother shall go in unto her, and take her to him to wife, and perform the duty of an husband's brother unto her.

25:6 And it shall be, that the firstborn which she beareth shall succeed in the name of his brother which is dead, that his name be not put out of Israel.

25:7 And if the man like not to take his brother's wife, then let his brother's wife go up to the gate unto the elders, and say, My husband's brother refuseth to raise up unto his brother a name in Israel, he will not perform the duty of my husband's brother.

25:8 Then the elders of his city shall call him, and speak unto him: and if he stand to it, and say, I like not to take her;

25:9 Then shall his brother's wife come unto him in the presence of the elders, and loose his shoe from off his foot, and spit in his face, and shall answer and say, So shall it be done unto that man that will not build up his brother's house.

25:10 And his name shall be called in Israel, The house of him that hath his shoe loosed [he is to be called a man of disgrace].

The book of Ruth shows that if the near kinsman rejected his duty, this duty of a husband's near kinsman would then pass on to the next nearest of kin

Below is not a reference to a loving fondling of her husband, but to an act of violence against another. The severity of the penalty is because such an injured man is to be cut off from the holy place through the blemish of the injury, and may be denied reproduction for the rest of his life due to the injury.

The spiritual allegory of this is that anyone preventing godly spiritual growth and the bearing of spiritual fruit (John 15) will not go unpunished. Today's elders destroy the brethren by preventing their spiritual growth and the bearing of spiritual fruit through their rejection of the knowledge of godliness, which knowledge of godliness God promised to increase in these latter days (Dan 12:4).

> **Hosea 4:6** My people are destroyed for lack of knowledge: because thou [today's elders] hast rejected knowledge, I will also reject thee, that thou shalt be no priest to me: seeing thou hast forgotten the law of thy God, I will also forget thy children.

Deuteronomy 25:11 When men strive together one with another, and the wife of the one draweth near for to deliver her husband out of the hand of him that smiteth him, and putteth forth her hand, and taketh him by the secrets: **25:12** Then thou shalt cut off her hand, thine eye shall not pity her.

Again the Law of Love for neighbour is seen. This is the issue of cheating others by manipulating measurements. The spirit of this law is that we are not to be deceitful or to use ANY method to be dishonest and to deceive others.

25:13 Thou shalt not have in thy bag divers [different weights and measures with which to cheat others] weights, a great and a small.

25:14 Thou shalt not have in thine house divers measures, a great and a small.

25:15 But thou shalt have a perfect and just weight, a perfect and just measure shalt thou have: that thy days may be lengthened in the land which the LORD thy God giveth thee.

25:16 For **all that do such things, and all that do unrighteously, are an abomination unto the LORD thy God.**

Later king Saul did much against Amalek, although he sinned in saving their cattle.

25:17 Remember what Amalek did unto thee by the way, when ye were come forth out of Egypt;

25:18 How he met thee by the way, and smote the hindmost of thee, even all that were feeble behind thee, when thou wast faint and weary; and he feared not God.

25:19 Therefore it shall be, when the LORD thy God hath given thee [victory over the Canaanites] rest from all thine enemies round about, in the land which the LORD thy God giveth thee for an inheritance to possess it, that thou shalt blot out the remembrance of [utterly destroy] Amalek from under heaven; thou shalt not forget it.

Deuteronomy 26

The law of the offering of the first fruits of the harvest

The Spring Wave Offering represents Jesus Christ the Lamb of God, and the first fruits represents the first fruits of the spiritual harvest of humanity.

The physical first fruits are holy to God, representing in type the first fruits of the spiritual harvest of humanity.

The spring harvest was to begin with the Wave Offering representing the resurrection, ascension and acceptance of Jesus Christ as the first of a harvest of many brethren.

The non sacrificial basket of first fruits of the first [barley] harvest was to be brought to the temple to be placed before the altar in rejoicing over the blessings of God for the physical harvest, and the spiritual harvests of humanity.

This ceremony is to take place after the Wave Sheaf ceremony during the Feast of Unleavened Bread.

Deuteronomy 26:1 And it shall be, when thou art come in unto the land which the LORD thy God giveth thee for an inheritance, and possessest it, and dwellest therein;

26:2 That thou shalt take of **the first of all the fruit of the earth**, which thou shalt bring of thy land [after the Wave Offering begins the harvest each year during the Feast of Unleavened Bread] that the LORD thy God giveth thee, and shalt put it in a basket, and shalt go unto the place which the LORD thy God shall choose to place his name there.

26:3 And thou shalt go unto the priest that shall be in those days, and say unto him, I profess this day unto the LORD thy God, that I am come unto the country which the LORD sware unto our fathers for to give us.

26:4 And the priest shall take the basket out of thine hand, and set it down before the altar of the LORD thy God.

26:5 And thou shalt speak and say before the LORD thy God, A Syrian ready to perish was my father, and he went down into Egypt, and sojourned there with a few, and became there a nation, great, mighty, and populous:

26:6 And the Egyptians evil entreated us, and afflicted us, and laid upon us hard bondage:

26:7 And when we cried unto the LORD God of our fathers, the LORD heard our voice, and looked on our affliction, and our labour, and our oppression:

26:8 And the LORD brought us forth out of Egypt with a mighty hand, and with an outstretched arm, and with great terribleness, and with signs, and with wonders:

26:9 And he hath brought us into this place, and hath given us this land, even a land that floweth with milk and honey.

26:10 And now, behold, I have brought the firstfruits of the land, which thou, O LORD, hast given me. And thou shalt set it before the LORD thy God, and worship before the LORD thy God:

26:11 And thou shalt rejoice in every good thing which the LORD thy God hath given unto thee, and unto thine house, thou, and the Levite, and the stranger that is among you.

Tithing for the poor

26:12 When thou hast made an end of tithing all the tithes of thine increase [at the end of the third year] **the third year**, which is the year of tithing, and hast given it unto the Levite, the stranger, the fatherless, and the widow, that they may eat within thy gates, and be filled;

26:13 Then thou shalt say before the LORD thy God, I have brought away the hallowed things out of mine house, and also have given them unto the [poor widows and orphans and handicapped among the tribe of Levi] Levite, and unto the stranger, to the fatherless, and to the widow, according to all thy commandments which thou hast commanded me: I have not transgressed thy commandments, neither have I forgotten them.

26:14 I have not eaten thereof in my mourning [during the burden of the tithing year], neither have I taken away ought thereof for any unclean use, nor given ought thereof for the dead: but I have hearkened to the voice of the LORD my God, and have done according to all that thou hast commanded me.

26:15 Look down from thy holy habitation, from heaven, and bless thy people Israel, and the land which thou hast given us, as thou swarest unto our fathers, a land that floweth with milk and honey.

Today many organizations of today's Ekklesia rob God and rob God's poor by misusing God's Poor Tithe for other purposes: God did not intend His poor tithe to become a cash cow for some corporate entity.

The book of Acts teaches us that it is the Deacons and not the elders or some corporate entity which is to care for the poor and to have jurisdiction over any poor fund.

While in the modern world there is some advantage in a church wide system to help the poor such a system should be run by non elders and be kept completely separate and totally independent from the preaching, teaching, study and counselling functions of the ministry.

The biblical example for deacons overseeing this matter is not only in the book of Acts but is a mirror of the Mosaic priests being helped by the other Levites.

Very soon now the tribulation will be upon us and there will be no tithing at all in a collapsed economy.

Our Baptismal Commitment

Our baptismal covenant is to live by every Word of God, in both the physical letter and in the spirit and intent of God's Word.

When we agree to be baptized we are committing ourselves to live by every Word of God and to follow no man no matter what that man claims about himself; if he does not faithfully teach us to be zealous to keep every Word of God.

Deuteronomy 26:16 This day the LORD thy God hath commanded thee to do these statutes and judgments: thou shalt therefore keep and do them with all thine heart, and with all thy soul.

26:17 Thou hast avouched the LORD this day to be thy God, and to walk in his ways, and to keep his statutes, and his commandments, and his judgments, and to hearken unto his voice:

26:18 And the LORD hath avouched thee this day to be his peculiar people, as he hath promised thee, and that thou shouldest keep all his commandments;

26:19 And to make thee high above all nations** [A faithful physical would be blessed as an allegory that the faithful of the New Covenant will be blessed in a resurrection to spirit, to become kings [rulers] and priests, teaching and leading all nations] **which he hath made, in praise, and in name, and in honour; and that thou mayest be an holy people unto the LORD thy God, as he hath spoken.**

Deuteronomy 27

The people are again encouraged to live by every Word of God, because possession of the physical promised land [and for the faithful New Covenant called out, possession of the spiritual Promised Land of Eternal Life] is absolutely dependent on living by every Word of God with enthusiastic passionate zeal and love for our LORD!

Deuteronomy 27:1 And Moses with the elders of Israel commanded the people, saying, **Keep all the commandments which I command you this day.**

27:2 And it shall be on the day when ye shall pass over Jordan unto the land which the LORD thy God giveth thee, that thou shalt set thee up great stones, and plaister them with plaister:

When they entered the land they were told to list the laws of God [the laws of the Land of God] on a monument at the border.

27:3 And **thou shalt write upon them all the words of this law, when thou art passed over, that thou mayest go in unto the land which the LORD thy God giveth thee**, a land that floweth with milk and honey; as the LORD God of thy fathers hath promised thee. **27:4** Therefore it shall be when ye be gone over Jordan, that ye shall set up these stones, which I command you this day, in mount Ebal, and thou shalt plaister them with plaister.

An altar is to be built at the entry of the promised land and peace offerings representing the people reconciled to and at peace with God, living by every Word of God are to be offered. This represents those resurrected to the promised land of eternal life being reconciled to God the Father and at peace with God.

Altars to God are to be built of whole stones, not cut out by the hand of man. The stones of the altar are representative of Messiah the Christ the Rock of our Salvation, who was the Implementing Creator of all things and who was not made by any man (John 1).

27:5 And there shalt thou build an altar unto the LORD thy God, **an altar of stones: thou shalt not lift up any iron tool upon them.**

27:6 Thou shalt build **the altar of the LORD thy God of whole stones: and thou shalt offer burnt offerings** [representative of wholehearted obedience and service to God] **thereon unto the LORD thy God:**

27:7 And **thou shalt offer peace offerings** [representative of being reconciled to and at peace with God], **and shalt eat** [the peace offerings] **there, and rejoice before the LORD thy God.**

Peace Offerings at their entry into the physical promised land given to them by God were an allegory of the entry of the New Covenant called out overcomers into the spiritual Promised Land of eternal life and their state of eternal peace with God.

The people of physical and spiritual Israel are never to forget that their place in the Promised Land is absolutely conditional on their faithful zeal to live by every Word of God.

27:8 And **thou shalt write upon the stones all the words of this law very plainly.**

Notice here very plainly, how hugely important the keeping of every Word of God is to our Great God.

Our baptismal commitment is to live by EVERY Word of God, as we enter voluntarily into a marriage covenant of espousal to a spiritual Husband.

Whether we are chosen to be changed to spirit and enter a final formal marriage with Christ the Lamb of God in eternal life or we are not chosen; is entirely dependent on whether we love God enough to zealously "be a DOER of the Word" and diligently faithfully live by every Word of God!

27:9 And Moses and the priests the Levites spake unto all Israel, saying, **Take heed, and hearken, O Israel; this day thou art become the people of the LORD thy God.**

27:10 Thou shalt therefore obey the voice of the LORD thy God, and do his commandments and his statutes, which I command thee this day.

Moses instructs the Levites to loudly declare blessings for obedience and cursing's for not diligently living by every Word of God.

27:11 And Moses charged the people the same day, saying,

27:12 These shall stand upon mount Gerizim to bless the people, when ye are come over Jordan; Simeon, and Levi, and Judah, and Issachar, and Joseph, and Benjamin:

27:13 And these shall stand upon mount Ebal to curse; Reuben, Gad, and Asher, and Zebulun, Dan, and Naphtali.

27:14 And **the Levites shall speak, and say unto all the men of Israel with a loud voice**,

27:15 Cursed be the man that maketh any graven or molten image, an abomination unto the LORD, the work of the hands of the craftsman, and putteth it in a secret place. And all the people shall answer and say, Amen.

Physical idolatry has its spiritual counterpart; the idolizing of corporate organizations, men and the false traditions of men; to follow them in place of living by every Word of God.

27:16 Cursed be he that setteth light by his father or his mother. And all the people shall say, Amen.

The spiritual lesson of obedience to physical parents is that we are to be submissive and obedient to God our Spirit Father, living by His every Word.

27:17 Cursed be he that removeth his neighbour's landmark. And all the people shall say, Amen.

This refers to stealing anything and to stealing land in particular.

27:18 Cursed be he that maketh the blind to wander out of the way. And all the people shall say, Amen.

Spiritually, leading the blind astray refers to teaching false doctrine leading folks astray spiritually.

27:19 Cursed be he that perverteth the judgment of the stranger, fatherless, and widow. And all the people shall say, Amen.

This refers to the perverting of godly judgment and not dealing justly with all people.

27:20 Cursed be he that lieth with his father's wife [since polygamy did exist at that time this would include but does not necessarily mean having one's own mother]; because he uncovereth his father's skirt. And all the people shall say, Amen.

This refers to shaming one's father, as a type of spiritual shame in sinning against God the Father.

27:21 Cursed be he that lieth with any manner of beast. And all the people shall say, Amen.

Spiritually this refers to our fidelity to our spiritual Husband Jesus Christ above all others, and the rejection of all false ways and sinful abominations.

27:22 Cursed be he that lieth with his sister, the daughter of his father, or the daughter of his mother. And all the people shall say, Amen.

This is a new law instituted by God through Moses, after humanity had reproduced enough that having one's sister was no longer needed [as it was in Adam's days, even Abraham having his own sister to wife]. This command separated Israel from the custom of the Egyptians at that time, which was to marry one's sister.

27:23 Cursed be he that lieth with his mother in law [his wife's mother]. And all the people shall say, Amen.

Here it is forbidden for a man to have a woman and her mother, which logically forbids a man to take a woman and her daughter. That is, a man having his own daughter is absolutely forbidden. The penalty for these things is to be cursed by God to utter and absolute destruction.

27:24 Cursed be he that smiteth his neighbour secretly. And all the people shall say, Amen. **27:25** Cursed be he that taketh reward to slay an innocent person. And all the people shall say, Amen.

Spiritual murder comes by the elders not rebuking all sin and not teaching people to live by every Word of God and by encouraging people to exalt the words of men above the Word of God in our thoughts and deeds.

Spiritually this refers to the sin of Balaam in taking a reward to lead the people astray from God into sin and so spiritually murdering them. This is a great sin in the Ekklesia today as many lead the people astray from God in pursuit of the reward of numbers and income.

Some foolish and ignorant people say that God's law is not a Law of Love! God's law is defined as "Love for God" and "Love for our neighbour" as Jesus Christ clearly defined the law from his own mouth!

God IS love; God's law IS love: BLESSED BE THE NAME OF THE LORD!!!

> **Matthew 22:36** Master, which is the great commandment in the law?

22:37 Jesus said unto him, Thou shalt love the Lord thy God with all thy heart, and with all thy soul, and with all thy mind.

22:38 This is the first and great commandment.

22:39 And the second is like unto it, Thou shalt love thy neighbour as thyself.

22:40 On these two commandments hang all the law and the prophets.

Deuteronomy 27:26 Cursed be he that confirmeth not all the words of this law to do them. And all the people shall say, Amen.

All those who refuse to live by every Word of God or to love anything including a preacher or a corporate church to obey it blindly without question are guilty of idolatry and spiritual adultery. Such people are under the curse of eternal death unless they sincerely repent and turn to passionately live by every Word of God and exalt the Eternal above all else.

Deuteronomy 28

In this latter day, Israel [primarily the British, American, Dutch and Scandinavian peoples] and Judah are receiving the blessings that God promised the descendants of Abraham, Isaac and Jacob.

We have been given choice blessings and we have responded by filling our lands with abominations and continual rebellion against the Word of our God.

Therefore, hear the warnings of God as recorded by Moses.

God will give Israel and Judah one last victory after which [if they do not repent and turn from their sin] they will be cast in to severe correction as soon as Peace and Safety is declared (1 Thess 5:3).

The Blessings for Obedience to every Word of God

We have been blessed and made the chief peoples on the earth for the past several hundred years. Now God is preparing to correct the nations of Israel and Judah one last time in preparation for the coming of Messiah the Christ.

Deuteronomy 28:1 And it shall come to pass, if thou shalt hearken diligently unto the voice of the LORD thy God, to observe and to do all his commandments which I command thee this day, that the LORD thy God will set thee on high above all nations of the earth:

28:2 And all these blessings shall come on thee, and overtake thee, if thou shalt hearken unto the voice of the LORD thy God.

28:3 Blessed shalt thou be in the city, and blessed shalt thou be in the field. **28:4** Blessed shall be the fruit of thy body, and the fruit of thy ground, and the fruit of thy cattle, the increase of thy kine, and the flocks of thy sheep. **28:5** Blessed shall be thy basket and thy store.

28:6 Blessed shalt thou be when thou comest in, and blessed shalt thou be when thou goest out. **28:7** The LORD shall cause thine enemies that rise up against thee to be smitten before thy face: they shall come out against thee one way, and flee before thee seven ways.

28:8 The LORD shall command the blessing upon thee in thy storehouses, and in all that thou settest thine hand unto; and he shall bless thee in the land which the LORD thy God giveth thee.

28:9 The LORD shall establish thee an holy people unto himself, as he hath sworn unto thee, if thou shalt keep the commandments of the LORD thy God, and walk in his ways. 28:10 And all people of the earth shall see that thou art called by the name of the LORD; and they shall be afraid of thee.

28:11 And the LORD shall make thee plenteous in goods, in the fruit of thy body, and in the fruit of thy cattle, and in the fruit of thy ground, in the land which the LORD sware unto thy fathers to give thee.

28:12 The LORD shall open unto thee his good treasure, the heaven to give the rain unto thy land in his season, and to bless all the work of thine hand: and thou shalt lend unto many nations, and thou shalt not borrow.

28:13 And the LORD shall make thee the head, and not the tail; and thou shalt be above only, and thou shalt not be beneath; **if that thou hearken unto the commandments of the LORD thy God**, which I command thee this day, to observe and to do them: **28:14** And thou shalt not go aside from any of the words which I command thee this day, to the right hand, or to the left, to go after other gods to serve them.

The curses for disobedience of the Word of God

The curses for disobedience, or compromising with any part of God's Word; which are even now beginning to fall upon the New Covenant spiritual Israel and upon the nations of physical Israel and Judah as a final warning; and which are about to climax with a final great correction.

Once Islamic Extremism in the Middle East is crushed and a regional peace deal is achieved; a man will be set up in the Vatican doing miracles, and when he goes to the Holy Place about 75 days after being set up, the correction of the nations will begin with the occupation of Jerusalem and will spread from there to include all nations over 42 months.

> **Daniel 12:7** And I heard the man clothed in linen, which was upon the waters of the river, when he held up his right hand and his left hand unto heaven, and sware by him that liveth for ever that it shall be for a time, times, and an half [42 prophetic 30 day months or 1260 days]; and when he shall have accomplished to scatter the power of the holy people, all these things shall be finished.

This is a long list of the horrors that will come upon us for the overspreading of our many abominations; which curses are already beginning.

Deuteronomy 28:15 But it shall come to pass, if thou wilt not hearken unto the voice of the LORD thy God, to observe to do all his commandments and his statutes which I command thee this day; that all these curses shall come upon thee, and overtake thee:

28:16 Cursed shalt thou be in the city, and cursed shalt thou be in the field. **28:17** Cursed shall be thy basket and thy store [harvest and storage]. **28:18** Cursed shall be the fruit of thy body, and the fruit of thy land, the increase of thy kine, and the flocks of thy sheep. **28:19** Cursed shalt thou be when thou comest in, and cursed shalt thou be when thou goest out.

28:20 The LORD shall send upon thee cursing, vexation, and rebuke, in all that thou settest thine hand unto for to do, until thou be destroyed, and until thou perish quickly; because of the wickedness of thy doings, whereby thou hast forsaken me.

28:21 The LORD shall make the pestilence cleave unto thee, until he have consumed thee from off the land, whither thou goest to possess it. **28:22** The LORD shall smite thee with a consumption [wasting away], and with a fever, and with an inflammation, and with an extreme burning, and with the sword, and with blasting, and with mildew; and they shall pursue thee until thou perish.

28:23 And thy heaven that is over thy head shall be brass, and the earth that is under thee shall be iron. **28:24** The LORD shall make the rain of thy land powder and dust: from heaven shall it come down upon thee, until thou be destroyed.

28:25 The LORD shall cause thee to be smitten before thine enemies: thou shalt go out one way against them, and flee seven ways before them: and shalt be removed into all the kingdoms of the earth. **28:26** And thy carcase shall be meat unto all fowls of the air, and unto the beasts of the earth, and no man shall fray them away.

28:27 The LORD will smite thee with the botch of Egypt, and with the emerods, and with the scab, and with the itch, whereof thou canst not be healed. **28:28** The LORD shall smite thee with madness, and blindness, and astonishment of heart:

28:29 And thou shalt grope at noonday [in confusion of mind], as the blind gropeth in darkness, and thou shalt not prosper in thy ways: and thou shalt be only oppressed and spoiled evermore, and no man shall save thee.

28:30 Thou shalt betroth a wife, and another man shall lie with her: thou shalt build an house, and thou shalt not dwell therein: thou shalt plant a vineyard, and shalt not gather the grapes thereof.

28:31 Thine ox shall be slain before thine eyes, and thou shalt not eat thereof: thine ass shall be violently taken away from before thy face, and shall not be restored to thee: thy sheep shall be given unto thine enemies, and thou shalt have none to rescue them.

28:32 Thy sons and thy daughters shall be given unto another people, and thine eyes shall look, and fail with longing for them all the day long; and there shall be no might in thine hand.

28:33 The fruit of thy land, and all thy labours, shall a nation which thou knowest not eat up; and thou shalt be only oppressed and crushed alway: **28:34** So that thou shalt be mad for the sight of thine eyes which thou shalt see. **28:35** The LORD shall smite thee in the knees, and in the legs, with a sore botch that cannot be healed, from the sole of thy foot unto the top of thy head.

28:36 The LORD shall bring thee, and thy king which thou shalt set over thee, unto a nation which neither thou nor thy fathers have known; and there shalt thou serve other gods, wood and stone. **28:37** And thou shalt become an astonishment, a proverb, and a byword, among all nations whither the LORD shall lead thee.

28:38 Thou shalt carry much seed out into the field, and shalt gather but little in; for the locust shall consume it. **28:39** Thou shalt plant vineyards, and dress them, but shalt neither drink of the wine, nor gather the grapes; for the worms [pests] shall eat them. **28:40** Thou shalt have olive trees throughout all thy coasts, but thou shalt not anoint thyself with the oil; for thine olive shall cast his fruit.

28:41 Thou shalt beget sons and daughters, but thou shalt not enjoy them; for they shall go into captivity. **28:42** All thy trees and fruit of thy land shall the locust consume.

28:43 The stranger that is within thee shall get up above thee very high; and thou shalt come down very low. **28:44** He shall lend to thee, and thou shalt not lend to him: he shall be the head, and thou shalt be the tail.

28:45 Moreover all these curses shall come upon thee, and shall pursue thee, and overtake thee, till thou be destroyed; because thou hearkenedst not unto the voice of the LORD thy God, to keep his commandments and his statutes which he commanded thee:

28:46 And they shall be upon thee for a sign and for a wonder, and upon thy seed for ever. **28:47 Because thou servedst not the LORD thy God with joyfulness, and with gladness of heart, for the abundance of all things;**

Because we will not zealously serve God during the abundance of God's blessings, we shall be given over to this curse of severe correction to humble us.

28:48 Therefore shalt thou serve thine enemies **which the LORD shall send against thee**, in hunger, and in thirst, and in nakedness, and in want of all things: and he shall put a yoke of iron upon thy neck, until he have destroyed thee.

28:49 The LORD shall bring a nation against thee from far, from the end of the earth, as swift as the eagle flieth; a nation whose tongue thou shalt not understand; **28:50** A nation of fierce countenance, which shall not regard the person of the old, nor shew favour to the young:

28:51 And he shall eat the fruit of thy cattle, and the fruit of thy land, until thou be destroyed: which also shall not leave thee either corn, wine, or oil, or the increase of thy kine, or flocks of thy sheep, until he have destroyed thee.

28:52 And he shall besiege thee in all thy gates, until thy high and fenced walls come down, wherein thou trustedst, throughout all thy land: and he shall besiege thee in all thy gates throughout all thy land, which the LORD thy God hath given thee.

28:53 And thou shalt eat the fruit of thine own body, the flesh of thy sons and of thy daughters, which the LORD thy God hath given thee, in the siege, and in the straitness, wherewith thine enemies shall distress thee:

28:54 So that the man that is tender among you, and very delicate [meek and timid], his eye shall be evil toward his brother, and toward the wife of his bosom, and toward the remnant of his children which he shall leave:

28:55 So that he will not give to any of them of the flesh of his children whom he shall eat: because he hath nothing left him in the siege, and in the straitness, wherewith thine enemies shall distress thee in all thy gates.

28:56 The tender and delicate woman among you, which would not adventure to set the sole of her foot upon the ground for delicateness and tenderness, her eye shall be evil toward the husband of her bosom, and toward her son, and toward her daughter,

28:57 And toward her young one that cometh out from between her feet, and toward her children which she shall bear: for she shall eat them for want of all things secretly in the siege and straitness, wherewith thine enemy shall distress thee in thy gates.

28:58 If thou wilt not observe to do all the words of this law that are written in this book, that thou mayest fear this glorious and fearful name, THE LORD THY GOD;

28:59 Then the LORD will make thy plagues wonderful **[great]**, and the plagues of thy seed, even great plagues, and of long continuance, and sore sicknesses, and of long continuance.

28:60 Moreover he will bring upon thee all the diseases of Egypt, which thou wast afraid of; and they shall cleave unto thee.

28:61 Also every sickness, and every plague, which is not written in the book of this law, them will the LORD bring upon thee, until thou be destroyed.

28:62 And ye shall be left few in number, whereas ye were as the stars of heaven for multitude; because thou wouldest not obey the voice of the LORD thy God.

28:63 And it shall come to pass, that as the LORD rejoiced over you to do you good, and to multiply you; so the LORD will rejoice over you to destroy you, and to bring you to nought; and ye shall be plucked from off the land whither thou goest to possess it.

28:64 And the LORD shall scatter thee among all people, from the one end of the earth even unto the other; and there thou shalt serve other gods, which neither thou nor thy fathers have known, even wood and stone.

28:65 And among these nations shalt thou find no ease, neither shall the sole of thy foot have rest: but the LORD shall give thee there a trembling heart, and failing of eyes, and sorrow of mind: **28:66** And thy life shall hang in doubt before thee; and thou shalt fear day and night, and shalt have none assurance of thy life:

28:67 In the morning thou shalt say, Would God it were even! and at even thou shalt say, Would God it were morning! for the fear of thine heart wherewith thou shalt fear, and for the sight of thine eyes which thou shalt see.

28:68 And the LORD shall bring thee into Egypt again with ships, by the way whereof I spake unto thee, Thou shalt see it no more again: and there ye shall be sold unto your enemies for bondmen and bondwomen, and no man shall buy you.

All of these were fulfilled in the past and a final similar correction is coming

Right now the nations of Israel, both physical and spiritual, think obedience to God is a little thing. Today the Israelite nations [including Spiritual Israel] are immersed wholeheartedly in sin and are about to receive God's just correction in its fullness.

Today's Spiritual Ekklesia continues to idolize men and false traditions; strangely counting their espousal to Christ as meaning that they are to obey lovers [idols of men] who claim to come in his name, rather than to keep their commitment to obey their God and to live by every Word of God.

Today's brethren are relying on their false traditions and corporate idols of men, instead of living by every Word of God.

Today's Spiritual Ekklesia of the New Covenant called out, is now facing the strong correction that Moses warned us of and that Jesus Christ warned us of in Revelation 3:14-22.

Deuteronomy 29

Moses recites more history and exhorts obedience to God

Deuteronomy 29:1 These are the words of the covenant, which the LORD commanded Moses to make with the children of Israel in the land of Moab, beside the covenant which he made with them in Horeb.

29:2 And Moses called unto all Israel, and said unto them, **Ye have seen all that the LORD did before your eyes in the land of Egypt unto Pharaoh, and unto all his servants, and unto all his land; 29:3** The great temptations [miraculous wonders] which thine eyes have seen, the signs, and those great miracles:

God revealed to Moses the need for a New and better Covenant as is later promised in Jeremiah 31:31 and Ezekiel 36:24.

Once Judah and Israel [mainly the British, American, Scandinavian and Dutch peoples] have been humbled in the final correction and are made ready to live by every Word of God; Messiah the Christ will come and deliver us.

> **Ezekiel 36:24** For I will take you from among the heathen, and gather you out of all countries, and will bring you into your own land.
>
> **36:25** Then will I sprinkle clean water upon you, and ye shall be clean: from all your filthiness, and from all your idols, will I cleanse you.

36:26 **A new heart also will I give you, and a new spirit will I put within you**: and I will take away the stony heart out of your flesh, and I will give you an heart of flesh.

36:27 And **I will put my spirit within you, and cause you to walk in my statutes, and ye shall keep my judgments, and do them**.

36:28 And ye shall dwell in the land that I gave to your fathers; and ye shall be my people, and I will be your God.

36:29 I will also save you from all your uncleannesses: and I will call for the corn, and will increase it, and lay no famine upon you.

Deuteronomy 29:4 Yet the LORD hath not given you an heart to perceive, and eyes to see, and ears to hear, unto this day [the day this was written].

The forty years in the wilderness

29:5 And I have led you **forty years in the wilderness**: your clothes are not waxen old upon you, and thy shoe is not waxen old upon thy foot.
29:6 Ye have not eaten [your own bread, but you ate manna] bread, neither have ye drunk wine or strong drink: that ye might know that I am the LORD your God.

29:7 And when ye came unto this place [Bashan (Golan); north of Moab on the east side of the Jordan river], Sihon the king of Heshbon, and Og the king of Bashan, came out against us unto battle, and we smote them: **29:8** And we took their land, and gave it for an inheritance unto the Reubenites, and to the Gadites, and to the half tribe of Manasseh.

29:9 Keep therefore the words of this covenant, and do them, that ye may prosper in all that ye do.

Remember that Moses is speaking just before his death and is rehearsing the history of Israel from the Exodus until they were ready to actually enter the land.

At this point Moses tells the people that their fathers did not enter the land forty years previously because of unbelief and disobedience, even though they were in a Covenant with God.

Moses then told the people that God was renewing the Mosaic Covenant that he had made with them at Sinai, and just before they enter the land Moses makes it clear that if they turn away like their fathers did, they will be removed from the land: Possession of the Promised Land is absolutely contingent upon faithful obedience to their Covenant to live by every Word of God.

This very same thing is true of the New Covenant called out of Spiritual Israel. Our entry into eternal life and receipt of the promises of God, is absolutely contingent on our faithful obedience to God our Father in heaven and to our New Covenant Husband.

Jesus Christ does not take spiritual adultery and a faithless wife lightly: He is a jealous God and will NOT tolerate the sin of doing what men and organizations say, above living by every Word of God.

If we turn back into spiritual Egypt and slavery to Satan the god-king of worldliness and wickedness: We shall surely be rejected by God as were all the ancients who sought to return to Egypt.

29:10 Ye stand this day all of you before the LORD your God; your captains of your tribes, your elders, and your officers, with all the men of Israel, **29:11** Your little ones, your wives, and thy stranger that is in thy camp, from the hewer of thy wood unto the drawer of thy water:

29:12 That thou shouldest enter into covenant with the LORD thy God, and into his oath, which the LORD thy God maketh with thee this day:
29:13 That he may establish thee to day for a people unto himself, and that he may be unto thee a God, as he hath said unto thee, and as he hath sworn unto thy fathers, to Abraham, to Isaac, and to Jacob.

29:14 Neither with you only do I make this covenant and this oath; **29:15** But with him that standeth here with us this day before the LORD our God, and also with him that is not here with us this day:

29:16 (For ye know how we have dwelt in the land of Egypt; and how we came through the nations which ye passed by; **29:17** And ye have seen their abominations, and their idols, wood and stone, silver and gold, which were among them:)

29:18 Lest there should be among you man, or woman, or family, or tribe, whose heart turneth away this day from the LORD our God, to go and serve the gods of these nations; lest there should be among you a root that beareth gall and wormwood;

Even if the New Covenant people of the Spiritual Ekklesia deceive ourselves that correction will not fall on us because we are such good folk in our own eyes and are called by the name of God's People; these things will still surely come upon us if we are zealous for our own ways and idols of men above any zeal to learn and to passionately live by every Word of God.

29:19 And it come to pass, when he heareth the words of this curse, that he bless himself in his heart, **saying, I shall have peace, though I walk in the imagination of mine heart**, to add drunkenness [intoxication with pride] to thirst [the lack of the waters of God's Spirit, and the Word of God]:

29:20 The LORD will not spare him, but then the anger of the LORD and his jealousy shall smoke against that man, and all the curses that are written in this book shall lie upon him, and the LORD shall blot out his name from under heaven. **29:21** And the LORD shall separate him unto evil out of all the tribes of Israel, according to all the curses of the covenant that are written in this book of the law:

29:22 So that the generation to come of your children that shall rise up after you, and the stranger that shall come from a far land, shall say, when they see the plagues of that land, and the sicknesses which the LORD hath laid upon it;

29:23 And that the whole land thereof is brimstone, and salt, and burning, that it is not sown, nor beareth, nor any grass groweth therein, like the overthrow of Sodom, and Gomorrah, Admah, and Zeboim, which the LORD overthrew in his anger, and in his wrath:

29:24 Even all nations shall say, Wherefore hath the LORD done thus unto this land? what meaneth the heat of this great anger?

Brethren, we, the spiritually called out of the New Covenant; have turned away from God our Father and from the Husband of our baptismal espousal to follow idols of men.

It is because of our great zeal to blindly obey our corporate gods, our idols of men and our false traditions; and our great LACK of zeal to follow and obey God our Father and the Husband of our baptismal commitment to live by every Word of God: that we will be rejected by Messiah the Christ (Rev 3:14-22) and cast into great tribulation, in the hope that by afflicting the flesh, God might perhaps save us spiritually.

29:25 Then men shall say, **Because they have forsaken the covenant of the LORD God of their fathers, which he made with them when he brought them forth out of the land of Egypt:**

29:26 For **they went and served other gods**, and worshipped them, gods whom they knew not, and whom he had not given unto them: **29:27** And the anger of the LORD was kindled against this land, to bring upon it all the curses that are written in this book: **29:28** And the LORD rooted them out of their land in anger, and in wrath, and in great indignation, and cast them into another land, as it is this day.

29:29 The secret things belong unto the LORD our God: **but those things which are revealed belong unto us and to our children for ever, that we may do all the words of this law.**

Deuteronomy 30

The compassion of God at the sincere repentance of many people after their humbling correction in this latter day, will bring Messiah the Christ to rule all nations and teach them the way to peace with each other and reconciliation with the God the Holy Father in heaven!

Deuteronomy 30:1 And it shall come to pass, when all these things are come upon thee [upon apostate physical and Spiritual Israel], the blessing and the curse, which I have set before thee, and thou shalt call them to mind among all the nations, whither the LORD thy God hath driven thee,

30:2 And [apostate physical and Spiritual Israel] **shalt return unto the LORD thy God, and shalt obey his voice according to all that I command thee this day, thou and thy children, with all thine heart, and with all thy soul;**

30:3 That then the LORD thy God will turn thy captivity, and have compassion upon thee, and will return and gather thee from all the nations, whither the LORD thy God hath scattered thee.

30:4 If any of thine be driven out unto the outmost parts of heaven, from thence will the LORD thy God gather thee, and from thence will he fetch thee: **30:5** And the LORD thy God will bring thee into the land which thy fathers possessed, and thou shalt possess it; and he will do thee good, and multiply thee above thy fathers.

This is the New Covenant prophesied by Moses and which was later prophesied in Jeremiah 31 and Ezekiel 36.

30:6 And **the LORD thy God will circumcise thine heart, and the heart of thy seed, to love the LORD thy God with all thine heart, and with all thy soul, that thou mayest live.** **30:7** And the LORD thy God will put all these curses upon thine enemies, and on them that hate thee, which persecuted thee [if they do not also sincerely repent].

30:8 And thou [apostate physical and Spiritual Israel will sincerely repent] **shalt return and obey the voice of the LORD, and do all his commandments which I command thee this day.**

30:9 And the LORD thy God will make thee plenteous in every work of thine hand, in the fruit of thy body, and in the fruit of thy cattle, and in the fruit of thy land, for good: for the LORD will again rejoice over thee for good, as he rejoiced over thy fathers:

This New Covenant is also conditional upon obedience to every Word of God.

God will save his wayward people of physical and spiritual Israel and God will also save all humanity by turning our hearts from stone to flesh and writing his law on their hearts, which hearts will be softened by the addition of his Holy Spirit as it is written in Joel 2:28.

> **Joel 2:28** And it shall come to pass afterward, that I will pour out my spirit upon all flesh;

Deuteronomy 30:10 If thou shalt [if apostate physical and Spiritual Israel sincerely repents and turns to live by every Word of God] **hearken unto the voice of the LORD thy God, to keep his commandments and his statutes which are written in this book of the law, and if thou turn unto the LORD thy God with all thine heart, and with all thy soul.**

If we commit to diligently learning and living by every Word of God, we shall be given the Holy Spirit of God which will enable us to keep the Word of God.

30:11 For this commandment which I command thee this day, it is not hidden from thee, neither is it far off. **30:12** It is not in heaven, that thou shouldest say, Who shall go up for us to heaven, and bring it unto us, that we may hear it, and do it?

30:13 Neither is it beyond the sea, that thou shouldest say, Who shall go over the sea for us, and bring it unto us, that we may hear it, and do it? **30:14** But the word is very nigh unto thee, in thy mouth, and in thy heart, that thou mayest do it.

> Possession of the physical Promised Land is absolutely CONDITIONAL on our obedience to every Word of God! Therefore lawbreakers WILL BE DRIVEN OFF THE LAND!
>
> This practical physical driving out of the wicked, is an allegory of the possession of the spiritual Promised Land of eternal life, which is also absolutely CONDITIONAL on our passionate love for God and our diligent obedience to live by every Word of God!

30:15 See, **I have set before thee this day life and good, and death and evil**; **30:16** In that **I command thee this day to love the LORD thy God, to walk in his ways, and to keep his commandments and his statutes and his judgments** [every WORD of God]**,** that thou mayest live and multiply: and the LORD thy God shall bless thee in the land whither thou goest to possess it.

30:17 But if thine heart turn away, so that thou wilt not hear, but shalt be drawn away, and worship other gods, and serve them; **30:18** I denounce unto you this day, that ye shall surely perish, and that ye shall not prolong your days upon the land, whither thou passest over Jordan to go to possess it.

> **God through Moses set before the people a choice to obey and live, or to turn away from godliness unto death.**
>
> **The choice was theirs:**
>
> **Today the choice is ours. Will we turn back to our God in diligent, faithful, zealous, passionate, obedient enthusiasm to live by every Word of God; or will we choose the easy way of wickedness that leads to our correction and the destruction of the unrepentant?**

30:19 I call heaven and earth to record this day against you, that I have set before you life and death, blessing and cursing: therefore choose life, that both thou and thy seed may live:

30:20 That thou mayest love the LORD thy God, and that thou mayest obey his voice, and that thou mayest cleave unto him: for he is thy life, and the length of thy days: that thou mayest dwell in the land which the LORD sware unto thy fathers, to Abraham, to Isaac, and to Jacob, to give them.

Deuteronomy 31

Moses gives his last instructions to the people and hands the leadership over to Joshua.

31:1 And Moses went and spake these words unto all Israel.

31:2 And he said unto them, **I am an hundred and twenty years old this day**; I can no more go out and come in: also the LORD hath said unto me, Thou shalt not go over this Jordan.

Joshua was faithful to live by every Word of God and no enemy could stand before him. If the New Covenant called out of spiritual Israel are faithfully diligent to live by every Word of God like Joshua was, we shall enter into the Promised Land of eternal life; for our Mighty God will go before us to conquer every sin and the grave itself.

31:3 The LORD thy God, he will go over before thee, and he will destroy these nations [as an instructional example of God destroying all sin and all of the unrepentant wicked in their due time] **from before thee, and thou shalt possess them:** and Joshua, he shall [Joshua will lead physical Israel] go over before thee, as the LORD hath said.

31:4 And the LORD shall do unto them [the Canaanites] as he did to Sihon and to Og, kings of the Amorites, and unto the land of them, whom he destroyed. **31:5** And the LORD shall give them up before your face, that ye may do unto them according unto all the commandments which I have commanded you.

Physical Israel was not to fear but was to trust in God; even so the brethren in today's Spiritual Ekklesia are not to fear what any man can do, but we are to be zealous to live by every Word of God; for the Almighty One is the Champion of all those who love him enough to follow him, to trust in him and to live by his every Word.

31:6 Be strong and of a good courage, fear not, nor be afraid of them: for the LORD thy God, he it is that doth go with thee; he will not fail thee, nor forsake thee.

Yes brethren, be strong for our LORD; to learn and to faithfully live by his every Word: Be strong my friends and do not fear what any man can do for our LORD is victorious over all, even over the grave itself!

31:7 And Moses called unto Joshua, and said unto him in the sight of all Israel, **Be strong and of a good courage: for thou must go with this people unto the land which the LORD hath sworn unto their fathers to give them; and thou shalt cause them to inherit it.**

31:8 And the LORD, he it is that doth go before thee; he will be with thee, he will not fail thee, neither forsake thee: fear not, neither be dismayed.

Moses wrote out [or caused to be written] a copy of this book of Deuteronomy and commanded that it be read to all the people every seventh year at the Feast of Tabernacles, to remind all the people in BOTH the Mosaic and the New Covenant of their imperative to obey their Covenant to live by every Word of God, so that they might prosper and receive the promised blessings.

This scriptural instruction to read Deuteronomy at the Fall Festival is widely ignored to this day. If only we would obey this instruction and read this book of Deuteronomy expounding its meaning regularly at the Feast of Tabernacles, we would be reminded of how far we have fallen from our baptismal commitment, and we would be warned of the correction which is soon coming upon us if we remain steadfast in our sins.

31:9 And Moses wrote this law, and delivered it unto the priests the sons of Levi, which bare the ark of the covenant of the LORD, and unto all the elders of Israel.

31:10 And Moses commanded them, saying, **At the end of every seven years, in the solemnity of the year of release, in the feast of tabernacles,**

31:11 When all Israel is come to appear before the LORD thy God in the place which he shall choose, thou shalt read this law before all Israel in their hearing.

31:12 Gather the people together, men and women, and children, and thy stranger that is within thy gates, that they may hear, and that they may learn, and fear the LORD your God, and observe to do all the words of this law:

31:13 And that their children, which have not known any thing, may hear, and learn to fear the LORD your God, as long as ye live in the land whither ye go over Jordan to possess it.

God then spoke to Moses and made Joshua God's leader over Israel. Moses and then Joshua were Judges over Israel as were the leaders of the book of Judges until the nation became a kingdom.

31:14 And the LORD said unto Moses, Behold, thy days approach that thou must die: call Joshua, and present yourselves in the tabernacle of the congregation, that I may give him a charge. And Moses and Joshua went, and presented themselves in the tabernacle of the congregation.

God speaks to Moses and Joshua

31:15 And the LORD appeared in the tabernacle in a pillar of a cloud: and the pillar of the cloud stood over the door of the tabernacle.

31:16 And the LORD said unto Moses, Behold, thou shalt sleep with thy fathers; . . .

God foretells the future of the people of physical Israel saying that they would fall away and suffer many things before ultimately [in this latter time] sincerely repenting and turning to serve God.

Despite this example for our instruction these same things have happened to today's Spiritual Ekklesia, which has also fallen away from any zeal to live by every Word of God.

. . . and **this people will rise up, and go a whoring after the gods of the strangers of the land, whither they go to be among them, and will forsake me, and break my covenant which I have made with them.**

31:17 Then my anger shall be kindled against them in that day, and I will forsake them, and I will hide my face from them, and they shall be devoured, and many evils and troubles shall befall them; so that they will say in that day, Are not these evils come upon us, because our God is not among us?

Because even today's New Covenant Spiritual Israel has forsaken the Eternal to follow their idols of men and false traditions; God will surely reject us into great tribulation (Rev 3:14-22), along with modern physical Israel and Judah.

31:18 And I will surely hide my face in that day for all the evils which they shall have wrought, in that they are turned unto other gods.

31:19 Now therefore write ye this song for you, and teach it the children of Israel: put it in their mouths, that this song may be a witness for me against the children of Israel.

31:20 For when I shall have brought them into the land which I sware unto their fathers, that floweth with milk and honey; and they shall have eaten and filled themselves, and waxen fat; then will they turn unto other gods, and serve them, and provoke me, and break my covenant.

31:21 And it shall come to pass, when many evils and troubles are befallen them, that this song shall testify against them as a witness; for it shall not be forgotten out of the mouths of their seed: for I know their imagination which they go about, even now, before I have brought them into the land which I sware.

Very soon God's two servants will surely remind physical and spiritual Israel to sincerely repent and turn to a zeal to live by every Word of God during great tribulation.

Moses encourages Joshua and commands that this book of Deuteronomy be placed in the Ark to be kept safe for a witness against the people who fall into sin.

31:22 Moses therefore wrote this song the same day, and taught it the children of Israel.

Where are the Joshua's of today who will help prepare and lead the brethren towards true godliness? Where are the Daniel's and Elijah's who are strong to cleave to their Mighty One as a Shining Light of example, to show the brethren the ways of the Eternal and the way to life eternal?

31:23 And he gave Joshua the son of Nun [of Ephraim] a charge, and said, **Be strong and of a good courage:** for thou shalt bring the children of Israel into the land which I sware unto them: and I will be with thee.

31:24 And it came to pass, when Moses had made an end of writing the words of this law in a book, until they were finished, **31:25** That Moses commanded the Levites, which bare the ark of the covenant of the LORD, saying,

31:26 Take this book of the law, and put it in the side of the ark of the covenant of the LORD your God, that it may be there for a witness against thee.

31:27 For I know thy rebellion, and thy stiff neck: behold, while I am yet alive with you this day, ye have been rebellious against the LORD; and how much more after my death?

It is so sad that human beings are driven to follow men; and that a supposedly godly people will quickly follow deceitful men away from God.

31:28 Gather unto me all the elders of your tribes, and your officers, that I may speak these words in their ears, and call heaven and earth to record against them.

31:29 For I know that after my death ye will utterly corrupt yourselves, and turn aside from the way which I have commanded you; and evil will befall you in the latter days; because ye will do evil in the sight of the LORD, to provoke him to anger through the work of your hands.

31:30 And Moses spake in the ears of all the congregation of Israel the words of this song, until they were ended.

Deuteronomy 32

Not to be confused with the Song of Moses' rejoicing over the crossing of the Red Sea this Song was given to Moses by God and is a warning from Almighty God to the people of physical Israel and the brethren of Spiritual Israel.

God is NOT a respecter of persons, just like he dealt with physical Israel; he WILL deal with spiritual Israel. Our strong correction is coming and is at the very door.

When physical and spiritual Judah and Israel have fallen into a final correction for all their abominations with which they have defiled themselves in the latter days, they will sincerely repent and turn to their God; and Messiah the Christ WILL come to deliver them.

The Song of Moses given to him by Almighty God as a witness against physical and spiritual Israel. Hear ye the Word of the LORD!

32:1 Give ear, O ye heavens, and I will speak; and hear, O earth, the words of my mouth.

32:2 My doctrine [the teachings of Holy Scripture] shall drop as the rain, my speech shall distil as the dew, as the small rain [dew and mist] upon the tender herb, and as the showers upon the grass: **32:3 Because I will publish the name of the LORD: ascribe ye greatness unto our God. 32:4 He is the Rock, his work is perfect: for all his ways are judgment: a God of truth and without iniquity, just and right is he.**

32:5 They have corrupted themselves, their spot [place] is not the spot [position or place of godly children] of his children [they are not God's children but rebellious people]: they are a perverse and crooked generation.

32:6 Do ye thus requite [is this how we reward God for delivering and blessing us] the LORD, **O foolish people and unwise? is not he thy father that hath bought thee? hath he not made thee, and established thee?**

32:7 Remember the days of old, consider the years of many generations: ask thy father, and he will shew thee; thy elders, and they will tell thee.

32:8 When the Most High divided to the nations their inheritance, when he separated the sons of Adam, he set the bounds of the people according to the number of the children of Israel.

Physical Israel [Jacob] is God's portion; how much more then is New Covenant Spiritual Israel to be the children of God?

32:9 For the LORD's portion is his people; Jacob is the lot of his inheritance.

Just as physical Israel was chosen by God to be God's people, God found us in the filth of our sins and called us to become a spiritual New Covenant Israel (Jer 51:31, Eze 36:26).

32:10 He found him in a desert land, and in the waste howling wilderness; he led him about, he instructed him, he kept him as the apple of his eye.
32:11 As an eagle stirreth up her nest, fluttereth over her young, spreadeth abroad her wings, taketh them, beareth them on her wings: **32:12** So the LORD alone did lead him, and there was no strange god with him.

32:13 He made him ride on the high places of the earth, that he might eat the increase of the fields; and he made him to suck honey out of the rock, and oil out of the flinty rock; **32:14** Butter of kine, and milk of sheep, with fat of lambs, and rams of the breed of Bashan, and goats, with the fat of kidneys of wheat; and thou didst drink the pure blood of the grape.

32:15 But Jeshurun waxed fat, and kicked: thou art waxen fat, thou art grown thick, thou art covered with fatness; then he forsook God which made him, and lightly esteemed the Rock of his salvation.

> **Jeshurun** (Hebrew: יְשֻׁרוּן), in the Hebrew Bible, is a poetic name for Israel, derived from a root word meaning upright, just or straight. Jeshurun appears four times in the Hebrew Bible — three times in Deuteronomy and once in Isaiah. It can mean the people of Israel (Deut. 32:15; 33:26), the Land of Israel (Deut. 33:5;), or the Patriarch Jacob (whom an Angel renamed Israel in Genesis 32:29):

New Covenant Spiritual Israel has also provoked God our Father in heaven and Jesus Christ the Husband of our baptismal commitment, by turning away to follow idols of men and rejecting truth and any zeal to live by every Word of God to cleave to our own false traditions.

32:16 They provoked him to jealousy with strange gods [which today's Spiritual Ekklesia does with idols of men and corporate entities, which we love more than we love to live by every Word of God], with abominations provoked they him to anger.

I will be very bold to write the truth here. Today's Ekklesia, the church of God groups, have been misled to exalt men and corporate church organizations as having the ultimate moral authority to bind and loose the Word of God.

I say straight out: This idea that men have authority over God's Word to decide what they want to keep [bind] or not keep [loose]: Is a Doctrine of Demons!

Almighty God decides and Almighty God teaches and commands; and we are to live by every Word of God; so says Jesus Christ!

> **Matthew 4:4** But he answered and said, It is written, **Man shall not live by bread alone, but by every word that proceedeth out of the mouth of God.**
>
> **1 John 2:4** He that saith, I know him, and **keepeth not his commandments, is a liar, and the truth is not in him.**
>
> **1 John 3:24** And **he that keepeth his commandments dwelleth in him, and he in him.** And hereby we know that he abideth in us, by the Spirit which he hath given us.
>
> **1 John 5:2** By this **we know that we love the children of God, when we love God, and keep his commandments.**
>
> **1 John 5:3** For **this is the love of God, that we keep his commandments**: and his commandments are not grievous.

Deuteronomy 32:17 They sacrificed unto devils [in spiritual terms we obey false teachings and do not live by every Word of God], not to God; to gods whom they knew not, to new gods that came newly up, whom your fathers feared not.

Brethren, today's Spiritual Ekklesia has forgotten any zeal to live by every Word of the Rock of our Salvation. We even call God's Sabbath's holy; condemning ourselves with our own mouths as we buy in restaurants and employ caterers and run businesses on God's Holy Time!

The longsuffering patience of God in giving us time to repent from our wickedness until now, does not mean that God's correction will never come! Our time of correction is now at hand!

32:18 Of the Rock that begat thee thou art unmindful, and hast forgotten God that formed thee.

The LORD is beginning to abhor today's Spiritual Ekklesia for our wicked rebellions against him in following our idols of men in place of any zeal to live by every Word of God (Rev 3:14-22).

32:19 And when the LORD saw it, he abhorred them, because of the provoking [rebelliousness] of his sons, and of his daughters. **32:20** And he said, I will hide my face from them, I will see what their end shall be: for they are a very froward [stubborn self-willed] generation, **children in whom is no faith**.

32:21 They have moved me to jealousy with [by serving idols of men] **that which is not God; they have provoked me to anger with their vanities:** and I will move them to jealousy with those which are not a people; I will provoke them to anger with a foolish nation.

32:22 For a fire is kindled in mine anger, and shall burn unto the lowest hell [God's anger will burn like the depths of the earth where the elements are molten], and shall consume the earth with her increase, and set on fire the foundations of the mountains [symbolically mountains represent governments: this speaking of the great tribulation wars].

32:23 I will heap mischiefs upon them; I will spend mine arrows upon them. **32:24** They shall be burnt with hunger, and devoured with burning heat, and with bitter destruction: I will also send the teeth of beasts upon them, with the poison of serpents of the dust.

32:25 The sword without, and terror within, shall destroy both the young man and the virgin, the suckling also with the man of gray hairs. **32:26** I said, I would scatter them into corners, I would make the remembrance of them to cease from among men:

God will then correct both Spiritual Ekklesia and the proud nations far and wide.

32:27 Were it not that I feared the wrath of the enemy, lest their adversaries should behave themselves strangely, and **lest they should say, Our hand is high, and the LORD hath not done all this.**

Rejecting any zeal to live by every Word of God, neither physical nor spiritual Israel today, has any wisdom or understanding of the things of God.

32:28 For they are a nation void of counsel, neither is there any understanding in them.

32:29 O that they were wise, that they understood this, that they would consider their latter end!

No nation could prevail against us IF we were pleasing God through living by every Word of God! Therefore if they excel over us it is because we are not faithful followers of our Mighty God.

32:30 How should one chase a thousand, and two put ten thousand to flight, except their Rock had sold them, and the LORD had shut them up? **32:31** For their rock is not as our Rock, even our enemies themselves being judges. **32:32** For their vine is of the vine of Sodom, and of the fields of Gomorrah: their grapes are grapes of gall, their clusters are bitter: **32:33** Their wine is the poison of dragons, and the cruel venom of asps. **32:34** Is not this laid up in store with me, and sealed up among my treasures?

The nations that will be used to correct the today's nations of apostate physical Israel and spiritual Israel, will themselves ultimately be corrected for their own wickedness.

32:35 To me belongeth vengeance and recompence; their foot shall slide in due time: for the day of their calamity is at hand, and the things that shall come upon them make haste.

When we see our idols and little gods of men and false traditions being destroyed; then we will sincerely repent and run to the Eternal, the Rock of our Salvation. When our great pride in ourselves broken and God sees our sincere repentance he will repent [stop] from correcting us and God will begin to show us mercy.

32:36 For the LORD shall judge his people, and repent himself for his servants, when he seeth that their power is gone, and there is none shut up, or left.

32:37 And he shall say, Where are their gods, their rock in whom they trusted,

God mocks our false idols of men, telling us to call upon them to save us. Can our idols of men to whom we give our substance and follow their false ways, save us? Not at all!

32:38 Which did eat the fat of their sacrifices, and drank the wine of their drink offerings? let them rise up and help you, and be your protection.

It is the Eternal who slays and who saves for all eternity; and not any corporate church organization or human being. Let us follow the Eternal to live by every Word of God alone, following men ONLY as they follow and live by every Word of God.

32:39 See now that I, even I, am he, and there is no god with me: I kill, and I make alive; I wound, and I heal: neither is there any that can deliver out of my hand.

32:40 For I lift up my hand to heaven, and say, I live for ever.

32:41 If I whet my glittering sword, and mine hand take hold on judgment; I will render vengeance to mine enemies, and will reward them that hate me.

32:42 I will make mine arrows drunk with blood, and my sword shall devour flesh; and that with the blood of the slain and of the captives, from the beginning of revenges upon the enemy.

32:43 Rejoice, O ye nations, with his people: for he will avenge the blood of his servants, and will render vengeance to his adversaries, and will be merciful unto his land, and to his people.

32:44 And Moses came and spake all the words of this song in the ears of the people, he, and Hoshea [Joshua] the son of Nun.

32:45 And Moses made an end of speaking all these words to all Israel:

32:46 And he said unto them, **Set your hearts unto all the words which I testify among you this day, which ye shall command your children to observe to do, all the words of this law.**

32:47 For it is not a vain thing for you; because it is your life: and through this thing [living by every Word of God] ye shall prolong your days in the land, whither ye go over Jordan to possess it.

The Song of Warning is Ended; Moses was told to go to Mt Nebo to see the promised land, and to go to the place where he would die.

32:48 And the LORD spake unto Moses that selfsame day, saying,

32:49 Get thee up into this mountain Abarim, unto mount Nebo, which is in the land of Moab, that is over against Jericho; and behold the land of Canaan, which I give unto the children of Israel for a possession: **32:50** And die in the mount whither thou goest up, and be gathered unto thy people; as Aaron thy brother died in mount Hor, and was gathered unto his people:

32:51 Because ye trespassed against me among the children of Israel at the waters of MeribahKadesh, in the wilderness of Zin; because ye sanctified me not in the midst of the children of Israel.

32:52 Yet thou shalt see the land before thee; but thou shalt not go thither unto the land which I give the children of Israel.

Deuteronomy 33

Moses before his death blessed the tribes of Israel and prophesied from God about their future. These things have happened only in part today, really being prophecies about the Millennium and beyond when these people will turn to a zeal for God and these blessings will come to the full.

33:1 And **this is the blessing, wherewith Moses the man of God blessed the children of Israel before his death.**

33:2 And he said, The LORD came from Sinai, and rose up from Seir unto them; he shined forth from mount Paran, and he came with ten thousands of saints: from his right hand went a fiery law for them. **33:3** Yea, he loved the people; all his saints are in thy hand: and they sat down at thy feet; every one shall receive of thy words.

33:4 Moses commanded us a law, even the inheritance of the congregation of Jacob. **33:5** And he [God] was king in Jeshurun [Israel], when the heads of the people and the tribes of Israel were gathered together.

I am going to add the Prophetic Blessings of Jacob in Genesis 49 beside the Prophetic Blessings of Moses, to give a fuller picture.

I will identify the locations of those tribes whose modern identity is certain. It is obvious that there has been a very substantial mixing of races and that tribal identity refers only to the primary founding peoples.

Reuben

Deuteronomy 33:6 Let Reuben live, and not die; and let not his men be few.

Genesis 49:3 Reuben, thou art my firstborn, my might, and the beginning of my strength, the excellency of dignity, and the excellency of power: **49:4** Unstable as water, thou shalt not excel; because thou wentest up to thy father's bed; then defiledst thou it: he went up to my couch.

Reuben is not to perish nor is Reuben to become an independent nation in his own right because of instability, yet Reuben is to have a large population in spite of being stateless.

The tribe of Reuben migrated from Palestine north into Scandinavia where they became known as North Men [Normans] and separating from Naphtali they then migrated southward and settled in Normandy, northern France.

Later most of them migrated from France to Louisiana which became a part of the US, and to Canada where they became the Quebecois and Acadians.

While Lower Louisiana had been settled by French colonists since the late 17th century, the Cajuns trace their roots to the influx of Acadian settlers after the Great Expulsion from their homeland in Maritime Canada during the French and British hostilities prior to the Seven Years' War (1756 to 1763). In the USA those deported by Britain to Louisiana are called Cajuns [French les Acadiens] or Accadians.

Reuben also inhabits the Canadian province of Quebec and teh french speaking Reubenites live in many other parts of modern Canada..

Reuben makes up a substantial part of the populations of the United States and Canada.

Judah

Deuteronomy 33:7 And this is the blessing of Judah: and he said, Hear, LORD, the voice of Judah, and bring him unto his people: let his hands be sufficient for him; and be thou an help to him from his enemies.

Genesis 49:8 Judah, thou art he whom thy brethren shall praise: thy hand shall be in the neck of thine enemies; thy father's children shall bow down before thee. **49:9** Judah is a lion's whelp: from the prey, my son, thou art gone up: he stooped down, he couched as a lion, and as an old lion; who shall rouse him up?

49:10 The sceptre shall not depart from Judah, nor a lawgiver from between his feet, until Shiloh come; and unto him shall the gathering of the people be. **49:11** Binding his foal unto the vine, and his ass's colt unto the choice vine; he washed his garments in wine, and his clothes in the blood of grapes: **49:12** His eyes shall be red with wine, and his teeth white with milk.

Judah has always been identified as the Jews, however today many Jews do not identify themselves racially, but by an affiliation to Rabbinic Judaism.

Messiah the Christ will come to Judah at Jerusalem and will bring with him the resurrected king David (Ezek 34 and 37) to whom the sceptre belongs.

Levi

Deuteronomy 33:8 And of Levi he said, Let thy Thummim and thy Urim be with thy holy one, whom thou didst prove at Massah, and with whom thou didst strive at the waters of Meribah;

33:9 Who said unto his father and to his mother, I have not seen him; neither did he acknowledge his brethren, nor knew his own children: for they have observed thy word, and kept thy covenant.

33:10 They shall teach Jacob thy judgments, and Israel thy law: they shall put incense before thee, and whole burnt sacrifice upon thine altar.

33:11 Bless, LORD, his substance, and accept the work of his hands; smite through the loins of them that rise against him, and of them that hate him, that they rise not again.

Levi was called out of the tribes of Israel to become the tribe of God. Therefore Levi is not considered to be one of the Twelve Tribes but remains scattered in both Judah and in the Ten Tribes of Israel. When the ten tribes were taken away from Judah and given to Jeroboam that wicked king cut the people off as much as he could from going to worship God at the temple in Jerusalem and set up a pagan religion in Israel. From that time on the Levites in the ten tribes either fled to Judah or were largely apostatized so that God called special prophets to teach godliness in Israel.

Simeon

Levi and Simeon were men with strong tempers and were not to become nations, they were to be divided and scattered through the tribes of Israel.

Genesis 49:5 Simeon and Levi are brethren; instruments of cruelty are in their habitations. **49:6** O my soul, come not thou into their secret; unto their assembly, mine honour, be not thou united: for in their anger they slew a man, and in their selfwill they digged down a wall. **49:7** Cursed be their anger, for it was fierce; and their wrath, for it was cruel: I will divide them in Jacob, and scatter them in Israel.

Benjamin

Benjamin was a war like people shedding much blood in Israel during the period of the Judges. Benjamin would remain attached to Judah and would not be considered to be one of the Ten Tribes of Israel, later - in the millennium - settling down and enjoying the riches of his inheritance and dwelling in a safe place.

Deuteronomy 33:12 And of Benjamin he said, The beloved of the LORD [Judah] shall dwell in safety by him [Benjamin and Judah will dwell together]; and the Lord shall cover [protect] him all the day long, and he shall dwell between his shoulders.

When God rent the Ten Tribes from Rehoboam, Judah and Benjamin were left together.

Genesis 49:27 Benjamin shall ravin as a wolf: in the morning he shall devour the prey, and at night he shall divide the spoil

Joseph

Joseph replaced Reuben as the first born, and was granted a double portion with his two sons each becoming a separate tribe in Israel.

Deuteronomy 33:13 And of Joseph he said, Blessed of the Lord be his land, for the precious things of heaven, for the dew, and for the deep that coucheth beneath [the riches under the land], **33:14** And for the precious fruits brought forth by the sun, and for the precious things put forth by the moon [blessings of great harvest from which came the wheat sheaf symbol], **33:15** And for the chief things of the ancient mountains, and for the precious things of the lasting hills [forestry, minerals and mining], **33:16** And for the precious things of the earth and fulness thereof, and for the good will of him that dwelt in the bush [God's blessings and protection]: let the blessing come upon the head of Joseph, and upon the top of the head of him that was separated from his brethren.

33:17 His glory is like the firstling of his bullock, and his horns are like the horns of unicorns [H7214 meaning "his strong bull:" due to the influence of James 1, this was mistranslated as unicorns in 1611]: with them he shall push the people together to the ends of the earth: and they are the ten thousands of Ephraim [H7233 great numbers], and they are the [many] thousands of Manasseh.

The term "strong bull" was deliberately mistranslated as "unicorn" by the king James translators, to insert the modern symbol of Scotland [unicorns] into the Bible, because James, a Scottish king, believed that he was a king from the line of David.

The riches of the British/American peoples are obvious and cannot be denied. They are truly descended from Joseph and have inherited these blessings. That does not mean that they are ruled by a monarch of the House of David today!

Joseph [the Anglo Saxon people who are the British and American people] would fight many, many wars, and receive mighty blessings of good things.

Genesis 49:22 Joseph is a fruitful bough, even a fruitful bough by a well; whose branches run over the wall: **49:23** [They will have many enemies and much war, but will be blessed by God with great strength over their enemies.] The archers have sorely grieved him, and shot at him, and hated him: **49:24** But his bow abode in strength, and the arms of his hands were **made strong by the hands of the mighty God of Jacob;**

49:25 Even by the God of thy father [Abraham], who shall help thee; and by the Almighty, who shall bless thee with blessings of heaven above, blessings of the deep that lieth under, blessings of the breasts, and of the womb:

49:26 The blessings of thy father have prevailed above the blessings of my progenitors unto the utmost bound of the everlasting hills: they shall be on the head of Joseph, and on the crown of the head of him that was separate from his brethren.

Zebulun

Zebulun is to dwell by the sea and is prophesied to be converted in the millennium.

Deuteronomy 33:18 And of Zebulun he said, Rejoice, Zebulun, in thy going out; and, Issachar, in thy tents. **33:19** They shall call the people unto the mountain [During the millennium they will call people to come to the Temple Mount; probably referring to Zebulun bringing people with ships.]; there [at the Ezekiel Temple] they shall offer sacrifices of righteousness:

for they shall suck of the abundance of the seas, and of treasures hid in the sand.

Genesis 49:13 Zebulun shall dwell at the haven of the sea; and he shall be for an haven of ships; and his border shall be unto Zidon.

Issachar

Genesis 49:14 Issachar is a strong ass couching down between two burdens: **49:15** And he saw that rest was good, and the land that it was pleasant; and bowed his shoulder to bear, and became a servant unto tribute.

Gad

Gad will be overcome during the tribulation but at the coming of Messiah he will overcome and sincerely repent.

Deuteronomy 33:20 And of Gad he said, Blessed be he that enlargeth Gad: he dwelleth as a lion, and teareth the arm with the crown of the head. **33:21** And he provided the first part for himself, because there, in a portion of the lawgiver, was he seated; and he came with the heads of the people, he executed the justice of the LORD, and his judgments with Israel.

Genesis 49:19 Gad, a troop shall overcome him: but he shall overcome at the last.

Dan

Dan shall leap from Bashan [the Golan], he shall have his own nation and he will vex his brothers. This speaking of the Irish [Dan] fight with the British [Ephraim].

The Patriarch Dan was born from the handmaid of Rachel, Bilhah. Rachel was in envy of her sister Leah and she wanted so badly to bear a child for Jacob, that she gave him her handmaid to bear a son. That son was Dan and when he was born she said, "God hath judged me, and hath also heard my voice, and hath given me a son: therefore she called his name Dan." (Gen 30:6). The meaning of the word "Dan" is "Judge" (Strong's #1777 "judge").

When Israel took possession of the promised land, the tribe of Dan was allotted its tribal inheritance in the South Western area on the

Mediterranean Sea, and included the busy port of Joppa, next to modern Tel-Aviv (Joshua 19:40-48).

Many Danes later left the land sailing from Joppa in ships while others migrated northwards to Laish, and called the city Dan, after their father, see Judges 18.

The northern city Laish, renamed Dan, by the tribe of Dan, was about thirty miles inland from the ancient busy port of Tyre.

Dan was divided into two halves as an early migration by ship to Ireland was later followed by a second migration with their Assyrian [Germanic] captors from Laish [Dan] ending up in Denmark.

Ephraim [The British] has tried to dominate the western Irish half tribe of Dan which in return has vexed Ephraim, while the eastern Danish half tribe has been a peaceable nation.

Deuteronomy 33:22 And of Dan he said, Dan is a lion's whelp: he shall leap from Bashan.

Genesis 49:16 Dan shall judge his people, as one of the tribes of Israel. Dan shall be a serpent by the way, an adder in the path, that biteth the horse heels, so that his rider shall fall backward.

Naphtali

Naphtali is to be known for wise words.

Deuteronomy 33:23 And of Naphtali he said, O Naphtali, satisfied with favour, and full with the blessing of the LORD: possess thou the west and the south.

The west and the south is a Hebraism for a long sea coast; Naphtali immigrated to Norway [the west] and /Sweden [south of Norway.

Genesis 49:21 Naphtali is a hind let loose: he giveth goodly words.

Asher

Asher shall be strong, wealthy and have access to oil.

Deuteronomy 33:24 And of Asher he said, Let Asher be blessed with children; let him be acceptable to his brethren, and let him dip his foot in oil. **33:25** Thy shoes shall be [he will walk on; possess] iron and brass; and as thy days, so shall thy strength be.

Genesis 49:20 Out of Asher his bread shall be fat, and he shall yield royal dainties.

All Israel and their nations will receive these blessings from the Eternal in the full in the soon coming Kingdom of God.

Brethren, these prophecies are only in part for now, given because God had promised these blessings to our forefathers. They are to be fulfilled in the Kingdom of God in their fullness, when all Israel repents and turns to the Eternal with a whole heart.

Jeshurun (Hebrew: יְשֻׁרוּן), in the Hebrew Bible, is a poetic name for Israel, derived from a root word meaning upright, just or straight. Jeshurun appears four times in the Hebrew Bible — three times in Deuteronomy and once in Isaiah. It can mean the people of Israel (Deut. 32:15; 33:26), the Land of Israel (Deut. 33:5;), or the Patriarch Jacob (whom an Angel renamed Israel in Genesis 32:29):

The blessings that have come so far are only a shadow of the future blessings coming to the repentant tribes when Messiah comes. When all Israel is sincerely repentant and Messiah comes the tribes will be united under the resurrected king David and will inherit all of these blessings in their fullness.

Deuteronomy 33:26 There is none like unto the God of Jeshurun, who rideth upon the heaven in thy help, and in his excellency on the sky. **33:27** The eternal God is thy refuge, and underneath are the everlasting arms: and he shall thrust out the enemy from before thee; and shall say, Destroy them.

33:28 Israel then shall dwell in safety alone: the fountain of Jacob shall be upon a land of corn and wine; also his heavens shall drop down dew. **33:29** Happy art thou, O Israel: who is like unto thee, O people saved by the LORD, the shield of thy help, and who is the sword of thy excellency! and thine enemies shall be found liars unto thee; and thou shalt tread upon their high places.

Deuteronomy 34

A scribe then writes a conclusion to this book concerning Moses death.

34:1 And Moses went up from the plains of Moab unto the mountain of Nebo, to the top of Pisgah, that is over against Jericho. And the LORD shewed him all the land of Gilead, unto Dan,

34:2 And all Naphtali, and the land of Ephraim, and Manasseh, and all the land of Judah, unto the utmost sea, **34:3** And the south, and the plain of the valley of Jericho, the city of palm trees, unto Zoar.

34:4 And the LORD said unto him, This is the land which I sware unto Abraham, unto Isaac, and unto Jacob, saying, I will give it unto thy seed: I have caused thee to see it with thine eyes, but thou shalt not go over thither.

34:5 So Moses the servant of the LORD died there in the land of Moab, according to the word of the LORD. **34:6** And he buried him in a valley in the land of Moab, over against Bethpeor: but no man knoweth of his sepulchre unto this day.

34:7 And Moses was an hundred and twenty years old when he died: his eye was not dim, nor his natural force abated. **34:8** And the children of Israel wept for Moses in the plains of Moab thirty days: so the days of weeping and mourning for Moses were ended.

34:9 And Joshua the son of Nun was full of the spirit of wisdom; for Moses had laid his hands upon him: and the children of Israel hearkened unto him, and did as the LORD commanded Moses.

34:10 And there arose not a prophet since in Israel like unto Moses, whom the LORD knew face to face, [until the coming of "That Prophet" Messiah the Christ].

34:11 In all the signs and the wonders, which the LORD sent him to do in the land of Egypt to Pharaoh, and to all his servants, and to all his land, **34:12** And in all that mighty hand, and in all the great terror which Moses shewed in the sight of all Israel.

Joshua

Joshua 1

Deuteronomy is about preparing to enter the physical promised land as an allegory on how to prepare to attain to the spiritual Promised Land of eternal life, and it is a warning that possession of the land is absolutely contingent on living by every Word of God.

Joshua is about the inheritance of the physical promised land being attained only by a hard struggle and closely following the Eternal; as an allegory that we may attain to the spiritual Promised Land of eternal life, only by an intensive struggle to overcome all sin through living by every Word of God

Egypt was an allegorical type of bondage to sin and the Canaanites were an allegorical type of unrepentant sinners who will be totally destroyed by Jesus Christ at the final judgment. This is a lesson for those who wrongly think that Jesus Christ will overlook willful sin because he is love and understands our weakness.

The scriptures were recorded for OUR instruction and reveal that Jesus will not permit any compromise with the Word of God or any lack of zeal to live by every Word of God: To follow him wherever he goes, precisely because he is love and wants to save us from the sorrow and death that sin brings.

The book of Joshua reveals the end of the unrepentant willful sinner typified by the Canaanites: Just as many of them were killed many of us will also surely die for unrepented self-justified willful sin.

Joshua 1:1 Now after the death of Moses the servant of the LORD it came to pass, that the LORD spake unto Joshua the son of Nun, Moses' minister [Joshua had been Moses servant, aide and assistant for many years], saying, **1:2** Moses my servant is dead; now therefore arise, go over this Jordan, thou, and all this people, unto the land which I do give to them, even to the children of Israel.

Joshua the faithful along with faithful Caleb was given every place that he had visited as a spy in the land; while the faithless who would not obey died in the wilderness.

All those who lacked faith to obey the Word of God and enter the land; DIED in the wilderness.

The death of the faithless in physical Israel was an example for today's spiritually called out yet faithless who are not zealous to live by every Word of God: They will not enter into the spiritual Promised Land of eternal life except they sincerely repent.

1:3 Every place that the sole of your foot shall tread upon, that have I given unto you, as I said unto Moses.

Joshua is reminded of the borders of the land given to Israel.

1:4 From the wilderness and this Lebanon even unto the great river, the river Euphrates, all the land of the Hittites, and unto the great sea toward the going down of the sun, shall be your coast.

Very many today fear men, they fear to question the words of men and to stand firmly on the Word of God: If we are zealous to live by every Word of God we will be delivered into that spiritual Promised Land of eternal life and NO MAN will be able to keep us out.

Following anyone contrary to God's Word or loving anything and allowing it to come between us and God, is idolatry and brings destruction. Only faithfully and zealously following the whole Word of God will bring the promise of eternal life.

Many elders also cling to false traditions because they fear rejection by their peers or by the brethren. It is only by learning to respect and to follow the whole Word of God that we may enter eternal life. Those who fear men so much that they cannot faithfully live by every Word of God are doomed to destruction by Jesus Christ.

God's encouragement to Joshua was recorded for US!

If we are full of faith and courage to follow the whole Word of our God: If we are strong and zealous to live by every Word of God, if we reject false traditions as we see them proved false by the Word of God; if we follow the Lamb whithersoever he goeth we may suffer trials in this life just like Israel did in conquering the land; but we WILL conquer sin and the grave through the might of our Master and we shall rise up into the Promised Land of Eternal Life when we hear our Master's call!

1:5 There shall not any man be able to stand before thee all the days of thy life: as I was with Moses, so I will be with thee: I will not fail thee, nor forsake thee. **1:6** Be strong and of a good courage: for unto this people shalt thou divide for an inheritance the land, which I sware unto their fathers to give them. **1:7 Only be thou strong and very courageous, that thou mayest observe to do according to all the law, which Moses my servant commanded thee: turn not from it to the right hand or to the left, that thou mayest prosper withersoever thou goest.**

1:8 This book of the law shall not depart out of thy mouth; but thou shalt meditate therein day and night, that thou mayest observe to do according to all that is written therein: for then thou shalt make thy way prosperous, and then thou shalt have good success.

My heart breaks for those who refuse to live by every Word of God and for those who even call the Word of God unreliable, because like the ten spies these men have no love or zeal for the Word of God and allow themselves to be intimidated by their fears.

Being fearful instead of being filled with the power of faith in following Almighty God and vainly leaning on their corporate idols and their false traditions, no matter what God's Word says and justifying their error in turning away from the truth: Dooms people to severe correction.

1:9 Have not I commanded thee? Be strong and of a good courage; be not afraid, neither be thou dismayed: for the LORD thy God is with thee [if we live by every Word of God] **whithersoever thou goest.**

Then Joshua commanded the people to prepare to enter the land.

1:10 Then Joshua commanded the officers of the people, saying, **1:11** Pass through the host, and command the people, saying, Prepare you victuals; for within three days ye shall pass over this Jordan, to go in to possess the land, which the LORD your God giveth you to possess it.

Joshua then reminded the people of Reuben, Gad and half of Manasseh, about their obligations.

1:12 And to the Reubenites, and to the Gadites, and to half the tribe of Manasseh, spake Joshua, saying, **1:13** Remember the word which Moses the servant of the LORD commanded you, saying, The LORD your God hath given you rest, and hath given you this land.

1:14 Your wives, your little ones, and your cattle, shall remain in the land which Moses gave you on this side Jordan; but ye shall pass before your brethren armed, all the mighty men of valour, and help them; **1:15** Until the LORD have given your brethren rest, as he hath given you, and they also have possessed the land which the LORD your God giveth them: then ye shall return unto the land of your possession, and enjoy it, which Moses the LORD's servant gave you on this side Jordan toward the sunrising.

1:16 And they answered Joshua, saying, **All that thou commandest us we will do, and whithersoever thou sendest us, we will go. 1:17** According as we hearkened unto Moses in all things, so will we hearken unto thee: only the LORD thy God be with thee, as he was with Moses.

The people of Gad, Reuben and the half of Manasseh pledged themselves to follow Joshua.

1:18 Whosoever he be that doth rebel against thy commandment, and will not hearken unto thy words in all that thou commandest him, he shall be put to death: only be strong and of a good courage.

Our deliverance into eternal life depends on our love for and our zeal to follow God our Father and for our espoused Husband, to live by every Word of God.

YES WE CAN conquer sin and enter the spiritual Promised Land of eternal life, just like Joshua conquered Canaan (a type of sin): Through the strength of our Mighty One, but ONLY by being faithful to live by every Word of God, to learn it and to keep it always!

Joshua 2

Two spies are saved by Rahab

This was probably a pub like, common public inn where food, drink, accommodations and company could be found by the traveler.

These two men would likely have eaten and taken a room at this establishment; this does not imply they were seeking company as well.

Joshua 2:1 And Joshua the son of Nun sent out of Shittim two men to spy secretly, saying, Go view the land, even Jericho. And they went, and came into an harlot's house, named Rahab, and lodged there.

Word comes to the ruler of the city that these men are spies and lodging at Rahab's house [inn].

2:2 And it was told the king of Jericho, saying, Behold, there came men in hither to night of the children of Israel to search out the country.

The ruler then demanded that Rahab the manager of the establishment, surrender the two men as spies.

2:3 And the king of Jericho sent unto Rahab, saying, Bring forth the men that are come to thee, which are entered into thine house [inn]: for they be come to search out all the country.

Doubtless the memory of the exodus from Egypt and the parting of the Red Sea [for Canaan had been dominated by Egypt before the end of pharaoh and his army] and the fame of Israel crossing the sea dry shod had spread across the city, and Rahab probably talked over these things with the two men. Rahab BELIEVED them and she added to that belief the works of faith!

She feared the God of Israel and believed; and she acted on that belief, which was FAITH in the Word of God: Believing that God's Word would be fulfilled and that the city and the people of Jericho would be destroyed.

Rahab believed God and she acted on her faith to save these two men! This shows that even the Canaanites (as types of sin) if they were to sincerely repent and add to repentance the works of godliness could be saved!

But Canaan as a whole refused to repent sincerely; they rejected God and trusted in their own idols and false teachings to save them!

If today's Ekklesia resists the Word of God to cling to their idols of men and their false traditions of men, we shall all likewise perish!

If we are zealous for the whole Word of God to learn it, to keep it, and to follow its author with zealous determination, fearing to turn away from God like Rahab: WE will be delivered just as Rahab was delivered!

This woman sheltered the two spies in her inn which was undoubtedly a capital offense worthy of death since she would be perceived as putting the whole city in grave danger; yet she risked the immediate danger and chose to fear God rather than men!

This whore had more faith and true repentance than very many of today's Spiritual Ekklesia who would not dare to stand up for the Word of God against the pollution of the Sabbath or other false teachings in today's assemblies!

No wonder this obscure Canaanite whore is an ancestor of David the zealous; and is accounted among the elect who will receive the promise of eternal life in the raising of the bride of Christ in Hebrews 11.

Oh my friends; where is our courage of FAITH coupled with actions, to stand on and keep the whole Word of God regardless of what others may say or do? Where is our zeal for the sanctity of the Sabbath and for the whole Word of God?

2:4 And the woman took the two men, and hid them, and said thus, There came men unto me, but I wist not whence they were: **2:5** And it came to pass about the time of shutting of the gate, when it was dark, that the men went out: whither the men went I wot not: pursue after them quickly; for ye shall overtake them. **2:6** But she had brought them up to the roof of the house, and hid them with the stalks of flax, which she had laid in order upon the roof. **2:7** And the men pursued after them the way to Jordan unto the fords: and as soon as they which pursued after them were gone out, they shut the gate. **2:8** And before they were laid down, she came up unto them upon the roof;

Rahab made a declaration of faith and coupled that declaration with the works of faith; saving the two men and placing her trust entirely in the hands of the Eternal.

Where is our faith and trust and belief in the Word of God and the promises of our loving LORD today?

Yes, other Canaanites also feared; but they would not repent!

Rahab feared and did sincerely repent and chose faith and trust in the Word of God above all else.

2:9 And she said unto the men, I know that the LORD hath given you the land, and that your terror is fallen upon us, and that all the inhabitants of the land faint because of you. **2:10** For we have heard how the LORD dried up the water of the Red sea for you, when ye came out of Egypt [forty years before]; and what ye did unto the two kings of the Amorites, that were on the other side Jordan, Sihon and Og, whom ye utterly destroyed. **2:11** And as soon as we had heard these things, our hearts did melt, neither did there remain any more courage in any man, because of you: **for the LORD your God, he is God in heaven above, and in earth beneath.**

God the Father and Jesus Christ are God indeed; why then do we not respect the sanctity of the Sabbath and the holiness of every Word of God? Why then do we fear men which are nothing but dust before our God? Why do we make idols of the men, false traditions and corporate entities that lead us away from Christ-like zeal for the Word of our God?

2:12 Now therefore, I pray you, swear unto me by the LORD, since I have shewed you kindness, that ye will also shew kindness unto my father's house, and give me a true token: **2:13** And that ye will save alive my father, and my mother, and my brethren, and my sisters, and all that they have, and deliver our lives from death.

The two men then agreed that she had spared them at the risk of her life and that she and her family should be saved.

My friends, put your trust in God in sincere repentance from all sin, going forward to live by every Word of God with loving enthusiastic zeal; regardless of any consequence, or what any person may say or do and Jesus Christ will spare you from the wages of unrepentant sin and raise you up to eternal life on that day!

2:14 And the men answered her, Our life for yours, if ye utter not this our business. And it shall be, when the LORD hath given us the land, that we will deal kindly and truly with thee.

She let them down from the wall by a rope, giving them a way to escape out of the city of sin; even so God will deliver all of his faithful who love God enough to keep his Word and to diligently seek out his truth.

2:15 Then she let them down by a cord through the window: for her house was upon the town wall, and she dwelt upon the wall.

Rahab tells the two men where the pursuers are seeking them, between Jericho and the Jordan river and shows them how to elude the pursuit. She is doing all this at the risk of her own life, just as we also should be living by every Word of God even if it costs us our physical lives.

2:16 And she said unto them, Get you to the mountain, lest the pursuers meet you; and hide yourselves there three days, until the pursuers be returned: and afterward may ye go your way.

The two men then gave her a way to save her house; telling her to use a scarlet thread [token, cloth] as a sign. How fascinating, that a scarlet thread was used; giving us a glimpse of the blood of the Passover Lamb on the doorposts of Israel in Egypt and the blood of the Lamb of God covering the sins of the repentant!

2:17 And the men said unto her, We will be blameless of this thine oath which thou hast made us swear. **2:18** Behold, when we come into the land, **thou shalt bind this line of scarlet thread in the window which thou didst let us down by: and thou shalt bring thy father, and thy mother, and thy brethren, and all thy father's household, home unto thee.**

Just as in Egypt, those who were outside the house during the destruction of Jericho would surely die; only those inside the house protected by the scarlet symbol of the blood of the Lamb of God would be spared.

This tells us that only those who are following Jesus Christ to faithfully live by every Word of God (Mat 4:4), with his blood atoning for their sin; will be saved spiritually.

2:19 And it shall be, that whosoever shall go out of the doors of thy house into the street, his blood shall be upon his head, and we will be guiltless: and whosoever shall be with thee in the house, his blood shall be on our head, if any hand be upon him.

Rahab is reminded to keep her word and promise to them; and warned that if she backslides she will surely die.

We, the spiritually called out of the New Covenant, must also keep our baptismal commitment of espousal to Jesus Christ to live by every Word of God and that we will do all that our LORD requires; and if we go back on our word and exalt any other instead of living by every Word of God: We will also surely die along with all other unrepentant sinners.

Notice that Rahab immediately bound the scarlet to her window, not waiting for a single day.

We must also immediately obey the Word of our God once we learn what is right. No delay, no vacillating, no forgetting; just immediate sincere repentance once we are made aware of any sin!

2:20 And if thou utter this our business, then we will be quit of thine oath which thou hast made us to swear. **2:21** And she said, According unto your words, so be it. And she sent them away, and they departed: and she bound the scarlet line in the window. **2:22** And they went, and came unto the mountain, and abode there three days, until the pursuers were returned: and the pursuers sought them throughout all the way, but found them not.

The two men give their good report.

2:23 So the two men returned, and descended from the mountain, and passed over, and came to Joshua the son of Nun, and told him all things that befell them: **2:24** And they said unto Joshua, Truly the LORD hath delivered into our hands all the land; for even all the inhabitants of the country do faint because of us.

Joshua 3

Joshua 3:1 And Joshua rose early in the morning; and they removed from Shittim [Acacia Wood], and came to Jordan, he and all the children of Israel, and lodged there before they passed over.

Three days after the people came to the Jordan river they were told to make ready to cross.

3:2 And it came to pass after three days, that the officers went through the host; **3:3** And they commanded the people, saying, When ye see the ark of the covenant of the LORD your God, and the priests the Levites bearing it, then ye shall remove from your place, and go after it. **3:4** Yet there shall be a space between you and it, about two thousand cubits by measure: come not near unto it, that ye may know the way by which ye must go: for ye have not passed this way heretofore.

The people were told to sanctify themselves, which means to repent, wash and be clean; to be separated from all sin and uncleanness.

This was an example for us, teaching us that all those who cross into the spiritual Promised Land of eternal life must be holy and free from all spiritual uncleanness and sin. Cleansed through sincere repentance and a genuine commitment to go and sin no more; thereby having the atoning sacrifice of Christ applied to us.

3:5 And Joshua said unto the people, Sanctify yourselves: for to morrow the LORD will do wonders among you.

In the morning Joshua commanded the priests to go forward over Jordan.

3:6 And Joshua spake unto the priests, saying, Take up the ark of the covenant, and pass over before the people. And they took up the ark of the covenant, and went before the people.

Jesus Christ then tells Joshua that he will demonstrate that he is with Joshua as he was with Moses.

3:7 And the LORD said unto Joshua, This day will I begin to magnify thee in the sight of all Israel, that they may know that, as I was with Moses, so I will be with thee.

Christ commands the priests to stop and stand still as soon as they enter the water.

3:8 And thou shalt command the priests that bear the ark of the covenant, saying, When ye are come to the brink of the water of Jordan, ye shall stand still in Jordan.

Joshua then declared to the people that God will give them a sign of a miracle to demonstrate that the God of Moses is with them and will lead then to inherit the land.

3:9 And Joshua said unto the children of Israel, Come hither, and hear the words of the LORD your God. **3:10** And Joshua said, Hereby ye shall know that the living God is among you, and that he will without fail drive out from before you the Canaanites, and the Hittites, and the Hivites, and the Perizzites, and the Girgashites, and the Amorites, and the Jebusites.

3:11 Behold, the ark of the covenant of the LORD of all the earth passeth over before you into Jordan. **3:12** Now therefore take you twelve men out of the tribes of Israel, out of every tribe a man. **3:13 And it shall come to pass, as soon as the soles of the feet of the priests that bear the ark of the LORD, the LORD of all the earth, shall rest in the waters of Jordan, that the waters** of Jordan shall be cut off from the waters that come down from above; and they shall stand upon an heap.

As long as the ark stood still over the water of Jordan, the swollen rushing river was held back and Israel crossed over dry-shod. This was a remarkable miracle of encouragement for Israel; and it must have been a very frightening exhibition of the power of God for the nearby Canaanites.

This crossing of the river was an instructional example that God's faithful will cross the river of death and rise from the grave entering the spiritual Promised Land of eternal life only by the power of God.

3:14 And it came to pass, when the people removed from their tents, to pass over Jordan, and the priests bearing the ark of the covenant before the people; **3:15** And as they that bare the ark were come unto Jordan, and the feet of the priests that bare the ark were dipped in the brim of the water, (for Jordan overfloweth all his banks all the time of [the Jordan overflowed during the early spring season] harvest,) **3:16** That the waters which came down from above stood and rose up upon an heap very far from the city Adam, that is beside Zaretan: and those that came down toward the sea of the plain, even the salt sea, failed, and were cut off: and the people passed over right against Jericho.

3:17 And the priests that bare the ark of the covenant of the LORD stood firm on dry ground in the midst of Jordan, and all the Israelites passed over on dry ground, until all the people were passed clean over Jordan.

Joshua 4

The God Being who later gave up his God-good to become flesh as Jesus Christ then commanded that twelve stones be taken from around the priests feet in the Jordan river and set up where they were to camp that evening, for a memorial so that Israel would always remember the power of God.

Joshua 4:1 And it came to pass, when all the people were clean passed over Jordan, that the LORD spake unto Joshua, saying, **4:2** Take you twelve men out of the people, out of every tribe a man, **4:3** And command ye them, saying, Take you hence out of the midst of Jordan, out of the place where the priests' feet stood firm, twelve stones, and **ye shall carry them over with you, and leave them in the lodging place, where ye shall lodge this night**.

A specially chosen man from each tribe [except Levi, the tribe of God] took a stone for his tribe out of Jordan.

4:4 Then Joshua called the twelve men, whom he had prepared of the children of Israel, out of every tribe a man: **4:5** And Joshua said unto them, Pass over before the ark of the LORD your God into the midst of Jordan, and take you up every man of you a stone upon his shoulder, according unto the number of the tribes of the children of Israel:

4:6 That this may be a sign among you, that when your children ask their fathers in time to come, saying, What mean ye by these stones? **4:7** Then ye shall answer them, That the waters of Jordan were cut off before the ark of the covenant of the LORD; when it passed over Jordan, the waters of Jordan were cut off: and **these stones shall be for a memorial unto the children of Israel for ever.**

This memorial of the power of God was set up near Jericho where the first camp in the physical promised land was established.

4:8 And the children of Israel did so as Joshua commanded, and took up twelve stones out of the midst of Jordan, as the LORD spake unto Joshua, according to the number of the tribes of the children of Israel, and **carried them over with them unto the place where they lodged, and laid them down there.** **4:9** And Joshua set up twelve stones in the midst of Jordan, in [from] the place where the feet of the priests which bare the ark of the covenant stood: and they are there unto this day.

The priests carrying the ark stood still in the river until all the people had passed over and then the twelve stones were gathered up; then as the priests marched out of the river the spring flood waters resumed.

The ark represented the presence of God opening the way for entry into the physical promised land; and the ceremony was symbolic of the fact that only by obedience to God and his Word, only by faithfully living by every Word of God and following God the Father and Jesus Christ can one pass over the spiritual boundary of death to rise up and enter the spiritual Promised Land of Eternal life.

4:10 For the priests which bare the ark stood in the midst of Jordan, until everything was finished that the LORD commanded Joshua to speak unto the people, according to all that Moses commanded Joshua: and the people hasted and passed over. **4:11** And it came to pass, when all the people were clean passed over, that the ark of the LORD passed over, and the priests, in the presence of the people.

Keeping their promise and doubtless eager to complete their mission and return to their families; the army of Reuben, Gad and half of Manasseh who had been given land east of the Jordan marched into the physical promised land, armed and ready for battle.

4:12 And the children of Reuben, and the children of Gad, and half the tribe of Manasseh, passed over armed before the children of Israel, as Moses spake unto them: **4:13** About forty thousand prepared for war passed over before the LORD unto battle, to the plains of Jericho.

This event magnified God before the people, and it also magnified Joshua by proving that he was with God and that God was with him!

4:14 On that day the LORD magnified Joshua in the sight of all Israel; and they feared him, as they feared Moses, all the days of his life.

Joshua was commanded by God, to command the priests to march forward.

4:15 And the LORD spake unto Joshua, saying, **4:16** Command the priests that bear the ark of the testimony, that they come up out of Jordan. **4:17** Joshua therefore commanded the priests, saying, Come ye up out of Jordan. **4:18** And it came to pass, when the priests that bare the ark of the covenant of the LORD were come up out of the midst of Jordan, and the soles of the priests' feet were lifted up unto the dry land, that the waters of Jordan returned unto their place, and flowed over all his banks, as they did before.

The first camp in the physical promised land where the twelve stones from Jordan were set up, was at Gilgal near Jericho.

4:19 And the people came up out of Jordan **on the tenth day of the first month, and encamped in Gilgal,** in the east border of Jericho. **4:20** And those twelve stones, which they took out of Jordan, did Joshua pitch in Gilgal.

This tent day of the first month was the day that the Passover lambs were to be selected

4:21 And he spake unto the children of Israel, saying, When your children shall ask their fathers in time to come, saying, What mean these stones? **4:22** Then ye shall let your children know, saying, Israel came over this Jordan on dry land.

Spiritually this is a tremendous lesson. The twelve stones are a memorial, showing that the way into the spiritual Promised Land is ONLY through faithfully living by every Word of God and following Jesus Christ the Lamb of God.

4:23 For the LORD your God dried up the waters of Jordan from before you, until ye were passed over, as the LORD your God did to the Red sea, which he dried up from before us, until we were gone over:

This memorial was about the entry of Israel into the physical promised land: When the resurrection of the chosen takes place and the children of faith who follow the Lamb whithersoever he goeth are raised up to that Promised Land of eternal life; the whole earth will know who is God indeed!

4:24 That all the people of the earth might know the hand of the LORD, that it is mighty: that ye might fear the LORD your God for ever.

Our God is Mighty to Deliver his faithful!

Why do we call his Sabbaths holy, and then pollute them; condemning ourselves? Why will people admit truths and then turn away from them to insist on their own false ways? Why do we idolize men and exalt the words of men above the whole Word of God? Why do we love men, corporations, social activities and friends; and we do NOT love God enough to DO what he says? Why are we zealous for our own false traditions, and condemn any zeal to keep the whole Word of God?

Today's Ekklesia is lukewarm and stands condemned by Jesus Christ (Rev 3:14-22) for our lack of zeal to live by every Word of God: We are ready to be vomited out of the body of Jesus Christ into severe correction for our lukewarmness to live by every Word of God (Rev 3:16)!

Why will you die, oh [spiritual] Israel? Why will you not choose LIFE eternal and cast your idols aside, to be zealous for the whole Word of God? Why do we fear men and not God? Why are we followers of false ways and we are not zealous to follow the whole Word of God?

Dare to be a Daniel, a Joshua; and to faithfully follow Jesus Christ in living by every Word of God with passionate zeal!

Rahab and False Witness

Why did God think highly of Rahab when she lied?

We all know that faith without works is dead and she had to do her part to prove her faith by her works. When the officers came to her door and demanded information about the two men, she deceived then to save the two men, some would condemn her calling this lying.

What does the scripture say? Clearly it says that we are not to bear false witness, yet Jesus came to reveal the purpose and intent, the spirit of the law; what did he teach?

Jesus taught that the foundation of the law was mercy; therefore he healed on the Sabbath day, and allowed that men could indeed lift an ox out of a pit on the Sabbath.

We are to obey the letter of the law, however in certain extremely rare emergency occasions the intent of the law - which is the spirit of mercy; may over-rule the letter of the law. Very rare emergencies are exceptions to the letter and such extremely rare exceptions should never become the norm.

> **Luke 14:3** And Jesus answering spake unto the lawyers and Pharisees, saying, Is it lawful to heal on the sabbath day? **14:4** And they held their peace. And he took him, and healed him, and let him go; **14:5** And answered them, saying, Which of you shall have an

ass or an ox fallen into a pit, and will not straightway pull him out on the sabbath day?

Jesus said that the Sabbath was made for the good of people and even animals, and that exceptions to resting on the holy weekly and annual Sabbaths could be made in exceptional cases, for the good, the life, health and safety of others.

Jesus used the situation of David when he had been fleeing from Saul's soldiers for three days without food and ate the Bread of Presence, saying that God desires mercy.

The vast majority of false witness is meant to deceive others (as is commonly done by the many elders today regarding their false teachings), or for personal gain, to pervert justice, or to harm others. She misled these officers to SAVE lives! This was an a situation where an exception to the letter of the law was necessary to obey the Greater Law of Mercy.

Joshua 5

Because of the miracle in stopping the spring flood of Jordan so that Israel could pass over, the local rulers were filled with the fear of God.

Joshua 5:1 And it came to pass, when all the kings of the Amorites, which were on the side of Jordan westward, and all the kings of the Canaanites, which were by the sea, heard that the LORD had dried up the waters of Jordan from before the children of Israel, until we were passed over, that their heart melted, neither was there spirit in them any more, because of the children of Israel.

After crossing the Jordan on the tenth day of the first month, Israel is commanded to be circumcised so that they would be properly prepared to take the Passover in the physical promised land.

Joshua 5:2 At that time the LORD said unto Joshua, Make thee sharp knives, and circumcise again the children of Israel the second time [because they had not circumcised their males in the wilderness]. **5:3** And Joshua made him sharp knives, and circumcised the children of Israel at the hill of the foreskins.

The people that came out of Egypt had not circumcised their children in the wilderness. Any who were circumcised in Egypt died in the wilderness because of their lack of faith to obey God. This is a lesson for us that baptism is no guarantee of salvation if we are not zealous to live by every Word of God.

5:4 And this is the cause why Joshua did circumcise: All the people that came out of Egypt, that were males, even all the men of war, died in the wilderness by the way, after they came out of Egypt. **5:5** Now all the people that came out [of Egypt] were circumcised: but all the people that were born in the wilderness by the way as they came forth out of Egypt, them they had not circumcised. **5:6** For the children of Israel walked forty years in the wilderness, till all the people that were men of war, which came out of Egypt, were consumed, because they obeyed not the voice of the LORD: unto whom the LORD sware that he would not shew them the land, which the LORD sware unto their fathers that he would give us, a land that floweth with milk and honey.

To enter the physical promised land it was essential to be physically circumcised according to the covenant that Melchizedek [Jesus Christ] made with Abraham.

> **Genesis 17:7** And I will establish my covenant between me and thee and thy seed after thee in their generations for an everlasting covenant, to be a God unto thee, and to thy seed after thee. **17:8** And I will give unto thee, and to thy seed after thee, the land wherein thou art a stranger, all the land of Canaan, for an everlasting possession; and I will be their God. **17:9** And God said unto Abraham, Thou shalt keep my covenant therefore, thou, and thy seed after thee in their generations. **17:10** This is my covenant, which ye shall keep, between me and you and thy seed after thee; Every man child among you shall be circumcised.

This was an instructional lesson, that ONLY those spiritually circumcised in heart and zealous to live by every Word of God will have the Passover sacrifice of the Lamb of God applied to them, atoning for all past sin and enabling them to enter the Promised Land of eternal life.

> To enter the spiritual Promised Land of eternal life, it is essential to be spiritually circumcised in heart removing the veil of sin which separates us from God.

> Physical circumcision is a type of spiritual conversion. Circumcision removes the barrier that protects and renders one sensitive. This is a type of the removal of the barrier of sin that comes between us and God, thereby making us sensitive to the spiritual things of God.

> In the New Covenant we are all to become circumcised in heart; that is, we are all to sincerely repent of sin and to become sensitive to the whole Word of God in order to enter the spiritual Promised Land of the resurrection to eternal life.

> **Deuteronomy 30:6** And the Lord thy God will circumcise thine heart, and the heart of thy seed, to love the Lord thy God with all thine heart, and with all thy soul, that thou mayest live.
>
> **Jeremiah 4:4** Circumcise yourselves to the Lord, and take away the foreskins of your heart, ye men of Judah and inhabitants of Jerusalem: lest my fury come forth like fire, and burn that none can quench it, because of the evil of your doings.
>
> **Colossians 2:11** In whom also ye are **circumcise**d with the circumcision made without hands, in putting off the body of the sins of the flesh by the circumcision of Christ:

Those who compromise and turn away from zeal to faithfully live by every Word of God commit sin; and sin comes between us and God, separating us from God and eternal life.

> **Isaiah 59:1** Behold, the Lord's hand is not shortened, that it cannot save; neither his ear heavy, that it cannot hear: **59:2** But your iniquities have separated between you and your God, and your sins have hid his face from you, that he will not hear.

Joshua 5:7 And their children, whom he raised up in their stead, them Joshua circumcised: for they were uncircumcised, because they had not circumcised them by the way. **5:8** And it came to pass, when they had done circumcising all the people, that they abode in their places in the camp, till they were whole. **5:9** And the LORD said unto Joshua, This day have I rolled away the reproach of Egypt from off you. Wherefore the name of the place is called Gilgal unto this day.

The people now being physically circumcised, could properly partake of the Passover in the physical promised land, since no uncircumcised person may take the Passover.

> **Exodus 12:48** And when a stranger shall sojourn with thee, and will keep the passover to the Lord, let all his males be circumcised, and then let him come near and keep it; and he shall be as one that is born in the land: **for no uncircumcised person shall eat thereof.**

This was an instructional allegory that only the spiritually circumcised in heart, the sincerely repentant and zealous to live by every Word of God; can be covered by the atoning blood of the Lamb of God and going and sinning no more; they can then enter the spiritual Promised Land of eternal life.

> **Romans 2:13** (For not the hearers of the law are just before God, but **the doers of the law shall be justified** [by the application of the Passover sacrifice of Jesus Christ].

Joshua 5:10 And the children of Israel encamped in Gilgal, **and kept the passover** on the fourteenth day of the month at even in the plains of Jericho.

The people began to eat of the OLD grain they found in the land the day after Passover, and on the day after that the manna ceased. This had nothing to do with starting the spring harvest [or setting the Wave Offering day] to eat of the NEW grain, they were eating the OLD grain found in storage in the land.

5:11 And they did eat of **the old corn of the land** on the morrow after the passover, unleavened cakes, and parched corn [grain] in the selfsame day. **5:12** And the manna ceased on the morrow after they had eaten of the old corn of the land; neither had the children of Israel manna any more; but they did eat of the fruit of the land of Canaan that year.

The one who later gave up his Godhood to be made flesh and become Jesus Christ appeared to Joshua; for no man has seen God the Father.

> **John 1:18** No man hath seen God at any time, the only begotten Son, which is in the bosom of the Father, he hath declared him.

Joshua 5:13 And it came to pass, when Joshua was by Jericho, that he lifted up his eyes and looked, and, behold, there stood a man over against him with his sword drawn in his hand: and Joshua went unto him, and said unto him, Art thou for us, or for our adversaries?

Joshua challenges a stranger, and then immediately falls down to worship Christ as soon as he understands who the stranger is.

5:14 And he said, Nay; but as captain of the host of the LORD am I now come. And Joshua fell on his face to the earth, and did worship, and said unto him, What saith my Lord unto his servant **5:15** And the captain of the LORD's host said unto Joshua, Loose thy shoe from off thy foot; for the place whereon thou standest is holy. And Joshua did so.

Joshua 6

When Israel crossed the Jordan river the city of Jericho had gone to a war footing and closed its gates.

Joshua 6:1 Now Jericho was straitly shut up because of the children of Israel: none went out, and none came in. **6:2** And the LORD said unto Joshua, See, I have given into thine hand Jericho, and the king thereof, and the mighty men of valour.

Joshua is given instructions for the taking of Jericho. Jericho is to be taken by God so that the fame and fear of God would be spread among the Canaanites.

Except for a few, the Canaanites would not repent but remained adamant in their sins. Therefore they are a type of sin in the Word of God.

The method of defeating Jericho by Christ was also an allegory of the plan of salvation for the early harvest.

How many of us have the faith of Joshua to follow Christ and trust in our God to deliver us from our spiritual enemies, Satan, sin and death? How many of us are just like the Canaanites and refuse to repent of our idolatry and lack of zeal for the Word of God?

Jericho as the first powerful city of Canaan reached by Israel represented the end of unrepentant sinners.

Just like Jerusalem was chosen to be the city of God; Jericho represented Satan and rebellion against God.

The Astounding Allegorical Prophecy of JERICHO

The people were to march around the city of Jericho which represented sin, for six days, remaining silent except for the blasting of the trumpets of God; and on the seventh day the trumpets were to sound and the people were to shout in rejoicing at the fall of Jericho.

The march around Jericho was reenacted at the Feast of Tabernacles from the Ezra restoration and revival, as an instructional allegory of the final victory over all sin being completed on the seventh and Last Great Day of the Feast of the Ingathering of Nations called Tabernacles!

Joshua 6:3 And ye shall compass the city, all ye men of war, and go round about the city once. Thus shalt thou do six days.

The priests were to sound their seven trumpets daily during the once daily march and they were to march around Jericho the city representing Sin, once each day; and then they were to march around the city seven times on the seventh day; and the city representing sin would come crashing down!

The sounding of trumpets and the shouting of rejoicing on the seventh day, the Last Great of the Feast of Tabernacles; pictures the end of God's plan for man as flesh and total victory over sin!

6:4 And seven priests shall bear before the ark seven trumpets of rams' horns: and **the seventh day ye shall compass the city seven times, and the priests shall blow with the trumpets.**

6:5 And it shall come to pass, **that when they make a long blast with the ram's horn, and when ye hear the sound of the trumpet, all the people shall shout with a great shout; and the wall of the city shall fall down flat, and the people shall ascend up every man straight before him.**

6:6 And Joshua the son of Nun called the priests, and said unto them, Take up the ark of the covenant, and let seven priests bear seven trumpets of rams' horns before the ark of the LORD. **6:7** And he said unto the people, Pass on, and compass the city, and let him that is armed pass on before the ark of the LORD.

6:8 And it came to pass, when Joshua had spoken unto the people, that the seven priests bearing the seven trumpets of rams' horns passed on before the LORD, and **blew with the trumpets: and the ark of the covenant of the LORD followed them. 6:9** And the armed men went before the priests that blew with the trumpets, and the rereward came after the ark, the priests going on, and blowing with the trumpets.

6:10 And Joshua had commanded the people, saying, **Ye shall not shout, nor make any noise with your voice, neither shall any word proceed out of your mouth, until the day I bid you shout; then shall ye shout.**

6:11 So the ark of the LORD compassed the city, going about it once: and they came into the camp, and lodged in the camp. **6:12** And Joshua rose early in the morning, and the priests took up the ark of the LORD. **6:13** And seven priests bearing seven trumpets of rams' horns before the ark of the LORD went on continually, and blew with the trumpets: and the armed men went before them; but the rereward [a rear guard followed the Ark of the Covenant] came after the ark of the LORD, the priests going on, and blowing with the trumpets. **6:14** And **the second day they compassed the city once, and returned into the camp: so they did six days.**

Right here please notice that the people OBEYED God, even though it would not have made any sense to them!

It is to the zealous faithful followers of Jesus Christ who live by every Word of God the Father in heaven; that the V I C T O R Y over DEATH; and the gift of the Promised Land of eternal life comes!

6:15 And it came to pass on the seventh day, that they rose early about the dawning of the day, and compassed the city after the same manner seven times: only on that day they compassed the city seven times. **6:16** And it came to pass at the seventh time, when the priests blew with the trumpets, Joshua said unto the people, Shout; for the LORD hath given you the city.

At the end of the main harvest of humanity all flesh now changed to spirit will Shout for Joy, for God has given us total victory over bondage to sin!

Which person having been changed to spirit and received the gift of eternal life in peace and prosperity, being brought into the family of God; will not be overflowing with joy and humility before the great power of our Mighty God on that day?

The word "accursed" means receiving total destruction. Nothing of Jericho representing sin was to be taken or saved; except the repentant Rahab and her family.

The city of Jericho was to be accounted accursed because it represented unrepentant sin and the wickedness of rebellion against God!

This symbolic city was accursed and destroyed, so shall all those who refuse to repent from acting contrary to the Word of God during their opportunity also be destroyed.

6:17 And the city shall be accursed, even it, and all that are therein, to the LORD: only Rahab the harlot shall live, she and all that are with her in the house, because she hid the messengers that we sent.

Joshua warns that to take of the accursed thing [a type of partaking in any sin] which was condemned to destruction; will make the partaker of the accursed thing accursed (condemned to destruction) himself. This is why Paul reminded Timothy not to be a partaker of other men's sins.

1 Timothy 5:22 . . . neither be **partaker of** [participate in] **other men's sins: keep thyself pure.**

Joshua 6:18 And ye, in any wise keep yourselves from the accursed thing, lest ye make yourselves accursed, when ye take of the accursed thing, and make the camp of Israel a curse, and trouble it.

When we partake of other men's sins like patronizing restaurants on Sabbaths and High Days, we make ourselves anathema to God Almighty!

On the Last Great Day of the Feast of Tabernacles when the priests circled the altar seven times on the seventh day, they sang with loud voices a song of repentance, redemption and salvation — **Save now, I pray, O Lord; O Lord, I pray, send now prosperity; Blessed is He who comes in the name of the Lord. . .**(Psalm 118:25-26).

The precious metals belonged to God for the victory he had wrought! Even so the precious things of this world will be inherited by Jesus Christ and his resurrected elect! Yet everything evil will be committed to total destruction!

The precious metals belonged to God for the victory he had wrought! Even so the precious things of this world will be inherited by Jesus Christ and his resurrected elect! Yet everything evil will be committed to total destruction!

6:19 But **all the silver, and gold, and vessels of brass and iron, are consecrated unto the LORD**: they shall come into the treasury of the LORD.

In these kinds of cities very many of the houses are built up against the outer wall, with the outer wall making up one of the four walls of the home. Therefore when the wall fell at Jericho so did a part of the houses, which opened up everything to the attack.

Israel OBEYED God and followed his instructions fully; thus being given a great victory! Even so, if we obey God the Father and Jesus Christ to fully and consistently live by every Word of God, God will grant us victory over sin and death!

6:20 So the people shouted when the priests blew with the trumpets: and it came to pass, when the people heard the sound of the trumpet, and the people shouted with a great shout, that the wall fell down flat, so that the people went up into the city, every man straight before him, and they took the city.

Everything was destroyed in Jericho, the city which represented sin and rebellion against the Word of God.

Yet, God can and will raise those people up in future and will then give them an opportunity to repent; and after learning and understanding this lesson they will probably repent.

This took place and was recorded as an object lesson FOR US; teaching us that if we depart from zeal for the Word of God we shall all also perish like Jericho did.

Yet, if we are faithful and zealous to keep the whole Word of God without compromise, we will be saved just as Rahab was saved!

6:21 And they utterly destroyed all that was in the city, both man and woman, young and old, and ox, and sheep, and ass, with the edge of the sword.

Joshua sends the two men back to Rahab's house to save her and her family as they had promised.

6:22 But Joshua had said unto the two men that had spied out the country, Go into the harlot's house, and bring out thence the woman, and all that she hath, as ye sware unto her. **6:23** And the young men that were spies went in, and brought out Rahab, and her father, and her mother, and her brethren, and all that she had; and they brought out all her kindred, and left them without the camp of Israel.

This is a lesson that we will be totally destroyed if we sin and choose to attempt to justify our sins instead of repenting; while the worst sinner who does repent will be saved.

6:24 And they burnt the city with fire, and all that was therein: only the silver, and the gold, and the vessels of brass and of iron, they put into the treasury of the house of the LORD. **6:25** And Joshua saved Rahab the harlot alive, and her father's household, and all that she had; and she dwelleth in Israel even unto this day; because she hid the messengers, which Joshua sent to spy out Jericho.

The city of sin was destroyed and Joshua cursed anyone who would build this city of sin again. In type he was teaching that spiritually anyone who goes back into the sin which they were delivered from will be cursed to destruction.

6:26 And Joshua adjured them at that time, saying, Cursed be the man before the LORD, that riseth up and buildeth this city Jericho: he shall lay the foundation thereof in his firstborn, and in his youngest son shall he set up the gates of it.

If we are faithful to God, he shall raise us up to positions of renown on that day; in direct proportion to our deeds of zeal for learning and keeping the whole Word of God during our physical lives!

6:27 So the LORD was with Joshua; and his fame was noised throughout all the country.

God justly decided that:

> **Ezekiel 18:20 The soul that sinneth, it shall die. The son shall not bear the iniquity of the father, neither shall the father bear the iniquity of the son: the righteousness of the righteous shall be upon him** [for righteousness], **and the wickedness of the wicked shall be upon him** [for judgment to death].

God then offers his mercy to all who sincerely repent!

> **18:21** But if the wicked will turn from all his sins that he hath committed, and keep all my statutes, and do that which is lawful and right, he shall surely live, he shall not die. **18:22** All his transgressions that he hath committed, they shall not be mentioned unto him: in his righteousness that he hath done he shall live.

God has no pleasure in the death of the wicked, but rather works to bring the wicked to sincere repentance and to save the wicked out of their wickedness.

> **18:23** Have I any pleasure at all that the wicked should die? saith the Lord GOD: and not that he should return from his ways, and live?

If we think that we are pleasing God and have it made if we obey our idols of men; Almighty God says the exact opposite!

The spiritually called out of the latter day Ekklesia have fallen into the wickedness of idolizing men and commit these sins in the spiritual sense.

If we will not sincerely repent and turn to a passionate zeal to learn and keep the whole Word of God and reject the false traditions of our idols of men we shall surely be corrected; and if we will still not repent we shall surely die for blindly following men contrary to the Word of God.

18:24 But when the righteous turneth away from his righteousness, and committeth iniquity, and doeth according to all the abominations that the wicked man doeth, shall he live? All his righteousness that he hath done shall not be mentioned: in his trespass that he hath trespassed, and in his sin that he hath sinned, in them shall he die.

According to this judgment; Jesus Christ will reject those who follow the false traditions of their idols of men and have no zeal to learn and to live by every Word of God.

How long will we pollute the Sabbath and High Days and follow idols of men contrary to God's Word?

18:25 Yet ye say, The way of the LORD is not equal. Hear now, O house of Israel; Is not my way equal? are not your ways unequal?

Those who teach that once baptized we can willfully commit some sin and that Christ knows how hard life is and will overlook that sin; those who teach the abominable "Primacy of Peter" LIE, that men have been placed in authority by God and must be obeyed without question even contrary to God: WILL SURELY DIE, along with those who follow them and are not zealous to live by every Word of God.

Ezekiel then speaks of sincere repentance and life, to which God is calling us.

18:26 When a righteous man turneth away from his righteousness, and committeth iniquity, and dieth in them; for his iniquity that he hath done shall he die.

18:27 Again, when the wicked man turneth away from his wickedness that he hath committed, and doeth that which is lawful and right, he shall save his soul alive.

18:28 Because he considereth, and turneth away from all his transgressions that he hath committed, he shall surely live, he shall not die.

18:29 Yet saith the house of Israel, The way of the LORD is not equal. O house of Israel, are not my ways equal? are not your ways unequal?

Every person will be judged by his own actions; NO ONE will be able to use the Nazi excuse that "I was just following the appointed leaders." Jesus Christ will respond to that excuse by saying that these men were not his appointed leaders at all and were allowed to come among us to TEST us, as to whether we will keep the Word of God or keep the words of men

(Deu 13)! And he will ask us why we did not follow God's Word and instead followed the false words of men!

Indeed God will allow false teachers to do wonders to TEST his people as to whether they will follow cunningly devised fables as is done in the congregations today or even miracles; to turn them away from zeal for keeping the Word of God and following the Eternal!

> **Deuteronomy 13:1** If there arise among you a prophet, or a dreamer of dreams [religious teacher or leader], and giveth thee a sign or a wonder,
>
> **13:2** And the sign or the wonder come to pass, whereof he spake unto thee, saying, Let us go after other gods [to follow Idols of men and to believe them contrary to the whole Word of God], which thou hast not known, and let us serve them

Those who teach people to serve men without question claiming that they are God's anointed; saying that we need not have any zeal for the Sabbath or for God and his Word (here comes the BIG LIE) because we are of God even though we teach falsely and depart from God's Word. If they were of God they would teach a passionate zeal for the whole Word of God; they would focus on God and would never focus anyone on themselves!

> **13:3** Thou shalt not hearken unto the words of that prophet, or that dreamer of dreams [religious leader or teacher]: **for the Lord your God proveth you, to know whether ye love the Lord your God with all your heart and with all your soul.**

Brethren, TODAY we are being Tested and Proven as to our loyalty and our zeal for God the Father and our espoused Husband our Mighty One. Will we blindly follow idols of men; or will we prove all things and hold fast only what is good by the whole Word of Almighty God?

> **1 Thessalonians 5:19** Quench not the Spirit [by sinning]
>
> **5:20** Despise not prophesyings [warnings and correction] .
>
> **5:21 Prove all things; hold fast that which is good**.
>
> **5:22** Abstain from all appearance of evil.

God calls today's Ekklesia to sincerely REPENT, lest we be destroyed for not proving all things by the Word of God and for our idolatry in obeying men and not God!

> **Ezekiel 18:30** Therefore I will judge you, O house of [physical and spiritual] Israel, every one according to his ways, saith the Lord GOD. Repent, and turn yourselves from all your transgressions; so iniquity shall not be your ruin

Let us sincerely repent of our Sabbath and High Day pollution, which we do because "the church says it is all right;" when Almighty God warns that he will destroy those who pollute his Sabbaths!

Let us sincerely repent of following the false traditions of our idols of men blindly and without questioning them or holding them up to the standard of God's Word.

Let us turn to a hot burning zeal to follow the Lamb whithersoever he goeth!

> **18:31 Cast away from you all your transgressions, whereby ye have transgressed; and make you a new heart and a new spirit: for why will ye die, O house of [physical and spiritual] Israel? 18:32 For I have no pleasure in the death of him that dieth, saith the Lord GOD: wherefore turn yourselves, and live ye.**

Joshua 7

The sin of Achan

Joshua 7:1 But the children of Israel committed a trespass in the accursed thing: for Achan, the son of Carmi, the son of Zabdi, the son of Zerah, of the tribe of Judah, took of the accursed thing: and the anger of the LORD was kindled against the children of Israel.

Spies are sent to view Ai

7:2 And Joshua sent men from Jericho to Ai, which is beside Bethaven, on the east of Bethel, and spake unto them, saying, Go up and view the country. And the men went up and viewed Ai.

Ai was a village near Jericho

7:3 And they returned to Joshua, and said unto him, Let not all the people go up; but let about two or three thousand men go up and smite Ai; and make not all the people to labour thither; for they are but few.

A few men from Ai defeated the three thousand of Israel and there was great mourning and concern because God had not been with the army.

7:4 So there went up thither of the people about three thousand men: and they fled before the men of Ai. **7:5** And the men of Ai smote of them about thirty and six men: for they chased them from before the gate even unto Shebarim, and smote them in the going down: wherefore the hearts of the people melted, and became as water.

Joshua and the elders humbled themselves before God to seek the reason. This is the first step in sincere repentance, which is to humble ourselves before God and seek understanding from him.

7:6 And Joshua rent his clothes, and fell to the earth upon his face before the ark of the LORD until the eventide, he and the elders of Israel, and put dust upon their heads.

Oh, that today's Spiritual Ekklesia would inquire of God in sincerity and truth like Joshua did, and not in self-justification of our sins.

7:7 And Joshua said, Alas, O LORD God, wherefore hast thou at all brought this people over Jordan, to deliver us into the hand of the Amorites, to destroy us? would to God we had been content, and dwelt on the other side Jordan! **7:8** O LORD, what shall I say, when Israel turneth their backs before their enemies! **7:9** For the Canaanites and all the inhabitants of the land shall hear of it, and shall environ us round, and cut off our name from the earth: and what wilt thou do unto thy great name?

Then Jesus Christ revealed the sin to them so that they might turn from it and be saved. Oh, if only today's Spiritual Ekklesia would sincerely seek out guidance and correction from Christ in genuine humility, then he would reveal God's truth to us and if we acted on that understanding in true sincere repentance; we would also be saved.

Let us seek to obey the Lord our God with all our hearts like Joshua, and not be corrupted to sin by partaking of wickedness like Achan.

Achan had stolen from the cursed things and from the precious metals consecrated to God and had deceitfully hidden them.

7:10 And the LORD said unto Joshua, Get thee up; wherefore liest thou thus upon thy face? **7:11** Israel hath sinned, and they have also transgressed my covenant which I commanded them: for they have even taken of the accursed thing, and have also stolen, and dissembled also, and they have put it even among their own stuff.

If we have any hidden unrepented sin and we try to justify it rather than sincerely repenting; we will be known by Christ and we will be destroyed if we do not sincerely repent.

7:12 Therefore the children of Israel could not stand before their enemies, but turned their backs before their enemies, because they were accursed: neither will I be with you any more, except ye destroy the accursed from among you.

When will we destroy the accursed thing; which is our idolatry to follow men and corporate organizations in place of following the whole Word of God?

Our massive sin is our idolatry of men and our overwhelming pride in our own false traditions, justifying them instead of turning to true zeal for the whole Word of God.

Because of the sins of today's Ekklesia we have been rejected by God the Father and Jesus Christ until we sincerely repent and expunge the evil from our midst.

7:13 Up, sanctify the people, and say, Sanctify yourselves against to morrow: for thus saith the LORD God of Israel, There is an accursed thing in the midst of thee, O Israel: thou canst not stand before thine enemies, until ye take away the accursed thing from among you.

Then the God who later gave up his Godhood to be made flesh as Jesus Christ made them cast lots to find the evildoer and he caused the lot to fall on the guilty person. Today many more than one is guilty, the vast majority of us are guilty of pride and idolatry to exalt the words of men above the Word of God.

7:14 In the morning therefore ye shall be brought according to your tribes: and it shall be, that the tribe which the LORD taketh shall come according to the families thereof; and the family which the LORD shall take shall come by households; and the household which the LORD shall take shall come man by man.

Achan is to be cast into the fire as a demonstration that those who love the pleasures and rewards of sin will be cast into the lake of fire if they will not repent.

Brethren, this idea that Jesus Christ is love and will allow us to compromise with the Word of God or justify committing sin against God by following the teachings of others is an ABOMINABLE LIE!

7:15 And it shall be, that he that is taken with the accursed thing **shall be burnt with fire, he and all that he hath: because he hath transgressed the covenant of the LORD,** and because he hath wrought folly in Israel.

Joshua obeyed God and did as he was commanded, finding and rooting wickedness out of the congregation! No, he did NOT tolerate diversity of doctrine (a fancy term for false teachings) or any sin, and neither does God the Father and Jesus Christ!

7:16 So Joshua rose up early in the morning, and brought Israel by their tribes; and the tribe of Judah was taken: **7:17** And he brought the family of

Judah; and he took the family of the Zarhites: and he brought the family of the Zarhites man by man; and Zabdi was taken: **7:18** And he brought his household man by man; and Achan, the son of Carmi, the son of Zabdi, the son of Zerah, of the tribe of Judah, was taken.

Joshua tells Achan to repent before God

7:19 And Joshua said unto Achan, My son, give, I pray thee, glory to the LORD God of Israel, and make confession unto him; and tell me now what thou hast done; hide it not from me.

Achan then admits his evil deeds

7:20 And Achan answered Joshua, and said, Indeed I have sinned against the LORD God of Israel, and thus and thus have I done: **7:21** When I saw among the spoils a goodly Babylonish garment, and two hundred shekels of silver, and a wedge of gold of fifty shekels weight, then I coveted them, and took them; and, behold, they are hid in the earth in the midst of my tent, and the silver under it.

Joshua very carefully sends officers to determine the truth of Achan's confession

7:22 So Joshua sent messengers, and they ran unto the tent; and, behold, it was hid in his tent, and the silver under it. **7:23** And they took them out of the midst of the tent, and brought them unto Joshua, and unto all the children of Israel, and laid them out before the LORD.

Then Achan and his whole family and all his possessions were stoned and burned to death.

Brethren, this was recorded as an example for us that if we harbor sins secretly, God knows and he will surely correct us most severely.

7:24 And Joshua, and all Israel with him, took Achan the son of Zerah, and the silver, and the garment, and the wedge of gold, and his sons, and his daughters, and his oxen, and his asses, and his sheep, and his tent, and all that he had: and they brought them unto the valley of Achor.

7:25 And Joshua said, Why hast thou troubled us? the LORD shall trouble thee this day. And all Israel stoned him with stones, and burned them with fire, after they had stoned them with stones. **7:26** And they raised over him a great heap of stones unto this day. So the LORD turned from the fierceness of his anger. Wherefore the name of that place was called, The valley of Achor, unto this day.

Joshua 8

Christ commands the destruction of Ai but grants Israel the spoil. Then the God who gave up his Godhood to be made flesh as Jesus Christ gave Joshua a stratagem by which he could take Ai in the next attempt, and Joshua again OBEYS the Eternal! If only we were full of the faithful obedience of Joshua!

Joshua 8:1 And the LORD said unto Joshua, Fear not, neither be thou dismayed: take all the people of war with thee, and arise, go up to Ai: see, I have given into thy hand the king of Ai, and his people, and his city, and his land: **8:2** And thou shalt do to Ai and her king as thou didst unto Jericho and her king: **only the spoil thereof, and the cattle thereof, shall ye take for a prey unto yourselves:** lay thee an ambush for the city behind it.

8:3 So Joshua arose, and all the people of war, to go up against Ai: and Joshua chose out thirty thousand mighty men of valour, and sent them away by night.

An Israelite army was hidden near Ai and then the strength of Ai was lured out by the main army of Israel. The army of Israel then fled drawing the men of Ai out to pursue them. Then the other band of Israel attacked Ai from the far side and when the pursuers from Ai looked back they saw their city burning as the five thousand of Israel attacked the city from another place.

8:4 And he commanded them, saying, Behold, ye shall lie in wait against the city, even behind the city: go not very far from the city, but be ye all ready: **8:5** And I, and all the people that are with me, will approach unto the city: **and it shall come to pass, when they come out against us, as at the first, that we will flee before them, 8:6 (For they will come out after us) till we have drawn them from the city; for they will say, They flee before us, as at the first: therefore we will flee before them.**

When the army of Ai has been distracted from the defense of Ai by Israel, the undefended city was then attacked from the rear by five thousand of Israel and taken.

8:7 Then ye shall rise up from the ambush, and seize upon the city: for the LORD your God will deliver it into your hand.

Israel then set the city on fire to destroy the Canaanite city as a lesson that we must destroy all sin, and as an example of the end of all unrepentant sinners.

Notice that it is our duty to obey not just the written law of the scriptures, but to obey and live by EVERY WORD of God!

> **Deuteronomy 8:3** And he humbled thee, and suffered thee to hunger, and fed thee with manna, which thou knewest not, neither did thy fathers know; that he might make thee know that man doth not live by bread only, but **by every word that proceedeth out of the mouth of the Lord doth man live**.

Joshua 8:8 And it shall be, when ye have taken the city, that ye shall set the city on fire: according to the commandment of the LORD shall ye do. See, I have commanded you.

In the morning Joshua prepared for the fight, numbering out the five thousand and separating the two forces.

8:9 Joshua therefore sent them forth: and they went to lie in ambush, and abode between Bethel and Ai, on the west side of Ai: but Joshua lodged that night among the people. **8:10** And Joshua rose up early in the morning, and numbered the people, and went up, he and the elders of Israel, before the people to Ai. **8:11** And all the people, even the people of war that were with him, went up, and drew nigh, and came before the city, and pitched on the north side of Ai: now there was a valley between them and Ai.

Five thousand were set to take the city from the west, while the main army was arrayed north of the city.

8:12 And he took about five thousand men, and set them to lie in ambush between Bethel and Ai, on the west side of the city.

8:13 And when they had set the people, even all the host that was on the north of the city, and their liers in wait on the west of the city, Joshua went that night into the midst of the valley.

Joshua advanced towards the city with the main army and the forces of Ai went out to meet Israel.

8:14 And it came to pass, when the king of Ai saw it, that they hasted and rose up early, and the men of the city went out against Israel to battle, he and all his people, at a time appointed, before the plain; but he wist not that there were liers in ambush against him behind the city.

Joshua then fled with the army of Israel and the strength of Ai pursued after them.

8:15 And Joshua and all Israel made as if they were beaten before them, and fled by the way of the wilderness. **8:16** And all the people that were in Ai were called together to pursue after them: and they pursued after Joshua, and were drawn away from the city. **8:17** And there was not a man left in Ai or Bethel, that went not out after Israel: and they left the city open, and pursued after Israel.

When the army of Ai was well distant from the city, God commanded Joshua to give the signal to his five thousand on the west of Ai.

8:18 And the LORD said unto Joshua, Stretch out the spear that is in thy hand toward Ai; for I will give it into thine hand. And Joshua stretched out the spear that he had in his hand toward the city. **8:19** And the ambush arose quickly out of their place, and they ran as soon as he had stretched out his hand: and they entered into the city, and took it, and hasted and set the city on fire.

The five thousand of Israel rushed into undefended Ai and set fire to the city and the army of Ai seeing their city destroyed behind them, went into panic and were destroyed as the main army of Israel turned back upon them.

8:20 And when the men of Ai looked behind them, they saw, and, behold, the smoke of the city ascended up to heaven, and they had no power to flee this way or that way: and the people [of Israel] that fled to the wilderness turned back upon the pursuers. **8:21** And when Joshua and all Israel saw that the ambush had taken the city, and that the smoke of the city ascended, then they turned again, and slew the men of Ai.

Then as the main army of Israel turned back on their pursuers, the five thousand of Israel who had set the city on fire came forth from the city to attack the army of Ai from the rear.

The army of Ai was then trapped between the main army of Israel before them and the five thousand now advancing out of the burning city on their rear.

8:22 And the other issued out of the city against them; so they were in the midst of Israel, some on this side, and some on that side: and they smote them, so that they let none of them remain or escape.

The wicked king was taken for judgment and his whole people were destroyed.

This destruction of the wicked Ai, is typical of the coming destruction of the wicked in today's Ekklesia who teach idolatry and Sabbath pollution and seek people to follow after themselves, not teaching the brethren any zeal to live by every Word of God! They will be cast into the affliction of great tribulation and ultimately unless they repent, all wicked persons will be cast into the eternal destruction of the lake of fire.

8:23 And the king of Ai they took alive, and brought him to Joshua.

8:24 And it came to pass, when Israel had made an end of slaying all the inhabitants of Ai in the field, in the wilderness wherein they chased them, and when they were all fallen on the edge of the sword, until they were consumed, that all the Israelites returned unto Ai, and smote it with the edge of the sword. **8:25** And so it was, that all that fell that day, both of men and women, were twelve thousand, even all the men of Ai. **8:26** For Joshua drew not his hand back, wherewith he stretched out the spear, until he had utterly destroyed all the inhabitants of Ai.

Complete destruction is the ultimate fate of all unrepentant sinners.

8:27 Only the cattle and the spoil of that city Israel took for a prey unto themselves, according unto the word of the LORD which he commanded Joshua. **8:28** And Joshua burnt Ai, and made it an heap for ever, even a desolation unto this day.

Here the author equates evening with sundown; demonstrating that the terms "evening" and "sun set" or "sun down" are synonymous.

Evening is not some ambiguous period; it is clearly sunset. If anyone tries to tell you that it is alright to work after sunset beginning Sabbath, because evening is a vague and ambiguous time period: Don't you believe them! They are false teachers tempting you and testing you, so that God can see how zealous you are for his Word!

At the same time some Rabbins teach that evening is at sunset for the Sabbath and is any time in the afternoon for other purposes because the sun is in process of going down; they are double minded and wrong: evening is sun set.

8:29 And the king of Ai **he hanged on a tree until eventide: and as soon as the sun was down**, Joshua commanded that they should take his carcase down from the tree, and cast it at the entering of the gate of the city, and raise thereon a great heap of stones, that remaineth unto this day.

The faithful followers of the God who later gave up his Godhood to become flesh as Jesus Christ [Hebrew: Yeshua Mashiach] were given the victory over the Canaanites at Ai; which was a type of God giving his faithful victory over Satan and sin.

If we are zealous and faithful to follow our Lord and his Word without compromise or turning aside; we will also be given a victory over sin and its king, Satan; through our zeal to obey and follow the Word of God, by God's power to keep his promises and deliver his called out faithful.

Joshua gave Burnt Offerings and Peace Offerings; and if we are at ONE in FULL UNITY to follow and live by every Word of God we will also be at peace with God the Father and with the Son! However if we are like the idolatrous Canaanites who followed the idols of their own ways, we will also be destroyed like they were destroyed!

8:30 Then Joshua built an altar unto the LORD God of Israel in mount Ebal, **8:31** As Moses the servant of the LORD commanded the children of Israel, as it is written in the book of the law of Moses, an altar of whole stones, over which no man hath lift up any iron: and they offered thereon burnt offerings unto the LORD, and sacrificed peace offerings.

Joshua then wrote a copy of the law of God on the altar stones; thus indicating that they had hearts of stone. If we are called and faithful we should be writing the law of God on our hearts by diligently studying to learn and internalize into our very natures the whole Word of God (Jer 31).

8:32 And he wrote there upon the stones a copy of the law of Moses, which he wrote in the presence of the children of Israel.

Then Israel stood one-half on Mount Gerizim and one-half on Mount Ebal

> **Deuteronomy 27:11** And Moses charged the people the same day, saying, **27:12** These shall stand upon mount Gerizim to bless the people, when ye are come over Jordan; Simeon, and Levi, and Judah, and Issachar, and Joseph, and Benjamin: **27:13** And these shall stand upon mount Ebal to curse; Reuben, Gad, and Asher, and Zebulun, Dan, and Naphtali.

Joshua 8:33 And all Israel, and their elders, and officers, and their judges, stood on this side the ark and on that side before the priests the Levites, which bare the ark of the covenant of the LORD, as well the stranger, as he that was born among them; half of them over against mount Gerizim, and half of them over against mount Ebal; as Moses the servant of the LORD had commanded before, that they should bless the people of Israel.

Then half the people declared the blessings for faithful obedience to live by every Word of God; and half the people declared the curses for living contrary to the Word of God. Then Joshua read the Book of the Law [Moses last words to the elders, the book of Deuteronomy, as recorded by the attending scribes.] to all the people.

Oh, that there was a Joshua among us today so that we would turn away from our lukewarm, lip-service only religion, and our lack of zeal for keeping the Word of God; and turn back to live by every Word of the Eternal Almighty God!

8:34 And afterward he read all the words of the law, the blessings and cursings, according to all that is written in the book of the law. **8:35** There was not a word of all that Moses commanded, which Joshua read not before all the congregation of Israel, with the women, and the little ones, and the strangers that were conversant among them.

God's message to today's Spiritual Ekklesia: Just as physical Israel was in bondage in physical Egypt, we were in a spiritual Egypt of bondage to Satan and sin. We must remember that from which we were delivered, and we must be faithful to follow our Deliverer and to never equate the words of men as above or equal to the Word of God.

Right now the nations of Israel, both physical and spiritual, seem to think that obedience to God is a little thing.

Today the Israelite nations [including spiritual Israel] are immersed wholeheartedly in sin and they are about to receive God's just correction in its fullness.

Today's brethren rely on their false traditions instead of standing on every Word of God. Today's physical nations as well as the Spiritual Ekklesia of the New Covenant called out, are now facing the strong correction that Moses warned us of and that Jesus Christ warned us of in Revelation 3:14-22.

Joshua 9

There are many good lessons that we can learn from the adventures of Joshua and Israel in entering the physical promised land.

When the rulers of many Canaanite cities in the land heard of the destruction of Jericho and Ai, they confederated together to come out to war against the common enemy, while the inhabitants of Gibeon invented a strategy to save themselves.

Joshua 9:1 And it came to pass, when all the kings which were on this side Jordan, in the hills, and in the valleys, and in all the coasts of the great sea over against Lebanon, the Hittite, and the Amorite, the Canaanite, the Perizzite, the Hivite, and the Jebusite, heard thereof; **9:2** That they gathered themselves together, to fight with Joshua and with Israel, with one accord.

The inhabitants of Gibeon were wiser than their neighbors and found a way to make peace with Israel through craftiness.

This teaches us that our spiritual enemy (Satan) may attack openly, or he may seek to influence us through craftiness. That is the main attack focus of Satan against the New Covenant people at this time.

Today we should follow the instructions of John Baptist and Jesus Christ, and demand the fruits [proofs of a change in belief and conduct] of sincere repentance and zeal for the whole Word of God before baptizing people.

Likewise those who do not have the fruits of zeal to live by every Word of God should be cast out of the assemblies.

9:3 And when the inhabitants of Gibeon heard what Joshua had done unto Jericho and to Ai, **9:4** They did work wilily, and went and made as if they had been ambassadors, and took old sacks upon their asses, and wine bottles, old, and rent, and bound up; **9:5** And old shoes and clouted upon their feet, and old garments upon them; and all the bread of their provision was dry and mouldy.

9:6 And they went to Joshua unto the camp at Gilgal, and said unto him, and to the men of Israel, We be come from a far country: now therefore make ye a league with us.

Israel asked them, how can we make a treaty with you in case you are found to dwell in the land: And the people of Gideon did their best to deceive them that they were indeed from a far county; and Israel believed them and did not properly investigate, neither did they inquire of God.

The people of Gibeon had heard of the might of God and believed the reports; they feared yet they acted with craft to avoid correction rather than repenting.

How could Israel have avoided this trap? By first inquiring of God for his instructions and will in the matter!

9:7 And the men of Israel said unto the Hivites, Peradventure [what if] ye dwell among us; and how shall we make a league with you? **9:8** And they said unto Joshua, We are thy servants. And Joshua said unto them, Who are ye? and from whence come ye? **9:9** And they said unto him, From a very far country thy servants are come because of the name of the LORD thy God: for we have heard the fame of him, and all that he did in Egypt, **9:10** And all that he did to the two kings of the Amorites, that were beyond Jordan, to Sihon king of Heshbon, and to Og king of Bashan, which was at Ashtaroth. **9:11** Wherefore our elders and all the inhabitants of our country spake to us, saying, Take victuals with you for the journey, and go to meet them, and say unto them, We are your servants: therefore now make ye a league with us.

These Gibeonites feared Joshua and Israel, and presented a superficial appearance to Israel which was false.

Today most of the tares in the assemblies are sincere but lack any real understanding and are zealous for a group and its leader, but are not zealous to live by every Word of God to learn it and to keep it. Instead they are idolaters of men and corporate entities; they hear the messages and then they exalt the messenger, the leader and the organization while having no zeal for God to enthusiastically keep his Word.

9:12 This our bread we took hot for our provision out of our houses on the day we came forth to go unto you; but now, behold, it is dry, and it is mouldy: **9:13** And these bottles of wine, which we filled, were new; and, behold, they be rent: and these our garments and our shoes are become old by reason of the very long journey.

Joshua and the elders looked at the physical evidence before them and did not ask the Lord about the spiritual reality and truth of the situation.

9:14 And the men took of their victuals, and **asked not counsel at the mouth of the LORD.**

This is one of the very few mistakes of Joshua, the Zealous, the Faithful; he believed them without first inquiring of God.

9:15 And Joshua made peace with them, and made a league with them, to let them live: and the princes of the congregation sware unto them.

After three days the truth came out

9:16 And it came to pass at the end of three days after they had made a league with them, that they heard that they were their neighbours, and that they dwelt among them.

Israel then marched to their cities

9:17 And the children of Israel journeyed, and came unto their cities on the third day. Now their cities were Gibeon, and Chephirah, and Beeroth, and Kirjathjearim.

Joshua and the leaders decide to make servants of them and call them out and give them an ultimatum to become servants

9:18 And the children of Israel smote them not, because the princes of the congregation had sworn unto them by the LORD God of Israel. And all the congregation murmured against the princes. **9:19** But all the princes said unto all the congregation, We have sworn unto them by the LORD God of Israel: now therefore we may not touch them. **9:20** This we will do to them; we will even let them live, lest wrath be upon us, because of the oath which we sware unto them. **9:21** And the princes said unto them, Let them live; but let them be hewers of wood and drawers of water unto all the congregation; as the princes had promised them.

Joshua demands an explanation and declares that they are to be servants.

9:22 And Joshua called for them, and he spake unto them, saying, Wherefore have ye beguiled us, saying, We are very far from you; when ye dwell among us? **9:23** Now therefore ye are cursed, and there shall none of you be freed from being bondmen, and hewers of wood and drawers of water for the house of my God.

The Gibeonites reply that they deceived Israel out of fear for their lives and promised to do whatever Joshua required for the sake of their lives.

9:24 And they answered Joshua, and said, Because it was certainly told thy servants, how that the LORD thy God commanded his servant Moses to give you all the land, and to destroy all the inhabitants of the land from before you, therefore we were sore afraid of our lives because of you, and have done this thing. **9:25** And now, behold, **we are in thine hand: as it seemeth good and right unto thee to do unto us, do.**

Joshua then spared their lives and made them servants of the Levites.

9:26 And so did he unto them, and delivered them out of the hand of the children of Israel, that they slew them not. **9:27** And Joshua made them that day hewers of wood and drawers of water for the congregation, and for the altar of the LORD, even unto this day, in the place which he should choose.

I want to say that in the case of Gibeon this was about the physical Mosaic Covenant, while in today's spiritual Ekklesia we have a somewhat similar problem on the spiritual level.

For decades we have sinned greatly in the spiritual Ekklesia by improperly baptizing anyone who will support the corporate church regardless of heir level of understanding or personal commitment to live by every Word of God.

First, it must be said that many of the tares in today's corporate Ekklesia, probably the majority, do not know that they are tares and are very sincere and very nice people. This is just NOT their time now.

For a long time it has been a habit in today's Ekklesia to baptize people who obviously have no understanding or zeal for the Word of God, simply because they are willing to follow and send money to the corporate entity.

One elder told me about 1985 that the majority of brethren were not converted and were brought in so that the corporate church could have their financial support and so that some good could rub off on them.

What is wrong with that? Have you not read that a little leaven leavens the whole lump? Do you not know that the unclean makes the clean unclean? These folks are very nice and very sincere, yet they have diluted us into a social club devoid of zeal to live by every Word of God!

Today, the spiritual Ekklesia is full of known and unknown tares [as well as outright weeds] who play follow the elder but have no zeal to live by every Word of God. The fruit of this ungodly policy of knowingly baptizing unqualified people is a general lack of zeal to live by every Word of God throughout the assemblies and the decline of today's assemblies into mere social club churches.

Just as the mixed multitude which left Egypt with Israel led them astray, just as Solomon's wives led him astray, the knowing and wilful improper baptizing of people obviously not zealous to live by every Word of God, just to swell numbers and increase income; has resulted in the decline of godliness in the organizations and brethren.

Often God allows Satan to sow tares in the congregations to test and prove the zeal of the brethren. That is one thing; but when we deliberately and wilfully baptize those who we know should not be baptized, it is a sin just like the sin of Solomon in bringing strange wives into his family (Neh 13:27, Ezra 10).

This is not about what God allows Satan to do; it is about our deliberate and willful actions against what God's Word teaches. Please see the lesson on "The Clean and Unclean".

Deliberately mixing the spiritually unclean with the spiritually clean, pollutes the clean with the unclean and leads them astray.

> **Haggai 2:11** Thus saith the Lord of hosts; Ask now the priests concerning the law, saying,
>
> **2:12** If one bear holy flesh in the skirt of his garment, and with his skirt do touch bread, or pottage, or wine, or oil, or any meat, shall it be holy? And the priests answered and said, No.
>
> **2:13** Then said Haggai, If one that is unclean by a dead body touch any of these, shall it be unclean? And the priests answered and said, It shall be unclean.
>
> **2:14** Then answered Haggai, and said, **So is this people, and so is this nation before me, saith the Lord; and so is every work of their hands; and that which they offer there is unclean.**

Joshua 10

Joshua 10:1 Now it came to pass, when Adonizedec king of Jerusalem had heard how Joshua had taken Ai, and had utterly destroyed it; as he had done to Jericho and her king, so he had done to Ai and her king; and how the inhabitants of Gibeon had made peace with Israel, and were among them; **10:2** That they feared greatly, because Gibeon was a great city, as one of the royal cities, and because it was greater than Ai, and all the men thereof were mighty.

The other rulers in Canaan hearing of all these things resolved to confederate together and come out to attack Gibeon for making peace with Israel.

10:3 Wherefore Adonizedec king of **Jerusalem**, sent unto Hoham king of **Hebron**, and unto Piram king of **Jarmuth**, and unto Japhia king of **Lachish**, and unto Debir king of **Eglon**, saying, **10:4** Come up unto me, and help me, **that we may smite Gibeon: for it hath made peace with Joshua and with the children of Israel.**

These five kings laid siege to Gibeon.

10:5 Therefore the five kings of the Amorites, the king of Jerusalem, the king of Hebron, the king of Jarmuth, the king of Lachish, the king of Eglon, gathered themselves together, and went up, they and **all their hosts, and encamped before Gibeon, and made war against it.**

Gibeon then asked for deliverance from Joshua. It occurs to me that Joshua could have seen this as deliverance from his Gibeonite problem and let the other Canaanites slaughter Gibeon; but Joshua had already given his word that the Gibeonites could be servants of the Levites.

10:6 And the men of Gibeon sent unto Joshua to the camp to Gilgal, saying, Slack not thy hand from thy servants; come up to us quickly, and save us, and help us: for all the kings of the Amorites that dwell in the mountains are gathered together against us.

Joshua was keeping his word and God was with him, informing him that God had worked the Gibeon problem out to bring destruction on the five kings of Canaan.

10:7 So Joshua ascended from Gilgal, he, and all the people of war with him, and all the mighty men of valour. **10:8** And the LORD said unto Joshua, Fear them not: for I have delivered them into thine hand; there shall not a man of them stand before thee.

Joshua marched all night and caught them by surprise in the early morning.

10:9 Joshua therefore came unto them suddenly, and went up from Gilgal all night.

The God who later gave up his Godhood to be made flesh as Jesus Christ, went before Israel and destroyed the five rulers and their armies.

No wimp who tolerates sin here, Jesus Christ is Mighty to Save his people: To save all those who are zealous and faithful to him and the Word of God!

10:10 And the LORD discomfited them before Israel, and slew them with a great slaughter at Gibeon, and chased them along the way that goeth up to Bethhoron, and smote them to Azekah, and unto Makkedah.

God rained great hailstones on them destroying many.

10:11 And it came to pass, as they fled from before Israel, and were in the going down to Bethhoron, that the LORD cast down great stones from heaven upon them unto Azekah, and they died: **they were more which died with hailstones than they whom the children of Israel slew with the sword.**

The God who became Jesus Christ even prolonged the hours of daylight so that Joshua could complete the job of destroying the five kings! Such is the power and the might and the glory of our Deliverer!

Why will we fear transitory physical temptations and persecutions when zeal for our Mighty One guarantees victory over Satan and sin and entry into the Promised Land of eternal life?

10:12 Then spake Joshua to the LORD in the day when the LORD delivered up the Amorites before the children of Israel, and he said in the sight of Israel, Sun, stand thou still upon Gibeon; and thou, Moon, in the valley of Ajalon. **10:13** And the sun stood still, and the moon stayed, until the people had avenged themselves upon their enemies. Is not this written in the book of Jasher? So the sun stood still in the midst of heaven, and hasted not to go down about a whole day. **10:14** And there was no day like that before it or after it, that the LORD hearkened unto the voice of a man: for the LORD fought for Israel. **10:15** And Joshua returned, and all Israel with him, unto the camp to Gilgal.

The five kings hid themselves and were sealed up in a cave by Israel until the battle was over and their army was destroyed.

10:16 But these five kings fled, and hid themselves in a cave at Makkedah. **10:17** And it was told Joshua, saying, The five kings are found hid in a cave at Makkedah. **10:18** And Joshua said, Roll great stones upon the mouth of the cave, and set men by it for to keep them: **10:19** And stay ye not, but pursue after your enemies, and smite the hindmost of them; suffer them not to enter into their cities: for the LORD your God hath delivered them into your hand.

A few of the enemy escaped into fenced cities but the slaughter had diminished them in a very big way.

10:20 And it came to pass, when Joshua and the children of Israel had made an end of slaying them with a very great slaughter, till they were consumed, that **the rest which remained of them entered into fenced cities.**

Then the fame of God, Joshua and Israel filled the land; and all the Canaanites were very afraid.

10:21 And all the people returned to the camp to Joshua at Makkedah in peace: none moved his tongue against any of the children of Israel.

Joshua then sent for the five kings

10:22 Then said Joshua, Open the mouth of the cave, and bring out those five kings unto me out of the cave. **10:23** And they did so, and brought forth those five kings unto him out of the cave, the king of Jerusalem, the king of Hebron, the king of Jarmuth, the king of Lachish, and the king of Eglon.

Joshua then proceeded to give a graphic lesson to the leaders of Israel. This graphic action was worth ten thousand words in strengthening the faith and heart of Israel to keep the Word of God and to follow Christ wherever he will lead us.

10:24 And it came to pass, when they brought out those kings unto Joshua, that Joshua called for all the men of Israel, and said unto the captains of the men of war which went with him, Come near, put your feet upon the necks of these kings. And they came near, and put their feet upon the necks of them.

Brethren, these words are for us today; fear God and do his will and zealously live by every Word of God and he will deliver us from death itself on that day! God our Father and our espoused Husband Jesus Christ; are Mighty, they are Worthy, and greatly to be exalted above all else!

10:25 And Joshua said unto them, Fear not, nor be dismayed, be strong and of good courage: for thus shall the LORD do to all your enemies against whom ye fight.

Again the word "evening" is used synonymously with sunset or sun down.

If anyone says that the word "evening" is ambiguous and that people can decide for themselves when to stop work for the Sabbath: They do not understand the Word of God. Evening is synonymous with sun down or sunset.

10:26 And afterward Joshua smote them, and slew them, and hanged them on five trees: and they were hanging upon the trees **until the evening. 10:27** And it came to pass at the **time of the going down of the sun, that Joshua commanded, and they took them down off the trees,** and cast them into the cave wherein they had been hid, and laid great stones in the cave's mouth, which remain until this very day.

Joshua totally destroyed Makkedah, which was the battle headquarters of the five kings and where they had hidden.

10:28 And that day Joshua took Makkedah, and smote it with the edge of the sword, and the king thereof he utterly destroyed, them, and all the souls that were therein; he let none remain: and he did to the king of Makkedah as he did unto the king of Jericho.

Joshua then proceeded to destroy the defenced cities of the five kings and their satellite towns.

10:29 Then Joshua passed from Makkedah, and all Israel with him, unto **Libnah**, and fought against Libnah: **10:30** And the LORD delivered it also, and the king thereof, into the hand of Israel; and he smote it with the edge of the sword, and all the souls that were therein; he let none remain in it; but did unto the king thereof as he did unto the king of Jericho.

10:31 And Joshua passed from Libnah, and all Israel with him, unto **Lachish**, and encamped against it, and fought against it: **10:32** And the

LORD delivered Lachish into the hand of Israel, which took it on the second day, and smote it with the edge of the sword, and all the souls that were therein, according to all that he had done to Libnah.

The king of Gezer came to help Lachish and was also defeated.

10:33 Then Horam king of Gezer came up to help Lachish; and Joshua smote him and his people, until he had left him none remaining.

Next was the city of Eglon one of the five great cities of the Canaanites.

10:34 And from Lachish Joshua passed unto **Eglon**, and all Israel with him; and they encamped against it, and fought against it: **10:35** And they took it on that day, and smote it with the edge of the sword, and all the souls that were therein he utterly destroyed that day, according to all that he had done to Lachish.

10:36 And Joshua went up from Eglon, and all Israel with him, unto **Hebron**; and they fought against it: **10:37** And they took it, and smote it with the edge of the sword, and the king thereof, and all the cities thereof, and all the souls that were therein; he left none remaining, according to all that he had done to Eglon; but destroyed it utterly, and all the souls that were therein.

Debir was also taken and all of the five great cities were destroyed

10:38 And Joshua returned, and all Israel with him, to **Debir**; and fought against it: **10:39** And he took it, and the king thereof, and all the cities thereof; and they smote them with the edge of the sword, and utterly destroyed all the souls that were therein; he left none remaining: as he had done to Hebron, so he did to Debir, and to the king thereof; as he had done also to Libnah, and to her king.

10:40 So Joshua smote all the country of the hills, and of the south, and of the vale, and of the springs, and all their kings: he left none remaining, but utterly destroyed all that breathed, as the LORD God of Israel commanded. **10:41** And Joshua smote them from Kadeshbarnea even unto Gaza, and all the country of Goshen, even unto Gibeon.

Joshua had succeeded in gaining possession of the south central core of the promised land in this series of battles; being completely victorious in all his battles because he was with Christ and Christ was with him. If we are likewise following Jesus Christ to live by every Word of God; we shall also be victorious over Satan and sin, continually overcoming and growing until the end.

If we follow our espoused spiritual Husband without compromise or turning aside from zeal to live by every Word of God; He will fight for us and deliver us!

Let us not try to fight our spiritual battles by compromising with sin and keeping our own ways to do what WE think is right! Let us follow God the Father and Jesus Christ to live by every Word of God, without any compromise, backsliding or turning aside!

10:42 And all these kings and their land did Joshua take at one time, **because the LORD God of Israel fought for Israel.**

10:43 And Joshua returned, and all Israel with him, unto the camp to Gilgal.

Joshua 11

After Israel's conquest of the south of the land, the northern Canaanites came together to fight against Israel and the campaign to control the land turned to the north.

Joshua 11:1 And it came to pass, when Jabin king of Hazor had heard those things, that he sent to Jobab king of Madon, and to the king of Shimron, and to the king of Achshaph, **11:2** And to the kings that were on the north of the mountains, and of the plains south of Chinneroth, and in the valley, and in the borders of Dor on the west, **11:3** And to the Canaanite on the east and on the west, and to the Amorite, and the Hittite, and the Perizzite, and the Jebusite in the mountains, and to the Hivite under Hermon in the land of Mizpeh.

11:4 And they went out, they and all their hosts with them, much people, even as the sand that is upon the sea shore in multitude, with horses and chariots very many. **11:5** And when all these kings were met together, they came and pitched together at the waters of Merom, to fight against Israel.

God promises to go before Israel and destroy the massed Canaanites.

11:6 And the LORD said unto Joshua, Be not afraid because of them: for to morrow about this time will I deliver them up all slain before Israel: thou shalt hough their horses, and burn their chariots with fire.

Joshua, encouraged by God's promise of victory, goes to the attack against a vastly superior force.

11:7 So Joshua came, and all the people of war with him, against them by the waters of Merom suddenly; and they fell upon them. **11:8** And the LORD delivered them into the hand of Israel, who smote them, and chased them unto great Zidon, and unto Misrephothmaim, and unto the valley of Mizpeh eastward; and they smote them, until they left them none remaining. **11:9** And Joshua did unto them as the LORD bade him: he houghed their horses, and burnt their chariots with fire.

Joshua then took Hazor which was the chief city of the Canaanites.

11:10 And Joshua at that time turned back, and took Hazor, and smote the king thereof with the sword: for Hazor beforetime was the head of all those kingdoms. **11:11** And they smote all the souls that were therein with the edge of the sword, utterly destroying them: there was not any left to breathe: and he burnt Hazor with fire.

Using the wicked Canaanites as a symbol of the unrepentant wicked and sin; the destruction of all the Canaanites was commanded by YHVH [who later became flesh as Jesus Christ], and Joshua obeyed in all things.

11:12 And all the cities of those kings, and all the kings of them, did Joshua take, and smote them with the edge of the sword, and he utterly destroyed them, as Moses the servant of the LORD commanded.

The cities that did not threaten war were not attacked or destroyed at that time.

11:13 But as for the cities that stood still in their strength, Israel burned none of them, save Hazor only; that did Joshua burn. **11:14** And all the spoil of these cities [which had come out against them], and the cattle, the children of Israel took for a prey unto themselves; but every man they smote with the edge of the sword, until they had destroyed them, neither left they any to breathe.

Joshua's zeal to keep the whole Word of YHVH was unquenchable; just like our zeal to live by every Word of God should be.

Our battle is not against flesh and blood but is spiritual and is against Satan and all sin and temptation to depart from our Christ-like zeal to live by every Word of God. Just as Joshua kept the whole Word of God, so we should also live by every Word of God (Mat 4:4).

> **Deuteronomy 8:3** And he humbled thee, and suffered thee to hunger, and fed thee with manna, which thou knewest not, neither did thy fathers know; that he might make thee know that **man doth not live by bread only, but by every word that proceedeth out of the mouth of the Lord doth man live.**

Joshua 11:15 As the LORD commanded Moses his servant, so did Moses command Joshua, and so did Joshua; he left nothing undone of all that the LORD commanded Moses.

The fight was long, but as long as they followed God the victory was assured.

11:16 So Joshua took all that land, the hills, and all the south country, and all the land of Goshen, and the valley, and the plain, and the mountain of Israel, and the valley of the same; **11:17** Even from the mount Halak, that goeth up to Seir, even unto Baalgad in the valley of Lebanon under mount Hermon: and all their kings he took, and smote them, and slew them. **11:18** Joshua made war a long time with all those kings.

It was the God who later became flesh as Jesus Christ, who hardened the hearts of the Canaanites so that they would not make peace!

WHY? To make them an example and an instruction for us so that we can learn that God the Father and Jesus Christ will not tolerate any sin; the unrepentant Canaanites being a type of sin.

11:19 There was not a city that made peace with the children of Israel, save the Hivites the inhabitants of Gibeon: all other they took in battle. **11:20** For it was of the LORD to harden their hearts, that they should come against Israel in battle, that he might destroy them utterly, and that they might have no favour, but that he might destroy them, as the LORD commanded Moses.

At that time the men of huge stature were destroyed out of Canaan, except for a few remaining in the Gaza area.

11:21 And at that time came Joshua, and cut off the Anakims [physical giants] from the mountains, from Hebron, from Debir, from Anab, and from all the mountains of Judah, and from all the mountains of Israel: Joshua destroyed them utterly with their cities. **11:22** There was none of the Anakims left in the land of the children of Israel: only in Gaza, in Gath, and in Ashdod, there remained. **11:23** So Joshua took the whole land, according to all that the LORD said unto Moses;

After conquering the land, Joshua divided the land for an inheritance unto Israel according to their divisions by their tribes. And the land rested from war.

Joshua 12

The cities which were destroyed by Moses on the east side of Jordan, which were given to Reuben, Gad and half of Manasseh.

Joshua 12:1 Now these are the kings of the land, which the children of Israel smote, and possessed their land on the other side Jordan toward the rising of the sun, from the river Arnon unto mount Hermon, and all the plain on the east: **12:2** Sihon king of the Amorites, who dwelt in **Heshbon**, and ruled from Aroer, which is upon the bank of the river Arnon, and from the middle of the river, and from half Gilead, even unto the river Jabbok, which is the border of the children of Ammon; **12:3** And from the plain to the sea of Chinneroth on the east, and unto the sea of the plain, even the salt sea on the east, the way to Bethjeshimoth; and from the south, under Ashdothpisgah:

12:4 And the coast [border] of **Og** king of Bashan, which was of the remnant of the giants, that dwelt at Ashtaroth and at Edrei, **12:5** And reigned in mount Hermon, and in Salcah, and in all Bashan, unto the border of the Geshurites and the Maachathites, and half Gilead, the border of Sihon king of Heshbon.

12:6 Them did Moses the servant of the LORD and the children of Israel smite: and Moses the servant of the LORD gave it for a possession unto the Reubenites, and the Gadites, and the half tribe of Manasseh.

The list of kings and cities that Joshua dispossessed for Israel on the west side of Jordan

12:7 And these are the kings of the country which Joshua and the children of Israel smote on this side Jordan on the west, from Baalgad in the valley of Lebanon even unto the mount Halak, that goeth up to Seir; which Joshua gave unto the tribes of Israel for a possession according to their divisions;

12:8 In the mountains, and in the valleys, and in the plains, and in the springs, and in the wilderness, and in the south country; **the Hittites, the Amorites, and the Canaanites, the Perizzites, the Hivites, and the Jebusites:**

12:9 The **king of Jericho,** one; **the king of Ai,** which is beside Bethel, one; **12:10 The king of Jerusalem,** one; **the king of Hebron,** one; **12:11 The king of Jarmuth**, one; **the king of Lachish,** one; **12:12 The king of Eglon**, one; **the king of Gezer**, one;

12:13 The king of Debir, one; **the king of Geder**, one; **12:14 The king of Hormah**, one; **the king of Arad**, one; **12:15 The king of Libnah**, one; **the king of Adullam**, one; **12:16 The king of Makkedah**, one; **the king of Bethel,** one;

12:17 The king of Tappuah, one; **the king of Hepher**, one; **12:18 The king of Aphek**, one; **the king of Lasharon**, one; **12:19 The king of Madon**, one; **the king of Hazor**, one; **12:20 The king of Shimronmeron**, one; **the king of Achshaph**, one;

12:21 The king of Taanach, one; **the king of Megiddo**, one; **12:22 The king of Kedesh**, one; **the king of Jokneam** of Carmel, one; **12:23 The king of Dor** in the coast of Dor, one; **the king of the nations of Gilgal**, one; **12:24 The king of Tirzah**, one: **all the kings thirty and one**.

The campaign lasted seven years and Joshua who had been the servant of Moses was now very old.

The first twelve chapters of Joshua cover the seven year military campaign to seize the land and contain many principles appropriate for our spiritual lives today.

The next twelve chapters cover the dividing of the land which took another seven years. For these fourteen years **until the first harvest planted by Israel** was reaped, they ate the grain in the land.

The Wave Offering and the Land Sabbath and Jubilee counts did not begin until the **first harvest of grain planted by Israel** at the beginning of the fifteenth year after they had entered the land; because it was the harvest of Israel and not the harvests of the Canaanites which were commanded to be offered after Israel began to till the land.

Joshua 13

Joshua 13:1 Now Joshua was old and stricken in years; and the LORD said unto him, Thou art old and stricken in years, and there remaineth yet very much land to be possessed.

The God who was later made flesh as Jesus Christ then revealed the remainder of the land he will give to Israel; and tells Joshua to divide the land he has already taken among the people..

13:2 This is the land that yet remaineth: all the borders of the Philistines [all Gaza], and all Geshuri,

Geshur lay upon the eastern side of the Jordan between Bashan [Gesher is more or less modern Golan], Maachah, and Mount Hermon, and within the limits of the Hebrew territory; but the Israelites did not expel its inhabitants, they ruled over Mount Hermon and Salecah and all Bashan (Golan), as far as the border of the Geshurites and the Maacathites, and half of Gilead, as far as the border of Sihon king of Heshbon.

The people of Geshur appear to have been brought under tribute, but to have retained their own kings. One of David's wives, Maachah the mother of Absalom, was daughter of Talmai king of Geshur; and it was here that Absalom found refuge after the murder of Amnon, and remained three years with his grandfather,

13:3 From Sihor, which is before Egypt,

Sihor "The river of Egypt," i.e., the Wadi el-Arish (1 Chronicles 13:5), which flows "before Egypt," i.e., in a north-easterly direction from Egypt, and enters the sea about 50 miles south-west of Gaza.

... even unto the borders of Ekron [a city of Philistia] northward, which is counted to the Canaanite: five lords of the Philistines; the Gazthites [Gaza] , and the Ashdothites [Ashdod], the Eshkalonites [Eschol] , the Gittites [Gath], and the Ekronites [Ekron ; also the Avites [Philistines of Gerar]:

The entire coast up to Sidon and then east including Mount Hermon and then slanting northeast and up to the Euphrates river.

13:4 From the south, all the land of the Canaanites, and Mearah that is beside the Sidonians [Sidon] unto Aphek, to the borders of the Amorites: **13:5** And the land of the Giblites, and all Lebanon, toward the sunrising, from Baalgad under mount Hermon unto the entering into Hamath [Euphrates].

Israel did not attain to dominance of all of the land given to them until the days of Solomon. Later all of the land of the ten tribes, that land north of Jerusalem was taken from the house of David until Christ comes with the resurrected David. Jesus Christ when he comes, will give the twelve tribes the whole of their physical promised land.

> **Ezekiel 34:23** And I will set up one shepherd over them, and he shall feed them, **even my servant David**; he shall feed them, and he shall be their shepherd. **34:24** And I the Lord will be their God, and my servant David a prince [the ruler] among them; I the Lord have spoken it.

The borders of millennial Israel will be from Al-Arish in Sinai up along the Mediterranean Sea to Sidon and then head east to Mount Hermon and up north to the Euphrates. The eastern border will then track due south to the river Arnon and will include all Bashan [modern Golan]. The southern border will be from the Dead Sea due south to Eilat and then a direct line north to Al Arish in Sinai. Israel will also dominate Lebanon, Syria, Jordan and Turkey.

Joshua 13:6 All the inhabitants of the hill country from Lebanon unto Misrephothmaim, and all the Sidonians, them will I drive out from before the children of Israel: only divide thou it by lot unto the Israelites for an inheritance, as I have commanded thee.

Ultimately after Christ comes, the inhabitants of Tyre and Sidon will be removed and given to the Sabeans (Joel 3:4-8).

Joshua is commanded to divide the land already taken.

13:7 Now therefore divide this land for an inheritance unto the nine tribes, and the half tribe of Manasseh, **13:8** With whom the Reubenites and the Gadites have received their inheritance, which Moses gave them, beyond Jordan eastward, even as Moses the servant of the LORD gave them;

Gad, Reuben and half of Manasseh were given the land from the river Arnon north to include the modern Golan and Lebanon east of Mount Hermon and part of Syria up to the Euphrates.

13:9 From Aroer, that is upon the **bank of the river Arnon**, and the city that is in the midst of the river, and all the plain of Medeba unto Dibon; **13:10** And all the cities of Sihon king of the Amorites, which reigned in Heshbon, **unto the border of the children of Ammon**; **13:11** And Gilead [Golan] , and the border of the Geshurites and Maachathites, and **all mount Hermon**, and all Bashan unto Salcah; **13:12** All the kingdom of Og in Bashan, which reigned in Ashtaroth and in Edrei, who remained of the remnant of the giants: for these did Moses smite, and cast them out.

Israel was not able to expel all the indigenous people, because after Joshua, they repeatedly turned away from God. This is an example that we cannot overcome Satan and sin, except through the power of God; which power is given ONLY to those who obey God and live by every Word of God [Acts 5:29, 5:32)

13:13 Nevertheless the children of Israel expelled not the Geshurites, nor the Maachathites: but the Geshurites and the Maachathites dwell among the Israelites until this day [the day this was written]. .

Levi received no land except for the forty-eight Levitical cities and their suburbs to live in.

13:14 Only unto the tribes of Levi he gave none inheritance; the sacrifices of the LORD God of Israel made by fire are their inheritance, as he said unto them.

The land of Reuben

13:15 And Moses gave unto the tribe of the children of Reuben inheritance according to their families. **13:16** And their coast was from Aroer, that is on the bank of the river Arnon, and the city that is in the midst of the river, and all the plain by Medeba; **13:17** Heshbon, and all her cities that are in the plain; Dibon, and Bamothbaal, and Bethbaalmeon, **13:18** And Jahaza, and Kedemoth, and Mephaath, **13:19** And Kirjathaim, and Sibmah, and Zarethshahar in the mount of the valley, **13:20** And Bethpeor, and Ashdothpisgah, and Bethjeshimoth, **13:21** And all the cities of the plain, and all the kingdom of Sihon king of the Amorites, which reigned in Heshbon, whom Moses smote with the princes of Midian, Evi, and Rekem, and Zur, and Hur, and Reba, which were dukes of Sihon, dwelling in the country.

Joshua executes God's judgment on Balaam: Balaam was NOT a prophet of God he was a pagan soothsayer and magician like Simon Magus! This is a lesson that all unrepentant wicked people and false teachers including those in today's Spiritual Ekklesia will pay the price for their sin.

13:22 Balaam also the son of Beor, the soothsayer, did the children of Israel slay with the sword among them that were slain by them.

The western border of Reuben was the Jordan

13:23 And the border of the children of Reuben was Jordan, and the border thereof. This was the inheritance of the children of Reuben after their families, the cities and the villages thereof.

The inheritance of Gad

13:24 And Moses gave inheritance unto the tribe of Gad, even unto the children of Gad according to their families.

Gad received the land from Ammon to the lake of Galilee

13:25 And their coast was Jazer, and all the cities of Gilead, and half the land of the children of Ammon, unto Aroer that is before Rabbah [Ammon]; **13:26** And from Heshbon unto Ramathmizpeh, and Betonim; and from Mahanaim unto the border of Debir; **13:27** And in the valley, Betharam, and Bethnimrah, and Succoth, and Zaphon, the rest of the kingdom of Sihon king of Heshbon, Jordan and his border, even unto the edge of the sea of Chinnereth [Sea of Galilee] on the other side Jordan eastward. **13:28** This is the inheritance of the children of Gad after their families, the cities, and their villages.

The inheritance of one half of the tribe of Manasseh; Manasseh being divided into two halves, one half on each side of the Jordan river.

13:29 And Moses gave inheritance unto the half tribe of Manasseh: and this was the possession of the half tribe of the children of Manasseh by their families. **13:30** And their coast was from Mahanaim, all Bashan [Golan with its heights and plains], all the kingdom of Og king of Bashan, and all the towns of Jair, which are in Bashan, threescore cities: **13:31** And half Gilead, and Ashtaroth, and Edrei, cities of the kingdom of Og in Bashan, were pertaining unto the children of Machir the son of Manasseh, even to the one half of the children of Machir by their families.

This is the dividing of the land east of Jordan between Gad, Reuben and half of Manasseh.

13:32 These are the countries which Moses did distribute for inheritance in the plains of Moab, on the other side Jordan, by Jericho, eastward.

13:33 But unto the tribe of Levi Moses gave not any inheritance: the LORD God of Israel was their inheritance, as he said unto them.

Joshua 14

The dividing of the land of Canaan on the WEST side of Jordan

Some may think that the record of the dividing of the land is meaningless dry history. In fact it is proof that God keeps his promises to those who are zealous to follow him and keep the whole Word of God.

This is also prophetic in that the descendants of these people will inherit the same lands in the millennial kingdom of God. Even if we do not know our genealogies Jesus Christ does: And he will give the land back to her proper inheritors during the millennial kingdom.

It is also an allegory that it is God who apportion offices in the Promised Land of eternal life as He sees fit.

Joshua 14:1 And these are the countries which the children of Israel inherited in the land of Canaan, which Eleazar the priest, and Joshua the son of Nun, and the heads of the fathers of the tribes of the children of Israel, distributed for inheritance to them. **14:2** By lot was their inheritance, as the LORD commanded by the hand of Moses, for the nine tribes, and for the half tribe. **14:3** For Moses had given the inheritance of two tribes and an half tribe on the other side Jordan: but unto the Levites he gave none inheritance among them.

Joseph had the birthright of a double portion through his two sons Ephraim and Manasseh.

14:4 For the children of **Joseph were two tribes, Manasseh and Ephraim:** therefore they gave **no part unto the Levites in the land, save**

cities to dwell in, with their suburbs for their cattle and for their substance.

14:5 As the LORD commanded Moses, so the children of Israel did, and they divided the land.

Judah was first called to receive their inheritance, and Caleb spoke to Joshua concerning the promise that he had received.

14:6 Then the children of Judah came unto Joshua in Gilgal: and Caleb the son of Jephunneh the Kenezite said unto him, Thou knowest the thing that the LORD said unto Moses the man of God concerning me and thee in Kadeshbarnea.

God kept his promise to Joshua and Caleb, that they would live to enter the land! Jesus Christ keeps his promises to those who wholly follow him to live by every Word of God!

14:7 Forty years old was I when Moses the servant of the LORD sent me from Kadeshbarnea to espy out the land; and I brought him word again as it was in mine heart. **14:8** Nevertheless my brethren that went up with me made the heart of the people melt: but I wholly followed the LORD my God. **14:9** And Moses sware on that day, saying, Surely the land whereon thy feet have trodden shall be thine inheritance, and thy children's for ever, **because thou hast wholly followed the LORD my God.**

14:10 And now, behold, the LORD hath kept me alive, as he said, these forty and five years, even since the LORD spake this word unto Moses, while the children of Israel wandered in the wilderness: and now, lo, I am this day fourscore and five years old. **14:11** As yet I am as strong this day as I was in the day that Moses sent me: as my strength was then, even so is my strength now, for war, both to go out, and to come in.

Caleb asks for his land of Hebron which had not yet been subdued, in faith that he would receive his portion according to the promise of God.

14:12 Now therefore give me this mountain, whereof the LORD spake in that day; for thou heardest in that day how the Anakims were there, and that the cities were great and fenced: if so be the LORD will be with me, then I shall be able to drive them out, as the LORD said.

Hebron was given to Caleb and his descendants

14:13 And Joshua blessed him, and gave unto Caleb the son of Jephunneh Hebron for an inheritance. **14:14** Hebron therefore became the inheritance of Caleb the son of Jephunneh the Kenezite unto this day, **because that he wholly followed the LORD God of Israel.**

Caleb subdues the giants that lived in Hebron at that time and there was peace.

14:15 And the name of Hebron before was Kirjatharba; which Arba was a great man among the Anakims. And the land had rest from war.

Judah was given the land to the south of Benjamin and later the royal city of Jerusalem which Benjamin surrounded. In the millennium this inheritance will be reversed with Benjamin receiving the south and Judah receiving the land surrounding Jerusalem.

Joshua 15

Joshua 15:1 This then was the lot of the tribe of the children of Judah by their families; even to the border of Edom the wilderness of Zin southward was the uttermost part of the south coast. **15:2** And their south border was from the shore of the salt sea, from the bay that looketh southward: **15:3** And it went out to the south side to Maalehacrabbim, and passed along to Zin, and ascended up on the south side unto Kadeshbarnea, and passed along to Hezron, and went up to Adar, and fetched a compass to Karkaa: **15:4** From thence it passed toward Azmon, and went out unto the river of Egypt; and the goings out of that coast were at the sea: this shall be your south coast. **15:5** And the east border was the salt sea, even unto the end of Jordan. And their border in the north quarter was from the bay of the sea at the uttermost part of Jordan:

15:6 And the border went up to Bethhogla, and passed along by the north of Betharabah; and the border went up to the stone of Bohan the son of Reuben: **15:7** And the border went up toward Debir from the valley of Achor, and so northward, looking toward Gilgal, that is before the going up to Adummim, which is on the south side of the river: and the border passed toward the waters of Enshemesh, and the goings out thereof were at Enrogel: **15:8** And the border went up by the valley of the son of Hinnom unto the south side of the Jebusite; the same is Jerusalem: and the border went up to the top of the mountain [Olivet] that lieth before the valley of Hinnom westward, which is at the end of the valley of the giants northward: **15:9** And the border was drawn from the top of the hill unto the fountain of the water of Nephtoah, and went out to the cities of mount Ephron; and the border was drawn to Baalah, which is Kirjathjearim:

15:10 And the border compassed from Baalah westward unto mount Seir, and passed along unto the side of mount Jearim, which is Chesalon, on the north side, and went down to Bethshemesh, and passed on to Timnah: **15:11** And the border went out unto the side of Ekron northward: and the border was drawn to Shicron, and passed along to mount Baalah, and went out unto Jabneel; and the goings out of the border were at the sea.

15:12 And the west border was to the great sea, and the coast thereof. This is the coast of the children of Judah round about according to their families.

The inheritance of Caleb

15:13 And **unto Caleb** the son of Jephunneh he gave a part among the children of Judah, according to the commandment of the LORD to Joshua, even **the city of Arba the father of Anak, which city is Hebron. 15:14** And **Caleb drove thence the three sons of Anak, Sheshai, and Ahiman, and Talmai, the children of Anak. 15:15** And he went up thence to the inhabitants of Debir: and the name of Debir before was Kirjathsepher.

15:16 And Caleb said, He that smiteth Kirjathsepher, and taketh it, to him will I give Achsah my daughter to wife. **15:17** And Othniel the son of Kenaz, the brother of Caleb, took it: and he gave him Achsah his daughter to wife.

Caleb gave his daughter, springs of water for a wedding present

15:18 And it came to pass, as she came unto him, that she moved him to ask of her father a field: and she lighted off her ass; and Caleb said unto her, What wouldest thou? **15:19** Who answered, Give me a blessing; for thou hast given me a south land; give me also springs of water. And he gave her the upper springs, and the nether springs.

The families of Judah and their inheritances

15:20 This is the inheritance of the tribe of the children of Judah according to their families.

15:21 And the uttermost cities of the tribe of the children of Judah toward the coast of Edom southward were Kabzeel, and Eder, and Jagur, **15:22** And Kinah, and Dimonah, and Adadah, **15:23** And Kedesh, and Hazor, and Ithnan, **15:24** Ziph, and Telem, and Bealoth,

15:25 And Hazor, Hadattah, and Kerioth, and Hezron, which is Hazor, **15:26** Amam, and Shema, and Moladah, **15:27** And Hazargaddah, and Heshmon, and Bethpalet, **15:28** And Hazarshual, and Beersheba, and Bizjothjah,

15:29 Baalah, and Iim, and Azem, **15:30** And Eltolad, and Chesil, and Hormah, **15:31** And Ziklag, and Madmannah, and Sansannah, 15:32 And Lebaoth, and Shilhim, and Ain, and Rimmon: all the cities are twenty and nine, with their villages: **15:33** And in the valley, Eshtaol, and Zoreah, and Ashnah,

15:34 And Zanoah, and Engannim, Tappuah, and Enam, **15:35** Jarmuth, and Adullam, Socoh, and Azekah, **15:36** And Sharaim, and Adithaim, and Gederah, and Gederothaim; fourteen cities with their villages: **15:37** Zenan, and Hadashah, and Migdalgad,

15:38 And Dilean, and Mizpeh, and Joktheel, 15:39 Lachish, and Bozkath, and Eglon, **15:40** And Cabbon, and Lahmam, and Kithlish, **15:41** And Gederoth, Bethdagon, and Naamah, and Makkedah; sixteen cities with their villages: **15:42** Libnah, and Ether, and Ashan,

15:43 And Jiphtah, and Ashnah, and Nezib, **15:44** And Keilah, and Achzib, and Mareshah; nine cities with their villages: **15:45** Ekron, with her towns and her villages: **15:46** From Ekron even unto the sea, all that lay near Ashdod, with their villages:

15:47 Ashdod with her towns and her villages, Gaza with her towns and her villages, unto the river of Egypt, and the great sea, and the border thereof: **15:48** And in the mountains, Shamir, and Jattir, and Socoh, 15:49 And Dannah, and Kirjathsannah, which is Debir, **15:50** And Anab, and Eshtemoh, and Anim, **15:51** And Goshen, and Holon, and Giloh; eleven cities with their villages:

15:52 Arab, and Dumah, and Eshean, 15:53 And Janum, and Bethtappuah, and Aphekah, **15:54** And Humtah, and Kirjatharba, which is Hebron, and Zior; nine cities with their villages:

15:55 Maon, Carmel, and Ziph, and Juttah, **15:56** And Jezreel, and Jokdeam, and Zanoah, **15:57** Cain, Gibeah, and Timnah; ten cities with their villages: **15:58** Halhul, Bethzur, and Gedor,

15:59 And Maarath, and Bethanoth, and Eltekon; six cities with their villages: **15:60** Kirjathbaal, which is Kirjathjearim, and Rabbah; two cities with their villages: **15:61** In the wilderness, Betharabah, Middin, and Secacah, **15:62** And Nibshan, and the city of Salt, and Engedi; six cities with their villages.

Jerusalem was later taken by David and made the capital of all Israel; and it was chosen by the God Being who later gave up his God-hood to be made flesh as Jesus Christ, to be the religious and secular capital of the whole earth during the millennial kingdom and forever more after the New Jerusalem comes down from heaven.

15:63 As for the Jebusites the inhabitants of Jerusalem, the children of Judah could not drive them out; but the Jebusites dwell with the children of Judah at Jerusalem unto this day [the day this was written].

Joshua 16

The land given to Joseph

Joshua 16:1 And the lot of the children of Joseph fell from Jordan by Jericho, unto the water of Jericho on the east, to the wilderness that goeth up from Jericho throughout mount Bethel, **16:2** And goeth out from Bethel to Luz, and passeth along unto the borders of Archi to Ataroth, **16:3** And goeth down westward to the coast of Japhleti, unto the coast of Bethhoron the nether, and to Gezer; and the goings out thereof are at the sea.

16:4 So the children of Joseph, Manasseh and Ephraim, took their inheritance.

The border of Ephraim

16:5 And the border of the children of Ephraim according to their families was thus: even the border of their inheritance on the east side was Atarothaddar, unto Bethhoron the upper; **16:6** And the border went out toward the sea to Michmethah on the north side; and the border went about eastward unto Taanathshiloh, and passed by it on the east to Janohah;

16:7 And it went down from Janohah to Ataroth, and to Naarath, and came to Jericho, and went out at Jordan. **16:8** The border went out from Tappuah westward unto the river Kanah; and the goings out thereof were at the sea. This is the inheritance of the tribe of the children of Ephraim by their families.

Ephraim also had some cities within the area of Manasseh

16:9 And the **separate cities for the children of Ephraim were among the inheritance of the children of Manasseh,** all the cities with their villages. **16:10** And they drave not out the Canaanites that dwelt in Gezer: but the Canaanites dwell among the Ephraimites unto this day [the day this was written], and serve under tribute.

Joshua 17

The land of Manasseh

One half of Manasseh, being the children of Manasseh the first born of Joseph; chose to stay on the east of Jordan and Galilee including the Golan heights and the fertile plains of modern Syria. The other half of Manasseh was on the west side along with Ephraim.

Joshua 17:1 There was also a lot for the tribe of Manasseh; for he was the firstborn of Joseph; to wit, **for Machir the firstborn of Manasseh,** the father of Gilead: because he was a man of war, therefore he had Gilead and Bashan [the area of the Golan Heights and plains of modern Syria.].

The firstborn son of Manasseh was given the Golan Heights and the fertile plains of Syria; while the other children of Manasseh were given land on the west of Jordan alongside Ephraim.

17:2 There was also a lot for the rest of the children of Manasseh by their families; for the children of Abiezer, and for the children of Helek, and for the children of Asriel, and for the children of Shechem, and for the children of Hepher, and for the children of Shemida: these were the male children of Manasseh the son of Joseph by their families.

The daughters of Zelophehad requested their inheritance as promised by Moses and by Christ.

17:3 But Zelophehad, the son of Hepher, the son of Gilead, the son of Machir, the son of Manasseh, had no sons, but daughters: and **these are the names of his daughters, Mahlah, and Noah, Hoglah, Milcah, and**

Tirzah. 17:4 And they came near before Eleazar the priest, and before Joshua the son of Nun, and before the princes, saying, The LORD commanded Moses to give us an inheritance among our brethren. Therefore according to the commandment of the LORD he gave them an inheritance among the brethren of their father.

The land of Manasseh on the west side of Jordan

17:5 And there fell ten portions to Manasseh, **beside the land of Gilead and Bashan**, which were on the other [east side] side Jordan; **17:6** Because the daughters of Manasseh had an inheritance among his sons: and the rest of Manasseh's sons had the land of Gilead.

17:7 And the coast of Manasseh was from Asher to Michmethah, that lieth before Shechem; and the border went along on the right hand unto the inhabitants of Entappuah.

The land of Tappuah was given to Manasseh, but the actual city being on the border was given to Ephraim

17:8 Now Manasseh had the land of Tappuah: but Tappuah on the border of Manasseh belonged to the children of Ephraim; **17:9** And the coast descended unto the river Kanah, southward of the river: these cities of Ephraim are among the cities of Manasseh: the coast of Manasseh also was on the north side of the river, and the outgoings of it were at the sea: **17:10** Southward it was Ephraim's, and northward it was Manasseh's, and the sea is his border; and they met together in Asher on the north, and in Issachar on the east.

Manasseh was also given some land in Issachar and Asher.

17:11 And Manasseh had in Issachar and in Asher Bethshean and her towns, and Ibleam and her towns, and the inhabitants of Dor and her towns, and the inhabitants of Endor and her towns, and the inhabitants of Taanach and her towns, and the inhabitants of Megiddo and her towns, even three countries.

After Joshua died, the tribes could not defeat the Canaanites because Israel had turned away from any zeal for God, which will be revealed in the Book of the Judges. They began to commit the sin of idolatry and follow other gods, exalting their idols of men above the whole Word of God.

17:12 Yet the children of Manasseh could not drive out the inhabitants of those cities; but the Canaanites would dwell in that land. **17:13** Yet it came to pass, when the children of Israel were waxen strong, that they put the Canaanites to tribute, but did not utterly drive them out.

As the tribe of Joseph, Ephraim and Manasseh were given only one joint lot and they complained about this to Joshua.

17:14 And the **children of Joseph** spake unto Joshua, saying, Why hast thou given me but one lot and one portion to inherit, [one piece of land for both Ephraim and Manasseh] seeing I am a great people, forasmuch as the LORD hath blessed me hitherto? **17:15** And Joshua answered them, If thou be a great people, then get thee up to the wood country, and cut down for thyself there in the land of the Perizzites and of the giants, if mount Ephraim be too narrow for thee.

17:16 And the children of Joseph said, The hill is not enough for us: and all the Canaanites that dwell in the land of the valley have chariots of iron, both they who are of Bethshean and her towns, and they who are of the valley of Jezreel.

Joshua then gave to the family of Joseph, a separate lot for Ephraim alone in addition to the lot given for Manasseh; so that Manasseh could have her own lot and Ephraim could have her own lot, receiving a double portion for the descendants of Joseph.

17:17 And Joshua spake unto the house of Joseph, even to Ephraim and to Manasseh, saying, Thou art a great people, and hast great power: thou shalt not have one lot only: **17:18** But the mountain [Mount Ephraim shall be for Ephraim] shall be thine; for it is a wood, and thou shalt cut it down: and the outgoings of it shall be thine: for thou shalt drive out the Canaanites, though they have iron chariots, and though they be strong.

Joshua 18

Until now the ark had traveled with the people and went with them into battle; now after seven years of war and seven years of dividing the land, the Tabernacle was "permanently" set up in Shiloh and the ark was placed inside the Most Holy Place. The laws of the land Sabbath, Jubilees and the Wave Offering then came into practical effect when Israel began to cultivate their own land.

The main job of the Levites had been preparing the Tabernacle for travel and assisting the priests. When the Tabernacle had a permanent place in the promised land and they would no longer travel, the chief task of the Levites was completed.

After that the synagogues [school] system of Israel was established in the 48 Levitical cities scattered throughout the tribes, and places of learning were established throughout the land along with traveling Levitical teachers. The Levites then taught basic education and the Word of God in every place; as long as they were faithful to God.

The synagogue was very much more than a place of worship on Sabbath as some have supposed. It was a place of basic and biblical education, and also a place of local Sabbath meetings.

Joshua 18:1 And the whole congregation of the children of Israel assembled together at Shiloh, and set up the tabernacle of the congregation there. And the land was subdued before them.

Joshua then commanded that three spies be sent out by each of the remaining tribes to search out the remaining land; 21 spies in all.

18:2 And there remained among the children of Israel seven tribes, which had not yet received their inheritance. **18:3** And Joshua said unto the children of Israel, How long are ye slack to go to possess the land, which the LORD God of your fathers hath given you? **18:4** Give out from among you three men for each tribe: and I will send them, and they shall rise, and go through the land, and describe it according to the inheritance of them; and they shall come again to me.

The remaining land was to be divided to the seven remaining tribes which have received no land as yet. Judah, Benjamin, Reuben, Gad and Joseph had their lands; and all the remaining land was to be divided into seven parts and each part apportioned to each of the seven remaining tribes by lot.

18:5 And they shall divide it into seven parts: Judah shall abide in their coast on the south, and the house of Joseph shall abide in their coasts on the north. **18:6** Ye shall therefore describe the land into seven parts, and bring the description hither to me, that I may cast lots for you here before the LORD our God.

The seven remaining tribes had their portion but no portion of land was sought for Levi, Levi having been given the Levitical cities amongst the lands of all the other tribes. In this way the Levites would be spread through ALL the tribes, so that every land would have Levites to teach them the whole Word of God.

David reveals that the land was filled with synagogues [Levitical schools] from the most ancient times in Psalm 74:8. From these Levitical synagogues [schools], Ezra restored the temple era synagogue system.

18:7 But the Levites have no part among you; for the priesthood of the LORD is their inheritance: and Gad, and Reuben, and half the tribe of Manasseh, have received their inheritance beyond Jordan on the east, which Moses the servant of the LORD gave them.

Joshua charged the spies to carefully scout and describe the land to him, so that he might cast lots before Christ at the Tabernacle in Shiloh.

18:8 And the men arose, and went away: and Joshua charged them that went to describe the land, saying, Go and walk through the land, and describe it, and come again to me, that I may here cast lots for you before the LORD in Shiloh. **18:9** And the men went and passed through the land, and described it by cities into seven parts in a book, and came again to Joshua to the host at Shiloh. **18:10** And Joshua cast lots for them in Shiloh before the LORD: and there Joshua divided the land unto the children of Israel according to their divisions.

Benjamin was to be between Judah which was south of Jerusalem and Joseph [in this case Manasseh].

The borders of Benjamin

18:11 And the lot of the tribe of the children of Benjamin came up according to their families: and the coast of their lot came forth between the children of Judah and the children of Joseph. **18:12** And their border on the north side was from Jordan; and the border went up to the side of Jericho on the north side, and went up through the mountains westward; and the goings out thereof were at the wilderness of Bethaven. **18:13** And the border went over from thence toward Luz, to the side of Luz, which is Bethel, southward; and the border descended to Atarothadar, near the hill that lieth on the south side of the nether Bethhoron.

18:14 And the border was drawn thence, and compassed the corner of the sea southward, from the hill that lieth before Bethhoron southward; and the goings out thereof were at Kirjathbaal, which is Kirjathjearim, a city of the children of Judah: this was the west quarter. **18:15** And the south quarter was from the end of Kirjathjearim, and the border went out on the west, and went out to the well of waters of Nephtoah: **18:16** And the border came down to the end of the mountain that lieth before the valley of the son of Hinnom, and which is in the valley of the giants on the north, and descended to the valley of Hinnom, to the side of Jebusi on the south, and descended to Enrogel,

18:17 And was drawn from the north, and went forth to Enshemesh, and went forth toward Geliloth, which is over against the going up of Adummim, and descended to the stone of Bohan the son of Reuben, **18:18** And passed along toward the side over against Arabah northward, and went down unto Arabah: **18:19** And the border passed along to the side of Bethhoglah northward: and the outgoings of the border were at the north bay of the salt sea at the south end of Jordan: this was the south coast.

18:20 And Jordan was the border of it on the east side. This was the inheritance of the children of Benjamin, by the coasts thereof round about, according to their families.

The cities of Benjamin

18:21 Now the cities of the tribe of the children of Benjamin according to their families were Jericho, and Bethhoglah, and the valley of Keziz, **18:22** And Betharabah, and Zemaraim, and Bethel, 18:23 And Avim, and Pharah, and Ophrah, **18:24** And Chepharhaammonai, and Ophni, and Gaba; twelve cities with their villages: **18:25** Gibeon, and Ramah, and Beeroth, 18:26 And Mizpeh, and Chephirah, and Mozah, **18:27** And Rekem, and Irpeel, and Taralah, **18:28** And Zelah, Eleph, and Jebusi, which is Jerusalem, Gibeath, and Kirjath; fourteen cities with their villages. This is the inheritance of the children of Benjamin according to their families.

Joshua 19

Simeon was to live in an enclave inside Judah in the far south.

Joshua 19:1 And the second lot came forth to Simeon, even for the tribe of the children of Simeon according to their families: and their inheritance was within the inheritance of the children of Judah.

The land of Simeon was Beersheba and the surrounding villages.

19:2 And they had in their inheritance Beersheba, and Sheba, and Moladah, **19:3** And Hazarshual, and Balah, and Azem, **19:4** And Eltolad, and Bethul, and Hormah, **19:5** And Ziklag, and Bethmarcaboth, and Hazarsusah, **19:6** And Bethlebaoth, and Sharuhen; thirteen cities and their villages: **19:7** Ain, Remmon, and Ether, and Ashan; four cities and their villages: **19:8** And all the villages that were round about these cities to Baalathbeer, Ramath of the south. This is the inheritance of the tribe of the children of Simeon according to their families.

19:9 Out of the portion of the children of Judah was the inheritance of the children of Simeon: for the part of the children of Judah was too much for them: therefore the children of Simeon had their inheritance within the inheritance of them.

The border of Zebulon

19:10 And the third lot came up for the children of Zebulun according to their families: and the border of their inheritance was unto Sarid: **19:11** And their border went up toward the sea, and Maralah, and reached to Dabbasheth, and reached to the river that is before Jokneam; **19:12** And turned from Sarid eastward toward the sunrising unto the border of Chislothtabor, and then goeth out to Daberath, and goeth up to Japhia, **19:13** And from thence passeth on along on the east to Gittahhepher, to Ittahkazin, and goeth out to Remmonmethoar to Neah;

19:14 And the border compasseth it on the north side to Hannathon: and the outgoings thereof are in the valley of Jiphthahel: **19:15** And Kattath, and Nahallal, and Shimron, and Idalah, and Bethlehem: twelve cities with their villages.

19:16 This is the inheritance of the children of Zebulun according to their families, these cities with their villages.

Issachar was by Jordan river.

19:17 And the fourth lot came out to Issachar, for the children of Issachar according to their families **19:18** And their border was toward Jezreel, and Chesulloth, and Shunem, **19:19** And Haphraim, and Shihon, and Anaharath, **19:20** And Rabbith, and Kishion, and Abez,

19:21 And Remeth, and Engannim, and Enhaddah, and Bethpazzez; **19:22** And the coast reacheth to Tabor, and Shahazimah, and Bethshemesh; and the outgoings of their border were at Jordan: sixteen cities with their villages. **19:23** This is the inheritance of the tribe of the children of Issachar according to their families, the cities and their villages.

Asher was on the Mediterranean Sea from Zebulon north to Carmel [Haifa].

19:24 And the fifth lot came out for the tribe of the children of Asher according to their families. **19:25** And their border was Helkath, and Hali, and Beten, and Achshaph, **19:26** And Alammelech, and Amad, and Misheal; and reacheth to Carmel westward, and to Shihorlibnath; **19:27** And turneth toward the sunrising to Bethdagon, and reacheth to Zebulun, and to the valley of Jiphthahel toward the north side of Bethemek, and Neiel, and goeth out to Cabul on the left hand,

19:28 And Hebron, and Rehob, and Hammon, and Kanah, even unto great Zidon; **19:29** And then the coast turneth to Ramah, and to the strong city Tyre; and the coast turneth to Hosah; and the outgoings thereof are at the sea from the coast to Achzib: **19:30** Ummah also, and Aphek, and Rehob: twenty and two cities with their villages. **19:31** This is the inheritance of the tribe of the children of Asher according to their families, these cities with their villages.

The land of Naphtali

19:32 The sixth lot came out to the children of Naphtali, even for the children of Naphtali according to their families. **19:33** And their coast was from Heleph, from Allon to Zaanannim, and Adami, Nekeb, and Jabneel, unto Lakum; and the outgoings thereof were at Jordan: **19:34** And then the coast turneth westward to Aznothtabor, and goeth out from thence to Hukkok, and reacheth to Zebulun on the south side, and reacheth to Asher on the west side, and to Judah upon Jordan toward the sunrising. **19:35** And the fenced cities are Ziddim, Zer, and Hammath, Rakkath, and Chinnereth,

19:36 And Adamah, and Ramah, and Hazor, **19:37** And Kedesh, and Edrei, and Enhazor, **19:38** And Iron, and Migdalel, Horem, and Bethanath, and Bethshemesh; nineteen cities with their villages. **19:39** This is the inheritance of the tribe of the children of Naphtali according to their families, the cities and their villages.

The lot of Dan

19:40 And the seventh lot came out for the tribe of the children of Dan according to their families. **19:41** And the coast of their inheritance was Zorah, and Eshtaol, and Irshemesh, **19:42** And Shaalabbin, and Ajalon, and Jethlah, **19:43** And Elon, and Thimnathah, and Ekron, **19:44** And Eltekeh, and Gibbethon, and Baalath, **19:45** And Jehud, and Beneberak, and Gathrimmon, 19:46 And Mejarkon, and Rakkon, with the border before Japho.

19:47 And the coast of the children of Dan went out too little for them: therefore the children of Dan went up to fight against Leshem, and took it, and smote it with the edge of the sword, and possessed it, and **dwelt therein, and called Leshem, Dan,** after the name of Dan their father. **19:48** This is the inheritance of the tribe of the children of Dan according to their families, these cities with their villages.

Joshua is given his lot in Ephraim

19:49 When they had made an end of dividing the land for inheritance by their coasts, the children of Israel gave an inheritance to Joshua the son of Nun among them: **19:50** According to the word of the LORD they gave him the city which he asked, even **Timnathserah in mount Ephraim**: and he built the city, and dwelt therein.

The end of the dividing of the land; next came the Levitical Cities including the Judicial Cities, followed by the farewell address of Joshua.

19:51 These are the inheritances, which Eleazar the priest, and Joshua the son of Nun, and the heads of the fathers of the tribes of the children of Israel, divided for an inheritance by lot in Shiloh before the LORD, at the door of the tabernacle of the congregation. So they made an end of dividing the country.

Joshua 20

Cities of Refuge

Joshua 20:1 The LORD also spake unto Joshua, saying, **20:2** Speak to the children of Israel, saying, Appoint out for you cities of refuge, whereof I spake unto you by the hand of Moses: **20:3** That the slayer that killeth any person unawares and unwittingly may flee thither: and they shall be your refuge from the avenger of blood.

These cities were places where an accused person could plead his case before authorities; hence they were cities of justice as well as of refuge. The command is for accused persons to come to these places for justice.

Here too it is also commanded that the judges or elders sit in the gates of the cities where they can be easily found and the case can be publicly heard.

20:4 And when he that doth flee unto one of those cities shall **stand at the entering of the gate of the city, and shall declare his cause in the ears of the elders of that city,** they shall take him into the city unto them, and give him a place, that he may dwell among them.

20:5 And if the avenger of blood pursue after him, then they shall not deliver the slayer up into his hand; because he smote his neighbour unwittingly, and hated him not beforetime.

The refugee must live in the city until an investigation has been conducted and a hearing takes place.

20:6 And **he shall dwell in that city, until he stand before the congregation for judgment**, and until the death of the high priest that shall be in those days: then shall the slayer return, and come unto his own city, and unto his own house, unto the city from whence he fled.

Three cities appointed west of Jordan

20:7 And they appointed **Kedesh in Galilee in mount Naphtali**, and **Shechem in mount Ephraim**, and Kirjatharba, which is **Hebron, in the mountain of Judah**.

Three cities appointed east of Jordan

20:8 And on the other side Jordan by Jericho eastward, they assigned **Bezer** in the wilderness upon the plain out **of the tribe of Reuben**, and **Ramoth in Gilead out of the tribe of Gad**, and **Golan in Bashan out of the tribe of Manasseh**.

20:9 These were the cities appointed for all the children of Israel, and for the stranger that sojourneth among them, that whosoever killeth any person at unawares might flee thither, and not die by the hand of the avenger of blood, until he stood before the congregation.

These six cities of refuge are Levitical cities to which 42 other Levitical cities are added; totaling 48 Levitical cities. The cities of refuge are run by the Levites and the judgments are made by the Priests and Levites.

The cities of refuge are more fully explained in Numbers 35:8-34.

Joshua 21

After the ark was settled in Shiloh and would move no more, the Levites were given cities scattered throughout all Israel so that they could act as teachers to all Israel.

Joshua 21:1 Then came near the heads of the fathers of the Levites unto Eleazar the priest, and unto Joshua the son of Nun, and unto the heads of the fathers of the tribes of the children of Israel; **21:2** And they spake unto them at Shiloh in the land of Canaan, saying, The LORD commanded by the hand of Moses to give us cities to dwell in, with the suburbs thereof for our cattle.

21:3 And the children of Israel gave unto the Levites out of their inheritance, at the commandment of the LORD, these cities and their suburbs.

First the priests, the family of Kohath, being of Levi, were given thirteen cities. These cities were in Judah, Simeon and Benjamin; because the priests would serve at Shiloh and later at the Temple which was built in Jerusalem.

21:4 And the lot came out for the families of the **Kohathites: and the children of Aaron the priest, which were of the Levites,** had by lot out of the **tribe of Judah**, and out of the **tribe of Simeon**, and out of the **tribe of Benjamin, thirteen cities.**

Then the descendants of Kohath [Levites that were not priests of Aaron], were given ten cities listed in Joshua 21:20-26.

21:5 And the rest of the children of Kohath had by lot out of the families of the **tribe of Ephraim**, and out of the **tribe of Dan** [the southern portion of Dan by the Med. Seacoast], and out of the [western] half **tribe of Manasseh**, ten cities.

The Levites descended from Gershon received thirteen cities

Listed in Joshua 21:27-33

21:6 And the children of Gershon had by lot out of the families of the **tribe of Issachar**, and out of the tribe of Asher, and out of the **tribe of Naphtali**, and out of the [eastern] **half tribe of Manasseh** in Bashan, thirteen cities.

The Levites descended from Merari were given twelve cities

Listed in Joshua 21:34-40

21:7 The children of Merari by their families had out of the **tribe of Reuben**, and out of the **tribe of Gad,** and out of the **tribe of Zebulun**, twelve cities.

21:8 And the children of Israel gave by lot unto the Levites these cities with their suburbs, as the LORD commanded by the hand of Moses.

The cities of the priests named

21:9 And they gave out of the tribe of the children of Judah, and out of the tribe of the children of Simeon, these cities which are here mentioned by name. **21:10 Which the children of Aaron, being of the families of the Kohathites, who were of the children of Levi, had: for theirs was the first lot.**

21:11 And they gave them the city of Arba the father of Anak, which city **is Hebron**, in the hill country of Judah, with the suburbs thereof round about it.

Hebron was given to the priests but the agricultural land surrounding Hebron remained the property of Caleb.

21:12 But the fields of the city, and the villages thereof, gave they to Caleb the son of Jephunneh for his possession.

The cities of the priests of Aaron the descendant of Levi

21:13 Thus they gave to the children of Aaron the priest Hebron with her suburbs, to be a city of refuge for the slayer; and **Libnah** with her suburbs, **21:14** And **Jattir** with her suburbs, and

Eshtemoa with her suburbs, **21:15** And **Holon** with her suburbs, and **Debir** with her suburbs, **21:16** And **Ain** with her suburbs, and **Juttah** with her suburbs, and **Bethshemesh** with her suburbs; **nine cities out of those two tribes. 21:17** And out of the tribe of Benjamin, **Gibeon** with her suburbs [Remember Gibeon who's people would be cutters of wood and drawers of water for the tabernacle and later the temple.], **Geba** with her suburbs, **21:18 Anathoth** with her suburbs, and **Almon** with her suburbs; **four cities.**

God in his wisdom [knowing that he would yet choose Jerusalem] gave the priests the Levitical cities nearest to Jerusalem where the priests would serve after the temple was built.

21:19 All **the cities of the children of Aaron, the priests, were thirteen cities with their suburbs.**

The list of Levitical/Priestly cities restated

21:20 And the families of the children of Kohath, the Levites which remained of the children of Kohath, even they had the **cities of their lot out of the tribe of Ephraim.**

21:21 For they gave them Shechem with her suburbs in **mount Ephraim**, to be a city of refuge for the slayer; and **Gezer** with her suburbs, **21:22** And **Kibzaim** with her suburbs, and **Bethhoron** with her suburbs; **four cities. 21:23** And out of **the tribe of Dan, Eltekeh** with her suburbs, **Gibbethon** with her suburbs, **21:24 Aijalon** with her suburbs, **Gathrimmon** with her suburbs; **four cities. 21:25** And out of the [western] half tribe of Manasseh, **Tanach** with her suburbs, and Gathrimmon with her suburbs; **two cities. 21:26 All the cities were ten** with their suburbs for the families of the children of Kohath that remained. [the families of Kohath the son of Levi, a part of which were not descendants of Aaron the priest]

The inheritance of Gershon the son of Levi

21:27 And unto the **children of Gershon**, of the families of the Levites, out of the other [eastern] half tribe of **Manasseh** they gave **Golan** in Bashan with her suburbs, to be a city of refuge for the slayer; and

Beeshterah with her suburbs; **two cities. 21:28** And out of the **tribe of Issachar, Kishon** with her suburbs, **Dabareh** with her suburbs, **21:29 Jarmuth** with her suburbs, **Engannim** with her suburbs; **four cities.**

21:30 And out of the **tribe of Asher, Mishal** with her suburbs, **Abdon** with her suburbs, **21:31 Helkath** with her suburbs, and **Rehob** with her suburbs; **four cities. 21:32** And out of the **tribe of Naphtali, Kedesh** in Galilee with her suburbs, to be a city of refuge for the slayer; and **Hammothdor** with her suburbs, and **Kartan** with her suburbs; **three cities.**

21:33 All the cities of the Gershonites according to their families were thirteen cities with their suburbs.

The inheritance of Merari the son of Levi

21:34 And unto **the families of the children of Merari, the rest of the Levites**, out of the **tribe of Zebulun, Jokneam** with her suburbs, and **Kartah** with her suburbs, **21:35 Dimnah** with her suburbs, **Nahalal** with her suburbs; **four cities. 21:36** And out of **the tribe of Reuben, Bezer** with her suburbs, and **Jahazah** with her suburbs, **21:37 Kedemoth** with her suburbs, and **Mephaath** with her suburbs; **four cities. 21:38** And out of **the tribe of Gad, Ramoth** in Gilead with her suburbs, to be a city of refuge for the slayer; and **Mahanaim** with her suburbs, **21:39 Heshbon** with her suburbs, **Jazer** with her suburbs; **four cities in all.**

21:40 So **all the cities for the children of Merari by their families, which were remaining of the families of the Levites, were by their lot twelve cities.**

The Levites [including the priests] were given forty eight cities, scattered in all Israel; six of which were cities of refuge.

21:41 All the cities of the Levites within the possession of the children of Israel were forty and eight cities with their suburbs. 21:42 These cities were every one with their suburbs round about them: thus were all these cities.

As long as the people diligently followed and lived by every Word of God, they had peace and blessings from their Mighty One; it was when they departed from zeal to live by every Word of God that they were greatly distressed.

It was the responsibility of the priesthood to offer sacrifices and make mediatorial intercession for the nation.

In the same way today it is the duty of the ministry to teach the people throughout all the congregations, a diligent passionate Christ-like zeal to live by every Word of God; in order that the people be accepted and not rejected by Christ for turning away from a zealous wholehearted keeping of the whole Word of God.

The modern concept of church Deacons sprang from the Levites whose job was to HELP the priests in all physical things pertaining to the holy things; and to teach the people throughout all the land a diligent passionate zeal for every Word of God.

Modern Deacons and Deaconesses are to be teachers of God's Word and are to care for the physical needs of the brethren, just as the Levites taught the people and took care of the physical needs of the priests.

A very large responsibility for the sins of physical Israel and Judah was because the priests and Levites went astray into idolatry first, and DID NOT TEACH the people zeal to learn and to live by every Word of God!

Today, a very large responsibility for the sins and lukewarm laxity for the zealous keeping of the whole Word of God and for today's gross idolatry in spiritual Israel; falls squarely on the leaders and elders who are leading the brethren into idolatry and DO NOT TEACH any zeal to learn and to live by every Word of God!

21:43 And the LORD gave unto Israel all the land which he sware to give unto their fathers; and they possessed it, and dwelt therein. **21:44** And the LORD gave them rest round about, according to all that he sware unto their fathers: and there stood not a man of all their enemies before them; the LORD delivered all their enemies into their hand. **21:45** There failed not ought of any good thing which the LORD had spoken unto the house of Israel; all came to pass.

After the death of Joshua and those who knew him, Israel fell into idolatry just as today's Spiritual Ekklesia has done; and they turned away from any zeal to keep the Word of God and followed their idols of men and corporations just as we do today.

When we study through Judges and the history of the kings we will see what becomes of the lukewarm for the Word of God who follow their idols and do what is right in their own eyes.

Joshua 22

Joshua speaks to the two and a half tribes which had chosen to live east of the Jordan River and releases them to cross back over to their land on the east side of the Jordan river.

Joshua 22:1 Then Joshua called the **Reubenites, and the Gadites, and the half tribe of Manasseh, 22:2** And said unto them, Ye have kept all that Moses the servant of the LORD commanded you, and have obeyed my voice in all that I commanded you: **22:3** Ye have not left your brethren these many days unto this day, but have kept the charge of the commandment of the LORD your God. **22:4** And now the LORD your God hath given rest unto your brethren, as he promised them: therefore now return ye, and get you unto your tents, and unto the land of your possession, which Moses the servant of the LORD gave you on the other side Jordan.

Joshua urges them to be diligent to live by every Word of God. This instruction to physical Israel is the very same for today's spiritual Israel in both the physical and the spiritual sense as taught by Jesus Christ. We must be zealous to learn and to live by every Word of God to receive the gift of entrance into the Promised Land of eternal life.

22:5 But take diligent heed to do the commandment and the law, which Moses the servant of the LORD charged you, to love the LORD your God, and to walk in all his ways, and to keep his commandments, and to cleave unto him, and to serve him with all your heart and with all your soul.

22:6 So Joshua blessed them, and sent them away: and they went unto their tents [went to their homes].

Joshua blesses the eastern half of the tribe of Manasseh.

22:7 Now to the one half of the tribe of Manasseh Moses had given possession in Bashan [Golan east of Galilee/Jordan]: but unto the other half thereof gave Joshua among their brethren on this side Jordan westward. And when Joshua sent them away also unto their tents, then he blessed them, **22:8** And he spake unto them, saying, Return with much riches unto your tents, and with very much cattle, with silver, and with gold, and with brass, and with iron, and with very much raiment: divide the spoil of your enemies with your brethren.

The two and one half tribes then departed to the east of Jordan

22:9 And the children of Reuben and the children of Gad and the half tribe of Manasseh returned, and departed from the children of Israel out of Shiloh, which is in the land of Canaan, to go unto the country of Gilead, to the land of their possession, whereof they were possessed, **according to the word of the LORD** by the hand of Moses.

Gad, Reuben and the east half of Manasseh honor God by building an altar to him.

22:10 And when they came unto the borders of Jordan, that are in the land of Canaan, the children of Reuben and the children of Gad and the half tribe of Manasseh built there an altar by Jordan, a great altar to see to.

The rest of Israel sees this as rebellion against God for God's altar was at Shiloh and they seek an explanation from the two and one half tribes, just as Jesus Christ later taught us to do in similar circumstances in Matthew 18.

22:11 And the children of Israel heard say, Behold, the children of Reuben and the children of Gad and the half tribe of Manasseh have built an altar over against the land of Canaan, in the borders of Jordan, at the passage of the children of Israel. **22:12** And when the children of Israel heard of it, **the whole congregation of the children of Israel gathered themselves together at Shiloh, to go up to war against them.**

Phinehas is sent with representatives of the tribes to speak with Reuben, Gad and Manasseh.

22:13 And the children of Israel sent unto the children of Reuben, and to the children of Gad, and to the half tribe of Manasseh, into the land of Gilead, Phinehas the son of Eleazar the priest, **22:14** And with him ten princes, of each chief house a prince throughout all the tribes of Israel; and each one was an head of the house of their fathers among the thousands of Israel. **22:15** And they came unto the children of Reuben, and to the children of Gad, and to the half tribe of Manasseh, unto the land of Gilead, and they spake with them, saying,

Phinehas seeks dialogue to know why Reuben, Gad and Manasseh have built this altar and apparently will not look to Shiloh.

22:16 Thus saith the whole congregation of the LORD, What trespass is this that ye have committed against the God of Israel, to turn away this day from following the LORD, in that ye have builded you an altar, that ye might rebel this day against the LORD? **22:17** Is the iniquity of Peor too little for us, from which we are not cleansed until this day, although there was a plague in the congregation of the LORD, **22:18** But that ye must turn away this day from following the LORD? and it will be, seeing ye rebel to day against the LORD, that to morrow he will be wroth with the whole congregation of Israel.

Phinehas tells them it would be better to return and possess land in the west of Jordan rather than to remain in the east and turn away from God.

22:19 Notwithstanding, if the land of your possession be unclean, then pass ye over unto the land of the possession of the LORD, wherein the LORD's tabernacle dwelleth, and take possession among us: but rebel not against the LORD, nor rebel against us, in building you an altar beside the altar of the LORD our God. **22:20** Did not Achan the son of Zerah commit a trespass in the accursed thing, and wrath fell on all the congregation of Israel? and that man perished not alone in his iniquity.

Reuben, Gad and Manasseh answer that they are not at all rebelling against God, but were setting up a memorial of their faithfulness and zeal for the whole Word of God.

22:21 Then the children of Reuben and the children of Gad and the half tribe of Manasseh answered, and said unto the heads of the thousands of Israel,

22:22 The LORD God of gods, the LORD God of gods, he knoweth, and Israel he shall know; if it be in rebellion, or if in transgression against the LORD, (save us not this day, [if we are in rebellion against the Word of God]) **22:23** That we have built us an altar to turn from following the LORD, or if to offer thereon burnt offering or meat offering, or if to offer peace offerings thereon, let the LORD himself require it;

Gad, Reuben and Manasseh answer that they have done this to prevent any apostasy by setting up a memorial that they are one people with one God and that there is no border or division between them and the rest of Israel.

22:24 And if **we have not rather done it for fear of this thing,** saying, In time to come your children might speak unto our children, saying, What have ye to do with the LORD God of Israel? **22:25** For the LORD hath made Jordan a border between us and you, ye children of Reuben and children of Gad; ye have no part in the LORD: so shall your children make our children cease from fearing the LORD.

This altar was not for sacrifice but was to be a memorial that the eastern tribes worshiped and obeyed the same God as the western tribes.

22:26 Therefore we said, Let us now prepare to build us an altar, not for burnt offering, nor for sacrifice: **22:27** But that it may be a witness [memorial] between us, and you, and our generations after us, that we might do the service of the LORD before him [at Shiloh and later at Jerusalem] with our burnt offerings, and with our sacrifices, and with our peace offerings; that your children may not say to our children in time to come, Ye have no part in the LORD. **22:28** Therefore said we, that it shall be, when they should so say to us or to our generations in time to come, that **we may say again, Behold the pattern of the altar of the LORD, which our fathers made, not for burnt offerings, nor for sacrifices; but it is a witness between us and you.**

These people without God's Spirit, put us to an open shame; for we claim to have God's Spirit and yet we have none of their zeal for the whole Word of God.

God forbid that the spiritual called out should worship and follow any other than God our Father in heaven and the Jesus Christ our Creator, through living by every Word of God and the Holy Scripture. It is time to turn back from our false traditions and idols of men and corporate entities, and to regain a true passionate zeal for the whole Word of God.

22:29 God forbid that we should rebel against the LORD, and turn this day from following the LORD, to build an altar for burnt offerings, for meat offerings, or for sacrifices, beside the altar of the LORD our God that is before his tabernacle.

These words brought peace under God between the eastern tribes and the western tribes.

Even so, if all in today's Spiritual Israel uttered the same commitments of zeal for God from the heart to serve the Eternal and keep all his Word with all their strength and minds; it would bring peace between them and God and between one another

22:30 And when Phinehas the priest, and the princes of the congregation and heads of the thousands of Israel which were with him, heard the words that the children of Reuben and the children of Gad and the children of Manasseh spake, it pleased them. **22:31** And Phinehas the son of Eleazar the priest said unto the children of Reuben, and to the children of Gad, and to the children of Manasseh, This day we perceive that the LORD is among us, because ye have not committed this trespass against the LORD: now ye have delivered the children of Israel out of the hand of the LORD.

Phinehas returned to Shiloh and reported to the leaders of the people.

22:32 And Phinehas the son of Eleazar the priest, and the princes, returned from the children of Reuben, and from the children of Gad, out of the land of Gilead, unto the land of Canaan, to the children of Israel, and **brought them word again**. **22:33** And the thing pleased the children of Israel; and the children of Israel blessed God, and did not intend to go up against them in battle, to destroy the land wherein the children of Reuben and Gad dwelt.

22:34 And the children of Reuben and the children of Gad called the altar Ed: for **it shall be a witness between us that the LORD is God.**

Joshua 23

The final address of Joshua

Joshua 23:1 And it came to pass a long time after that the LORD had given rest unto Israel from all their enemies round about, that Joshua waxed old and stricken in age. **23:2** And **Joshua called for all Israel, and for their elders, and for their heads, and for their judges, and for their officers**,

Joshua disclaims any military success, and credits God for all victories over the Canaanites.

The Canaanites were a type of sin and the spiritually called out cannot overcome sin except by zeal for and relying upon: every Word of God.

It is because of our idolatry and our turning aside to our own ways that we are guaranteed failure to overcome sin, and failure to attain to the resurrection to spirit and the spiritual Promised Land of eternal life.

and said unto them, I am old and stricken in age: **23:3** And ye have seen all that the LORD your God hath done unto all these nations because of you; for **the LORD your God is he that hath fought for you.**

If we follow our Mighty One without any compromise, to zealously live by every Word of God; all sin would be conquered by the indwelling of the One who conquered all sin; and the Promised Land of Eternity will be divided among us as each receives his office from our Lord.

The dividing of the land was a type of dividing the offices of the eternal kingdom among the chosen overcomers; for all these things are decided according to our zeal for the whole Word of God and NOT by our zeal for our idols or our own ways.

23:4 Behold, I have divided unto you by lot these nations that remain, to be an inheritance for your tribes, from Jordan, with all the nations that I have cut off, even unto the great sea westward. **23:5** And the LORD your God, he shall expel them [those remaining] from before you, and drive them from out of your sight; and ye shall possess their land, as the LORD your God hath promised unto you.

Be strong and courageous to follow the Word of our Mighty One and to cleave exclusively to God; do not follow any idol of men or corporate entity away from a Christ-like zeal to live by every Word of God.

Today we are spiritually lukewarm, being filled with zeal for our false traditions and idols of men, and we seem to have no zeal to learn and to live by every Word of God to please our LORD.

We call the Sabbath holy and then pollute it; we refuse to preach the commanded gospel of warning and repentance, and instead preach what people want to hear: which is not battling against sin! It is accommodating sin!

23:6 Be ye therefore very courageous to keep and to do all that is written in the book of the law of Moses, that ye turn not aside therefrom to the right hand or to the left; **23:7** That ye come not among these nations, these that remain among you; neither make mention of the name of their gods, nor cause to swear by them, neither serve them, nor bow yourselves unto them: **23:8** But cleave unto the LORD your God, as ye have done unto this day.

If we were zealous for the whole Word of God and faithfully following our Master, NOTHING could prevent us from overcoming all sin and standing in the resurrection to spirit.

23:9 For the LORD hath driven out from before you great nations and strong: but as for you, no man hath been able to stand before you unto this day.

If we are zealous to live by every Word of God the godly faithful can drive out all sin by the power of God the Father and the Master Overcomer, Jesus Christ; and Satan could not turn us aside from our Beloved One.

23:10 One man of you shall chase a thousand: **for the LORD your God, he it is that fighteth for you, as he hath promised you.**

If we truly loved God the Father and Jesus Christ; we would DO what they teach and what they command us to do, with passionate enthusiasm to please them!

23:11 Take good heed therefore unto yourselves, that ye love the LORD your God.

If we turn aside to idols and false traditions, we will surely fail to conquer sin and we will not be chosen to enter the Promised Land of eternity.

If we in any way turn aside to sin and join together in trying to marry false doctrine with the truth, mixing the profane with the holy and thereby polluting the whole lump; Jesus Christ will no longer go before us to drive sin out of us and he will correct us just as he did to physical Israel.

23:12 Else if ye do in any wise go back, and cleave unto the remnant of these nations, even these that remain among you, and shall **make marriages with them** [a type of becoming ONE with sin], and go in unto them, and they to you: **23:13** Know for a certainty that the LORD your God will no more drive out any of these nations from before you; but they shall be snares and traps unto you, and scourges in your sides, and thorns in your eyes, until ye perish from off this good land which the LORD your God hath given you.

If the spiritually converted knowingly marry the unconverted; God's Spirit will leave us because we have become one flesh with the unconverted.

23:14 And, behold, this day I am going the way of all the earth: and **ye know in all your hearts and in all your souls, that not one thing hath failed of all the good things which the LORD your God spake concerning you; all are come to pass unto you, and not one thing hath failed thereof.**

God blesses all those who are zealously faithful to live by every Word of God.

23:15 Therefore it shall come to pass, that as all good things are come upon you, which the LORD your God promised you; so shall the LORD bring upon you all evil things, until he have destroyed you from off this good land which the LORD your God hath given you.

When we do something that God forbids and we justify ourselves by saying, "the church said this is OK;" we have made that man or organization our idol and we have exalted it above the Word of God.

In doing that we have turned aside from any zeal for our God, and into zeal for an idol of men! We have transgressed our baptismal covenant to become fully ONE with God the Father and Jesus Christ.

23:16 When ye have transgressed the covenant of the LORD your God, which he commanded you, and have gone and served other gods, and bowed yourselves to them; then shall the anger of the LORD be kindled against you, and ye shall perish quickly from off the good land which he hath given unto you.

Joshua 24

Then all the people gathered together [not just the leaders as in Joshua 23] so that Joshua could address the whole nation.

Joshua 24:1 And Joshua gathered all the tribes of Israel to Shechem, and called for the elders of Israel, and for their heads, and for their judges, and for their officers; and they presented themselves before God.

Joshua then repeats the Word of the God who later became flesh as Jesus Christ to all the people, rehearsing the history of the nation and its relationship with God.

In the beginning of Israel, Jesus Christ first revealed himself to Abraham and called him out of his city and then revealed himself to Isaac, Jacob and Joseph; and then they went down into Egypt to become an allegory of the spiritually called out.

24:2 And Joshua said unto all the people, **Thus saith the LORD God of Israel,** Your fathers dwelt on the other side of the flood in old time, even Terah, the father of Abraham, and the father of Nachor: and they served other gods. **24:3** And I took your father Abraham from the other side of the flood, and led him throughout all the land of Canaan, and multiplied his seed, and gave him Isaac. **24:4** And I gave unto Isaac Jacob and Esau: and I gave unto Esau mount Seir, to possess it; but Jacob and his children went down into Egypt.

Physical Egypt was a type of bondage to sin and was defeated by Jesus Christ, picturing Christ destroying spiritual bondage to Satan and sin by his atoning sacrifice as the ultimate Lamb of God.

Then Israel was called out of physical Egypt and crossed the Red Sea by the power of Christ; in a kind of baptism in the Red Sea, rising up out of a symbolic death to a total victory and a new life as a new nation. This event symbolically represents the death and resurrection of the spiritually called out and total victory over bondage to Satan and sin.

Physical Israel then celebrated a total victory over bondage to the spiritual pharaoh Satan on the last and High Holy Day of the Feast of Unleavened Bread.

This is also an allegorical lesson about a resurrection of the spiritually called out from bondage to Satan, sin and death at the end of six thousand years [pictured by the end of the sixth day when Israel crossed the Sea] since the creation of humanity, after which the High Holy [seventh] Day of that Feast representing the millennial Sabbath of rest is celebrated.

The seven days of Unleavened Bread picture the calling out of certain people over six thousand years of human history, followed by the High Day picturing the millennial Sabbath of Rest.

24:5 I sent Moses also and Aaron, and I plagued Egypt, according to that which I did among them: and afterward I brought you out. **24:6** And I brought your fathers out of Egypt: and ye came unto the sea; and the Egyptians pursued after your fathers with chariots and horsemen unto the Red sea.

When Israel sought deliverance from pharaoh; God delivered Israel from pharaoh and opened up the sea of death [picturing death and the resurrection] allowing physical Israel to cross over: This pictured God the Father and Jesus Christ calling a people out if sin and delivering them from the bondage of sin and death in a resurrection to eternal life.

24:7 And when they [Israel] cried unto the LORD, he put darkness between you and the Egyptians, and brought the sea upon them, and covered them; and your eyes have seen what I have done in Egypt: and ye dwelt in the wilderness a long season.

Then Christ gave them victory over their enemies [a type of victory over sin] and led them into the physical land of promise; just as he will give ultimate victory over sin and over death itself to his faithful who are zealous to live by every Word of God the Father and to follow Christ the Lamb of God in all things.

24:8 And I brought you into the land of the Amorites, which dwelt on the other side Jordan; and they fought with you: and I gave them into your hand, that ye might possess their land; and I destroyed them from before you. **24:9** Then Balak the son of Zippor, king of Moab, arose and warred against Israel, and sent and called Balaam the son of Beor to curse you: **24:10** But I would not hearken unto Balaam; therefore he blessed you still: so I delivered you out of his hand.

Jesus Christ delivered Jericho that great city into the hands of Joshua and Israel and gave Israel a great victory over the city; which represented a spiritual victory over sin and death itself.

24:11 And you went over Jordan, and came unto Jericho: and the men of Jericho fought against you, the Amorites, and the Perizzites, and the Canaanites, and the Hittites, and the Girgashites, the Hivites, and the Jebusites; and I delivered them into your hand.

If the spiritually called out are diligent to learn and zealously keep the whole Word of God like Joshua was: We will be given total victory over sin through the One who has already attained total victory over sin. But if we turn aside from zeal to live by every Word of God, if we begin to compromise with the Word of God and to follow idols of men, we shall all likewise perish spiritually just like Jericho perished physically.

24:12 And I sent the hornet before you, which drave them out from before you, even the two kings of the Amorites; but not with thy sword, nor with thy bow.

Physical Israel was given a land of promise and if they had obeyed God in all things they would have remained in the land forever. This history is a solemn warning and lesson for us that entry into the Promised Land of eternal life, is entirely contingent on our zeal to faithfully live by every Word of God.

24:13 And I have given you a land for which ye did not labour, and cities which ye built not, and ye dwell in them; of the vineyards and oliveyards which ye planted not do ye eat.

This message is for BOTH physical AND spiritual Israel: It is for us today!

Let us fear, respect and obey our God, Our Master, Our Redeemer; and turn away from fearing men and following them contrary to the Word of God.

24:14 Now therefore **fear the LORD, and serve him in sincerity and in truth: and put away the gods which your fathers served on the other side of the flood, and in Egypt; and serve ye the LORD.**

Choose whether you will serve idols of men, false traditions and corporate church groups, or whether you will prove all things and hold fast to and live by every Word of God.

24:15 And if it seem evil unto you to serve the LORD, choose you this day whom ye will serve; whether the gods which your fathers served that were on the other side of the flood, or the gods of the Amorites, in whose land ye dwell: but **as for me and my house, we will serve the LORD.**

Like the Israel of Joshua we should also declare that we will serve the Eternal and no other.

Remember the might of our Deliverer and remember that the idols of men are as nothing before Almighty God: Follow men, ONLY as they live by every Word of God! We should all be as faithful to God as Joshua was.

24:16 And the people answered and said, God forbid that we should forsake the LORD, to serve other gods; 24:17 For the LORD our God, he it is that brought us up and our fathers out of the land of Egypt, from the house of bondage, and which did those great signs in our sight, and preserved us in all the way wherein we went, and among all the people through whom we passed: 24:18 And the LORD drave out from before us all the people, even the Amorites which dwelt in the land: therefore will we also serve the LORD; for he is our God.

In ancient times the people could not keep their promises to God. Neither has most of today's Spiritual Ekklesia kept our baptismal promise to enter into a Marriage Covenant to obey our espoused Husband Jesus Christ who commands us to live by every Word of God the Father.

Just as physical Israel was corrected for their turning aside into idolatry; so we of Spiritual Israel will also be corrected for our turning aside from zeal to follow our LORD.

24:19 And Joshua said unto the people, Ye cannot [The people say they will follow God, but they cannot keep their word.] serve the LORD: for he is an holy God; he is a jealous God; he will not forgive your transgressions nor your sins. **24:20** If ye forsake the LORD, and serve strange gods, then he will turn and do you hurt, and consume you, after that he hath done you good.

Just as they insisted that they would follow and obey God we also claim to be followers of God the Father and every Word of God; yet we call the Sabbath holy and then pollute it, therefore we also condemn ourselves with our own mouths.

24:21 And the people said unto Joshua, Nay; but we will serve the LORD.

Dear brethren, we are indeed witnesses against ourselves when we declare that we follow God and then we exalt and follow our idols of men.

24:22 And Joshua said unto the people, Ye are witnesses against yourselves that ye have chosen you the LORD, to serve him. And they said, We are witnesses.

Let us put away our idols of men and false ways; and open up our Bibles to learn and to keep the whole Word of God.

24:23 Now therefore put away, said he, the strange gods which are among you, and incline your heart unto the LORD God of Israel.

The people declared that they would follow the Word of God; just as we also declare that we will follow the Word of God and then we refuse any zeal to live by every Word of God.

24:24 And the people said unto Joshua, The LORD our God will we serve, and his voice will we obey.

Joshua then set a stone [reminiscent of the Chief Corner Stone] as a witness that the people had indeed pledged themselves to obey and follow the Eternal and to live by every Word of God.

This physical stone was a type of the ROCK of our Salvation, Jesus Christ; who has heard our baptismal pledge to follow him and to be zealous to live by every Word of God, regardless of any trial or temptation! Therefore if we grow lax and lukewarm, sinning against zeal for our lord and our Covenant with him: HE, Jesus Christ, the espoused Husband of our baptismal vow: will judge us.

24:25 So Joshua made a covenant with the people that day, and set them a statute and an ordinance in Shechem. **24:26** And Joshua wrote these words in the book of the law of God, and took a great stone, and set it up there under an oak, that was by the sanctuary of the LORD. **24:27** And Joshua said unto all the people, Behold, this stone shall be a witness unto us; for it hath heard all the words of the LORD which he spake unto us: it shall be therefore a witness unto you, lest ye deny your God. **24:28** So Joshua let the people depart, every man unto his inheritance.

Joshua the faithful dies

24:29 And it came to pass after these things, that Joshua the son of Nun, the servant of the LORD, died, being **an hundred and ten years old**. **24:30** And they buried him in the border of his inheritance in Timnathserah, which is in mount Ephraim, on the north side of the hill of Gaash.

Joshua was such a powerful example of faithfulness and obedience to God that his influence continued and the people obeyed God during his leadership and for years after his death.

Every elder and leader will have to give an account for leading the brethren away from zeal for God and into a zeal for following men.

It would be better to have never lived than to stand before our Mighty Judge and have to answer for turning people into idolatry and away from any zeal to live by every Word of God.

24:31 And Israel served the LORD all the days of Joshua, and all the days of the elders that overlived Joshua, and which had known all the works of the LORD, that he had done for Israel.

Then the bones of Joseph were buried in Shechem

24:32 And the bones of Joseph, which the children of Israel brought up out of Egypt, buried they in Shechem, in a parcel of ground which Jacob bought of the sons of Hamor the father of Shechem for an hundred pieces of silver: and it became the inheritance of the children of Joseph.

Later Eleazar the high priest during the leadership of Joshua also died and the era of Joshua ended, beginning the book of the Judges.

24:33 And Eleazar the son of Aaron died; and they buried him in a hill that pertained to Phinehas his son, which was given him in mount Ephraim.

Visit Our Website
theshininglight.info

www.ingramcontent.com/pod-product-compliance
Lightning Source LLC
Chambersburg PA
CBHW081348230426
43667CB00017B/2758